BRITISH ARMED FORCES
SPECIAL VOUCHERS

CW01656266

IMPORTANT NOTICE

- Although all information contained herein is obtained from sources believed to be reliable, no responsibility whatsoever is assumed for any omissions, errors or their consequences.

- All illustrations of vouchers have been reduced to fit the surrouding text. No standard reductions rate has been applied nor is the actual reduction rate given.

BRITISH ARMED FORCES SPECIAL VOUCHERS

Theo van Elmpt

ELRAN PRESS
THE NETHERLANDS

ACKNOWLEDGEMENTS

- Vouchers © British Crown copyright /MOD. Reproduced with the permission of the Controller of Her Britannic Majesty's Stationary Office.
- Figures 1 and 6 © Crown copyright - Reproduced by permission of the Controller of Her Brittanic Majesty's Stationery Office - file WO 32/16765, PRO, London.
- Figures 23 and 44 © Reproduced by permission of Thomas De La Rue and Company Limited

CIP-DATA KONINKLIJKE BIBLIOTHEEK, DEN HAAG

Elmpt, Theo van

British Armed Forces special vouchers / Theo van Elmpt. -
Uithoorn : Elran Press. - Ill., fig., tab.
1st ed.: 1994. With ref.
ISBN 90-801808-2-3
NUGI 648
Subject headings: militairy currency ; British Armed Forces
; 1946-1979.

ISBN 90-801808-2-3

First published 1994 97 96 95 94 2 3 4

Second Impression February 1994

Published by ELRAN PRESS - The Netherlands

Copyright © T.F.A. van Elmpt 1994

All rights reserved. No part of this publication may be reproduced, stored in a retrieval system, or transmitted in any form, electronic, chemical, optical, photocopying, recording or otherwise, without the prior permission of the copyright owner or the publisher.

Design and lay out : Rob Aantjes and Arjen Verschoor
Cover design: Arjen Verschoor
Printed in The Netherlands by Drukkerij Tulp BV - Zwolle

CONTENTS

PREFACE

This book would not have been written had it not been for Richard and Claire Lobel. Not only are they responsible for the author's interest in numismatics in general, but also for his interest in the British Armed Forces issues in particular. A number of other individuals and institutions should also be thanked for the assistance given in the preparation of this book, particularly Dr. John R. Bullen of the Imperial War Museum who put me on the right track to start my research, the Public Record Office and its Reading Room Staff, and the Archivist of the Bank of England, Henry Gillett, and his staff for the assistance they gave me in pursuing and uncovering the right information. Also I should like to thank in particular Rob Aantjes and Arjen Verschoor, who spent many a free day patiently and professionally coping with what must have seemed an endless stream of corrections, additions and deletions to the text and the layout of this book. Finally, I should like to thank all those at the Ministry of Defence, Messrs. De La Rue and the Public Record Office who were so helpful in permitting the reproduction of the various illustrations, at such short notice.

LIST OF ILLUSTRATIONS

LIST OF TABLES

LIST OF ABBREVIATIONS

AMC	Allied Military Currency
AMM	Allied Military Marks (in use in occupied Germany)
AMS	Allied Military Schillings (in use in occupied Austria)
BAFSV	British Armed Forces Special Voucher
BAOR	British Army of the Rhine
BCOF	British Commonwealth Occupation Force
BETFOR	British Element Trieste Forces
BoE	Bank of England
BTA	British Troops in Austria
CDB	Currency Destruction Board
COGA	Control Office for Germany and Austria
DPIC	Deputy Paymaster-in-Chief
F1	War Office Department General Finance & Currency Control
F9	War Office Department - Organisation & Methods
FRO	Force Routine Order
GRO	General Routine Order
HQ	Headquarters
MoD	Ministry of Defence
NAAFI	Navy, Army and Air Force Institutes
NCO	Non Commisioned Officer
PIC	Paymaster-in-Chief
PO	Postal Order
PUS	Permanent Under-Secretary
RAPC	Royal Army Pay Corps
RE	Royal Engineers
Sgd	Signed
SNCO	Senior Non Commisioned Officer
WO	War Office
WO	Warrant Officer

INTRODUCTION

In 1946, in an attempt to combat black market dealings between the British Occupation Forces[1] and the local population, particularly in Germany and Austria, the British Government introduced special-vouchers and tokens to be used in the NAAFI canteens instead of normal currency. Although these vouchers were intended as a temporary measure they were kept in use until November 1959 and, in West Berlin, the only potential black market spot left, even until 31 December 1979, when their use could finally be abandoned. It was in 1990 that the Ministry of Defence started looking for a way of disposing of their surplus vouchers and they decided to sell off their stock via public auction. This auction was held on 14 February 1991 and, in a single lot, over 17 million vouchers were sold by Phillips of London. The notes included in this lot were reportedly the very last of the government's holdings. A previous batch of notes had been disposed of in 1980, when the Ministry of Defence had approached a number of British note dealers to put in a tender for an undisclosed quantity of notes that were in shillings and pence and that could no longer be used due to the decimalisation of the £ s d system[2] in 1971. Only one of the dealers responded and bought some of the notes available.

This book traces the history of the British Armed Forces Special Vouchers from the first preparations in 1946 to their final demise in 1979 and, although there are still a great many gaps in our knowledge, a lot of previously unknown details have come to light.

[1] For a short description of the role and organisation of the British Occupation Forces see Appendix J

[2] For those readers not familiar with the £ s d system a short explanation has been provided in Appendix H

2

HOW IT ALL STARTED

On the fifth of March 1946 a meeting was held at the War Office, chaired by Sir Eric Bourne Bentinck Speed, the Permanent Under-Secretary of State for War and Secretary of the Army Command Council, to discuss a knotty problem. A problem that had cost the British taxpayer many millions of pounds in the course of little more than a year.

In the past months it had become clear to the War Office that British soldiers overseas, notably those serving in the British Army of the Rhine (BAOR), with their access to NAAFI canteens, were doing a roaring trade in food, cigarettes and consumer goods with the local population. They would sell the goods they had bought at low prices from the canteens, at greatly inflated prices for local currency, at black market rates of up to 800 DM to the £ sterling. The local currency would then be changed back to sterling at the official exchange rate of 40 DM to the £, thus leaving the British taxpayer to pay the difference. Besides the sale of black market goods, there was also substantial traffic in currency itself at similar, exhorbitant rates. In the case of the liberated territories such as France, Holland, Denmark and Belgium, the governments concerned tended to set the exchange rates at levels which considerably over-valued their currencies in terms of sterling, as against the relative purchasing power in the months following liberation. This was prompted by the hope that, as things became more normal, these rates would be justified. A desire to restrict the purchasing power of troops' pay may also have played an important role in this decision. A further reason for this over-valuation, certainly in the case of Germany, was the distrust which these countries themselves felt for their own currency, which meant that, despite the official prohibition against the holding of foreign currency, there was a very ready market for sterling and Allied notes at a rate out of all proportion to the official rate.

Finally, besides traffic in goods and currencies, the troops also acquired very substantial quantities of illicit currency, at least in the early days. It was not so much a question of large-scale black market dealings as of a multitude of small transactions between large numbers of officers and men, and even larger numbers of civilians. The administrative problem, therefore, was to prevent the illicitly acquired currency from being converted into sterling or into goods which the British taxpayer had paid for in sterling. On the whole this problem was virtually confined to Germany and Austria.

PROVISIONAL MEASURES

This problem had, of course, not gone unnoticed and some provisional measures had already been taken long before the March 1946 meeting took place.

- A limit had been imposed on the amount of currency which could be exchanged by British troops returning home to the UK. This limit was set at the amount actually drawn as pay in the final two months, less the amount converted into Postal Orders.

- The sales of Postal Orders had been confined to currency actually drawn as pay at the pay table. So it would not be possible to draw, for example, 10 Allied Military Marks and send the equivalent of 100 Allied Military Marks home by Postal Order.

- Canteens were prohibited from accepting Deutsch Marks, which had obviously been acquired illegally, since the currency that was used to pay the troops was the Allied Military Mark. Also, notes with a value higher than 50 Allied Military Marks were not accepted by the NAAFI canteens. This also held true for the AM note for 1,000 marks as put into circulation by the Russians.

There were still serious loopholes, however. For example, there was nothing to prevent the troops from illicitly acquiring Reichsmark notes for canteen purchases and underdrawing their pay or indeed drawing no pay at all. There was also the problem that *all* Allied forces serving in Germany used the British canteens, where available. These forces were all paid (by their own governments) in Allied Military Marks. When used for purchasing goods in British canteens these marks would not return any real value to the British government (i.e. the British taxpayer) for the subsidised canteen goods which had been specially imported into Germany.

THE DAMAGE

The extent of the losses to the British taxpayer was not easy to assess. Up to February 1946, however, the British Pay Services had acquired currency in excess of the amounts issued by them as follows:

Dutch Guilders	£15 million
German Marks	£ 6 million
Norwegian Kronor	£ 0.25 million

Normally these surpluses could, of course, be changed back into sterling via the Dutch, German and Norwegian central banks, but the Treasury had a strong suspicion that these governments would refuse to do this and was, understandably, rather annoyed about the matter, especially in the case of the £15 million owed by the Dutch. What had actually happened was that, on 26 September 1945 the Dutch Government had introduced a very stringent currency reform in which all Dutch notes were demonetised suddenly and without much warning. Following this demonetisation, large holdings of Dutch money, often illegally acquired, found their way to the British Treasury via black market transactions by the troops. Since the object of the Dutch Government had been to eliminate such holdings, it would, from their point of view, defeat the object of the exercise if they were to change these amounts back into sterling because they happened to be in the coffers of the British Treasury. Of course, in the case of the German Reichsmarks there was no hope at all of recouping any value whatsoever since these were virtually valueless.

By 1947 a clearer picture had emerged of the scale of the black market dealings and the total losses incurred was estimated at £58 million, a large enough amount for the Public Defence Committee of the House of Commons to question Sir Eric Speed on the matter during a special hearing in April 1947.

THE SOLUTION

In the view of the War Office, the only real remedy for the problem would be to prohibit the acceptance of any currency in the canteens, or any form of remittance to the UK. This, of course, implied the necessity of introducing a whole new currency to be used exclusively in the canteens and for buying Postal Orders. In Germany, this 'canteen money' would then be freely convertible into marks through the official channels, but no conversion would be made from marks into canteen money or pounds sterling. In this way the troops would be unable to benefit from their illicitly-acquired marks. They could neither buy canteen goods with them nor could they send them home via Postal Order. (Of course they could send the notes home, but in Britain these would not be exchanged for sterling either since it was illegal to bring in continental currencies.)

The War Office acknowledged the fact that all Allied Forces personnel using British canteens would also need to be supplied with this special 'canteen money' and that such an operation would be very costly. Not only would it be necessary to design, print and distribute a new currency, but it would be impossible, in the initial conversion stage (in which the troops could change their holdings in marks for the new canteen money), to prevent large amounts of illicitly-acquired 'black' marks being 'laundered'. The scheme would also involve considerable manpower. The total commitment was estimated by the War Office at £3 million pounds, and a staff of 80 people would be involved in getting the scheme off the ground. Given the fact that the total turnover in British canteens was estimated at £20 million a year, much of which would be in black market currency, it was felt, however, that the canteen money scheme would more than pay for itself.

THE START OF THE PROJECT

The proposal to introduce canteen money, when put forward during the March 1946 meeting, was immediately welcomed by all concerned, including the Treasury, the Air Ministry, the NAAFI, the Paymaster-in-Chief, the Admiralty, the British Army of the Rhine and the various War Office departments, so the meeting got off to a flying start.

There were, of course, difficulties to be resolved. In order to handle the canteen money on behalf of the British Paymasters the German banks would need to be involved and the Americans, Canadians, and other Allied Forces would also need to have access to the canteen money since they used the British canteen facilities. When the question was raised as to what denomination the new currency should have, it did not take long to decide that, since the British were issuing the money, the denomination should be in sterling. Although it was initially felt that notes should be issued with the values of 3d, 6d, 1/-, 2/-, 2/6, 5/-, 10/- and £1, the 2/- note never materialised because of the proximity of this value to the 2/6 note.

The question of small change, such as a ½d and a 1d, used to buy cups of tea and other small items, was also addressed and it was decided to use tokens like the ones already in use in NAAFI canteens. The Treasury felt that Allied Forces contingents, who would also have to use the new currency if they were to purchase goods in NAAFI canteens, would have to pay sterling in London, before being issued with the canteen money they required. It was left to the War Office to arrange with the Control Office for Germany and Austria to involve the German banks as far as was practicable.

THE SCHEME GETS UNDER WAY

From the moment the decision was taken to go ahead with the scheme, everything moved along with great speed and precision. The very next day, on 6 March 1946, Ministerial approval was obtained. Given the scale and importance of the operation, Sir Eric Speed thought it prudent to seek the personal approval of the Chancellor of the Exchequer, approval which was apparently granted.

The whole operation was co-ordinated and organised by C.E. Key C.B.E, the Assistant Secretary Financial Staff at the War Office and Paymaster-in-Chief, who had also been in charge of the British

Military Authority notes operation a few years earlier. The Principle Civilian Staff Officers, J.R. Trevaldwyn and O.H. Wagstaff, were to be in charge of the day-to-day operational work.

There was a lot to be done and not a moment's time was wasted. On 11 March, Trevaldwyn had already contacted J.S. Lithiby of the Bank of England, and the Bank was asked to act as advisor on the various aspects of the new note issue, and as liaison with the printer, Thomas De La Rue and Company. Although the War Office would normally order its own supplies, in this case they asked the Bank to order the notes on their behalf. The reason for this was to avoid endless delay since the rules provided that, if the order were to be placed by the War Office, such an order must be the result of a competitive tender. The way round this was to have the Bank of England order the notes from an outside printing firm instead of the order being placed by the War Office. This arrangement with the Bank was unofficially mentioned to the relevant departments and apparently approved. A rough typewritten sketch of a 5/- note had already been prepared by the War Office and sent to the Bank of England. This sketch was, of necessity, a fairly rough draft. (Figure 1) and a long way from the final version of that same note (Figure 2)

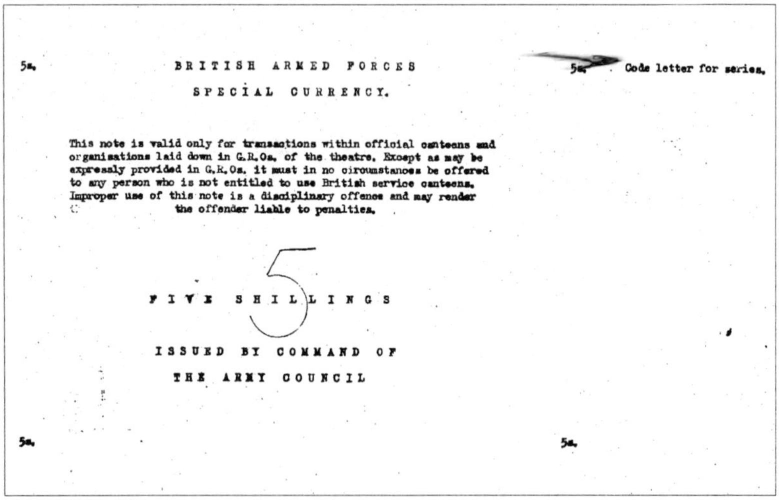

5s. BRITISH ARMED FORCES SPECIAL CURRENCY. 5s. Code letter for series.

This note is valid only for transactions within official canteens and organisations laid down in G.R.Os. of the theatre. Except as may be expressly provided in G.R.Os. it must in no circumstances be offered to any person who is not entitled to use British service canteens. Improper use of this note is a disciplinary offence and may render the offender liable to penalties.

5

FIVE SHILLINGS

ISSUED BY COMMAND OF THE ARMY COUNCIL

5s. 5s.

Figure 1. The 5/- preliminary sketch as produced by the War Office

Figure 2. The 5/- voucher as it was finally produced

It is interesting to note that the text in the sketch still reads 'British Armed Forces Special *Currency*' as compared to *Voucher*. It was the intention at the time that Sir Eric Speed's signature should appear below the words 'Issued by Command of the Army Council'.

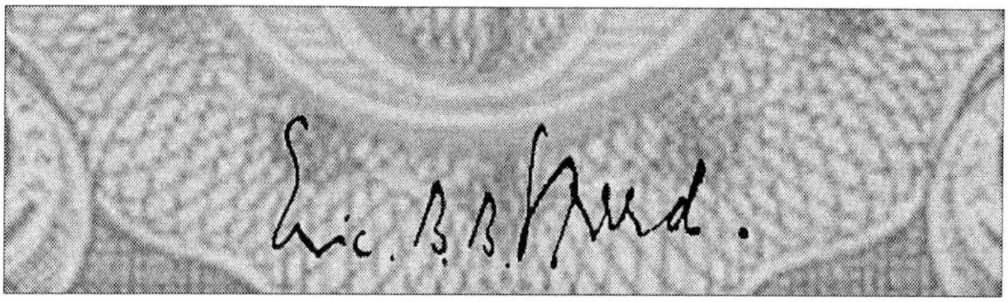

Figure 3. The signature of Sir Eric B.B. Speed as it was to grace the BAFSV (simulated composition)

10

THE FIRST SERIES

DESIGN AND PRODUCTION OF THE BAFSV AND NAAFI TOKENS

While discussing the preliminary design, a number of objections were raised by the Bank of England. The Bank's primary concern was that the vouchers should resemble real money as little as possible. But, although the Bank was obviously bothered by the fact that another organisation was about to issue something very akin to its own banknotes, it loyally supported the War Office in its efforts to produce the vouchers, in a period when there must have been extreme shortages of every conceivable resource necessary to complete the job.

THE DESIGN OF THE NOTES

On the basis of the War Office's sketch for the 5/- note, the Bank initiated a first attempt at a design[1] by De La Rue. This design was received by Trevaldwyn on 23 March 1946 together with a number of recommendations from the Bank. One of the points the Bank mentioned was that they disliked the word 'currency' and they suggested the use of the word 'token' or 'voucher' as being a more accurate description of the note. They also thought that the four lines of print on the face, containing the instructions, should be moved to the back of the voucher. It would then be possible to print on the front in a larger type, 'For use only as detailed on the reverse'.

[1] It would appear that de De La Rue incorporated a considerable number of features from the design for the 5 Franc and 10 Franc notes which they designed and printed in 1944 for the Belgian National Bank.

As we now know, both these suggestions were incorporated in the final design. Some suggestions were not incorporated, however, such as that of making the notes square instead of rectangular. Although the War Office agreed with the Bank about '*... this phoney stuff looking like banknotes...*', they felt that the rectangular shape of banknotes had presumably been adopted in view of the convenience in counting, sorting etc, a reasoning with which the Bank of England could hardly disagree. As to the substitution of the text 'British Armed Forces' by "British Service Canteens' which the Bank suggested, the War Office felt that, since the NAAFI had no responsibility whatsoever over the canteen money, the text should remain 'British Armed Forces'. The Bank also thought it would be preferable not to introduce a £1 note, apparently for fear of confusion with the bank's own £1 note. The War Office, however, felt that, from the point of view of production costs and handling, it would be too awkward not to have a one pound denomination and insisted that a £1 voucher be included.

And so, on 25 March 1946, less than three weeks after the initial meeting, all the major decisions that were to shape the BAFSVs as we know them had been taken.

Others too, contributed some constructive thinking to the project. The Deputy Paymaster-in-Chief, Brigadier H. Golding, proposed an alternative name for the notes-to-be. He suggested that they be called 'British Armed Forces Local Money' or BAFLM - pronounced "baffle'em". It would have been a rather apt name given the purpose of it all. Brigadier Golding thought so too, because, although his suggestion was turned down, he did not easily abandon his attempts to gain acceptance for 'his' name. A suggestion of his which *was* accepted was the printing of the denomination on all four corners on the face and on the back of the voucher. According to the Brigadier it was the omission of this in the Allied Militairy Currency that made that currency very difficult to handle, both for sorting and for counting.

Although the Bank had allowed for the incorporation of a signature, as requested, the War Office apparently had second thoughts about this and asked the Bank for its opinion on the matter. The Bank advised against a signature mainly because it preferred to see as little resemblance as possible to real bank notes. The

Bank had such a strong aversion to any such resemblance that it actually instructed the printer to make the design and colour scheme look less like real currency by using a '..*rather startling band of colour which no self-respecting note printer would dream of using...*', an instruction the printer did not ignore. Looking at the notes with hindsight, however, it is remarkable how the printers made use of the same hues which are used today in the new 'E'-Series notes for the Bank of England... .

On 11 April 1946 Trevaldwyn received a new (second) design made by De La Rue. It was for the face and back of the 5/- voucher and incorporated all the various points that had been agreed upon in the past three weeks. It was also understood that all vouchers would be designed along the same general lines with a diagonal band of colour formed by a rainbow printing. In the words of the Bank these vouchers '*...had the charm of simplicity ... coupled with the lack of security ... which no self-respecting note-printer would dream of submitting for use as currency...*".

Once this design had been approved the engraving for the whole Series would be immediately put in hand by the Bank and final proofs for the 2/6 and 5/- vouchers would be submitted. The Bank promised to send paste-up designs for the three lowest denominations and for the 10/- and the £1 vouchers, and also provided the specifications set out below for the whole Series, later to become known as 'the First Series'. The notes were divided into groups according to their sizes.

GROUP 1	*3d, 6d and 1/-*
size	: 4 1/2" x 2 1/4"
face	: 2 lithographic printings (main design and tint)
back	: 1 ditto (bearing denomination)
numbering	: no numbering. Cipher letter E, F & G
design	: all three denominations to bear identical structural designs on face. The three back designs will also be identical.
colours	: different colours for each denomination; 'end' colour of face and back of each denomination to be in same or similar colour.

GROUP 2 *2/6 and 5/-*

size	: 5" x 2 1/2"
face	: 2 lithographic printings (main design and tint)
back	: 1 ditto (bearing denomination)
numbering	: numbered in one position with prefix ciphers D/1 and C/1 respectively
design	: both denominations to bear identical structural-designs on face and back, as above, (differing from those of both lower and higher denominations
colours	: different colours for each denomination; 'end' colour of face and back of each denomination to be in same or similar colour.

GROUP 3 *10/- and £1*

size	: 5 1/2" x 2 3/4"
face	: 2 lithographic printings (main design and tint)
back	: 2 ditto (bearing denomination)
numbering	: numbered in two positions with prefix ciphers B/1 and A/1 respectively. Colour of numbering to differ.
design	: to differ from each other, both face and back.
colours	: different colours for each denomination; 'end' colour of face and back of each denomination to be in same or similar colour.

THE PAPER

With everything in very short supply just after the war, securing a large enough quantity of high quality banknote paper was not a simple task. The first idea was to see whether banknote paper might be available from the stocks used to print the Allied Military Currency (Austrian schillings) in America. On 14 March 1946 the Control Office for Germany and Austria made an inventory of the supplies which were available and as it transpired 1,230 reams of paper were stored in Hull, 950 reams in Dublin and 1,070 reams in the USA. The Control Office also managed to secure a sample of the paper in question which Trevaldwyn sent to the Bank of England on 18 March 1946, asking for its advice. The Bank had no objection to the use of this paper but pointed out that perhaps the War Office or Allied Command might object to the fact that the paper contained a clearly legible watermark reading 'Allied Military Currency'. The printer would have to go to considerable lengths to avoid the watermark, if necessary, which might then influence the size of the notes to be printed.

The War Office decided, naturally enough, on a course involving the least possible delay so looked further and, quite by accident, stumbled on a solution to the problem. As it turned out, the War Office had purchased a supply of paper for £6,077 in October 1945. This paper was to have been used in printing special BMA notes denominated in Bahts to be used as liberation money for Siam should military action take the British into that country. This order fell through because it was decided at the last moment to use existing Baht notes still in stock, and the paper was still waiting at the printer. It seems that everybody had forgotten about these supplies until, on 26 April 1946, the Bank advised the War Office that it had taken the liberty of using 69 reams of this paper to print an Issue of Tax Certificates, as fresh supplies of the commercial paper normally used for this purpose were not available at the time. The Bank estimated that the cost of the 69 reams used would be £73 14s 10d for which it enclosed a cheque. Part of the original stock of paper had also been used to print notes for the Dutch Government in 1945[2] and the value of the paper for this order was £1,330. These figures make it possible to estimate the total quantity of paper still available, which must have been around 6,000 reams. The Bank also recommended that the War Office might store this paper instead of pulping it as it could well be very useful one day, being '*... a plain unwatermarked paper...*'.

This signal came at exactly the right moment and the remaining 'Siam' paper was immediately designated for use in the first printing of the BAFSVs.

[2] These are quite probably the notes listed in Pick, 6th Edition, The Netherlands numbers 70 and 71

Sir Eric Speed was not at all happy about the lack of security features in the notes but as the production of new, watermarked, paper would take at least three months this was not a viable option. He finally settled for the additional security of threaded paper for the 10/- and £1 notes, for which the Bank and De La Rue could provide sufficient paper[3], and plain 'Siam' paper for the other denominations. After approval had been secured from the Treasury it was decided to go ahead with this first printing but to consider better security measures in print runs to come.

THE NUMBERS NEEDED

Meanwhile, in order to establish the total number of vouchers to be printed, Trevaldwyn contacted the Deputy Paymaster-in-Chief of the British Army of the Rhine, Brigadier Golding, to ask him for an estimate of the amounts needed.

The Brigadier produced an estimate per denomination on the assumption that about £7 per head would be needed initially, based on 11,000 individuals on pay in August 1946, rising to 19,500 individuals in January 1947 and the total amount was estimated at £10 million, broken down as follows:

Table 1. Estimated initial number of vouchers needed

denomination	value	no. of notes
£1	£2,250,000	2,250,000
10/-	£4,000,000	8,000,000
5/-	£2,000,000	8,000,000
2/6	£1,000,000	8,000,000
1/-	£400,000	8,000,000
6d	£250,000	10,000,000
3d	£100,000	8,000,000
TOTAL	£10,000,000	52,250,000

[3] These 10/- and £1 notes were printed at 24 notes (eight up, three across) to a sheet of threaded paper, with each sheet measuring 24 1/4" x 18 3/4".

In order to facilitate handling and counting it was considered that these notes were best packed in boxes with only one denomination per box and with a total of 50,000 notes per box. The total number of boxes needed for packing purposes would therefore be more than one thousand.

THE PRINTING

The printer received the 'all-clear' from the Bank to go ahead on Monday, 6 May 1946 and by 25 June 1946, only seven weeks later, De La Rue had finished printing the first order of 52,250,000 notes. The War Office received 6 complete sets of specimen notes on 9 July 1946. De La Rue was a little concerned, however, that future orders might also be placed at such short notice[4] and asked the Bank to relay to the War Office that any further order would require at least twelve week's notice before delivery could commence. De La Rue felt that for ' .... [the order] *under production everybody had been... very fortunate since there happened to be the large stock of* [Siam] *paper and also a fairly big fleet of printing machines required as well as the appropriate staff. Notwithstanding all this, night work had been necessary and the greatest difficulty was experienced in producing over 50 million notes in so short a time.*'

For obvious reasons the cost of printing the notes never seemed to have played a significant role in the negotiations. It was only after the notes were actually printed that a quote was given by De La Rue to Trevaldwyn via the Bank's printing works (see Table 2).

From the details of the quote it transpires that only the 3d, 6d, 2/6, and the 5/- denominations were printed on the Siam paper. The prices of these denominations, therefore, excluded the price of the paper. The 1/-, 10/- and £1 notes were printed on paper supplied by De La Rue and the prices quoted included this paper. This explains the price difference between the 1/- and the 6d vouchers which are, after all, the same size. The reason for the 3d voucher being more expensive than the 6d one is because fewer of the former were printed.

[4] As it transpired later their fears were justified - the Second and Third Series vouchers would be commissioned with the same urgency.

Table 2. Quoted printing costs of First Series per 1,000 vouchers

denomination	number of notes	price
3d	8,000,000	9/- per 1000
6d	10,000,000	8/10 per 1000
1/-	8,000,000	12/6 per 1000
2/6	8,000,000	13/8 per 1000
5/-	8,000,000	13/8 per 1000
10/-	8,000,000	22/9 per 1000
£1	2,250,000	24/6 per 1000

Based on this quote Trevaldwyn arrived at the following actual costs:

Table 3. Total printing costs of First Series vouchers

denomination	total price
3d	£3,600
6d	£4,416 13s 4d
1/-	£5,000
2/6	£5,466 13s 4d
5/-	£5,466 13s 4d
10/-	£9,100
£1	£3,062 10s
TOTAL PRINTING COST	£36,112 10s

To this must be added the initial cost of £850 for designing, engraving, plate-making and other preliminary work.

The total cost for the 52,250,000 notes, therefore, was about £37,000 excluding the £6,000 already paid for the Siam paper in 1945. This would bring the grand total up to £43,000 for the first printing of 52,250,000 notes of what was later to be known as the 'First Series'.

As can be seen from the actual First Series vouchers, the initial intention of marking the 3d, 6d and the 1/- note with the letters E, F and G respectively, which were to appear in the top right hand corner of the face, had been abandoned. This decision was taken in May 1946 when it became clear that such marking would jeopardise the final delivery date and it was decided to number only the four highest denominations.

In the end the first print run delivered by the printer in June 1946 consisted of:

Table 4. Number of First Series vouchers delivered initially

denomination	value	no. of notes	prefixes
£1	£2,250,000	2,250,000	A/1-A/3
10/-	£4,000,000	8,000,000	B/1-B/8
5/-	£2,000,000	8,000,000	C/1-C/8
2/6	£1,000,000	8,000,000	D/1-D/8
1/-	£400,000	8,000,000	none
6d	£250,000	10,000,000	none
3d	£100,000	8,000,000	none
TOTAL	£10,000,000	52,250,000	

THE GOOD-OVERS

When, in 1947, the supply of First Series notes was running out and De La Rue were asked to print a Second Series of BAFSVs, a number of notes were found in their storage room which had been left over from the print run of the first order. These were so-called 'good-overs', the excess notes produced during a print run in case of mishaps during the numbering and cutting process. Rather than destroying them at the time the printer had put them into storage. The numbers which were still available are shown in Table 5.

These notes were offered to the War Office in May 1947 at half the original cost. The War Office decided to take the £1 and the

10/- notes, but not the others which were subsequently destroyed by the printer.

Table 5. First Series vouchers good-overs

denomination	no. of notes	prefixes
£1	100,000	A/3
10/-	50,000	B/9
5/-	50,000	C/9
2/6	125,000	D/9
1/-	750,000	none
6d	45,000	none
3d	none	none
TOTAL	1,120,000	

The maximum number of First Series notes destined for circulation can therefore be put at:

Table 6. Total number of First Series vouchers available for circulation

denomination	value	no. of notes	prefixes
£1	£2,350,000	2,350,000	A/1-A/3
10/-	£4,025,000	8,050,000	B/1-B/9
5/-	£2,000,000	8,000,000	C/1-C/8
2/6	£1,000,000	8,000,000	D/1-D/8
1/-	£400,000	8,000,000	none
6d	£250,000	10,000,000	none
3d	£100,000	8,000,000	none
TOTAL	£10,125,000	52,400,000	

While coping with the complexities of the vouchers, Trevaldwyn also turned his attention to the issue of small change: the tokens. This issue had already been addressed in the meeting of 5 March 1946 and it had been decided that tokens of ½d and 1d should be used, similar to tokens already used by the NAAFI at the time. These tokens basically came in two types. The hexagonal 'French' tokens made of a brown plastic laminate called CP3 and imprinted with '½ franc' and '1 franc' which were used in France, and hexagonal plastic tokens for 10 and 20 Groschen, coloured yellow and red respectively, which were used in Austria.

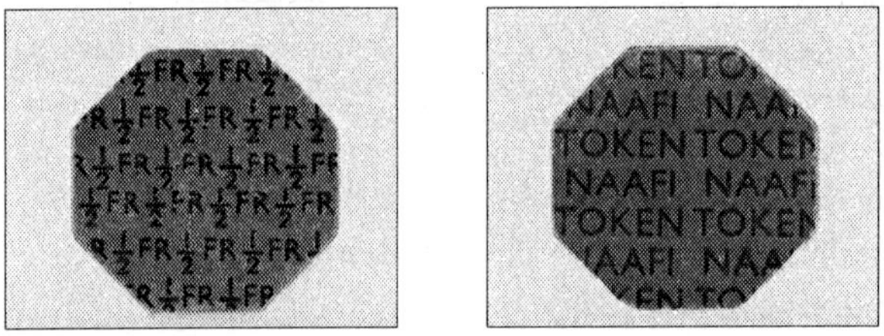

Figure 4. French hexagonal NAAFI token made of CP3

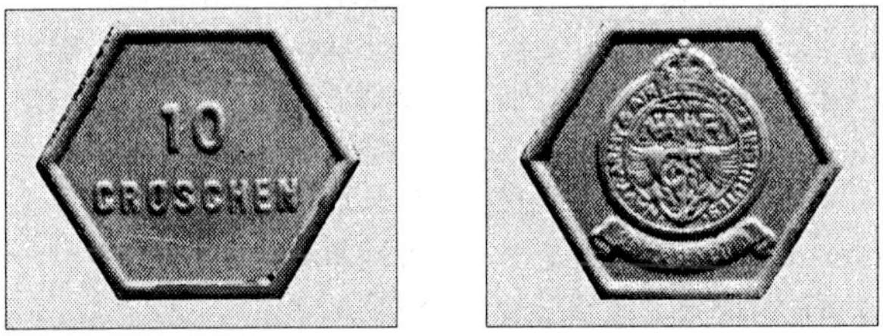

Figure 5. Austrian NAAFI token made of plastic

Since it was known that De La Rue had printed the brown French CP3 laminate tokens Trevaldwyn invited two De La Rue representatives to discuss delivery of tokens. The meeting took place on 22 March 1946 during which samples of both the French and the Austrian tokens were examined. When the representatives saw the Austrian tokens they did not recall ever having come across them before and they were quite certain that De La Rue had not produced them[5]. This Groschen-type token was considered by the representatives to be too easy to counterfeit '... *in any back room..*' and De La Rue advised against using this type. As for the French laminate tokens which De La Rue itself had produced, they thought that using the special laminate known as CP3 with a special pattern engraved on it, would provide enough security. It would not be necessary to have a metal thread running though them as well, which was apparently one of the suggestions made by the War Office. De La Rue felt that it should be possible to deliver 2 million pieces in a fairly short time at a cost of 7/- per 1,000. It also advised Trevaldwyn, however, that it was not the only manufacturer of this type of item nor was it the largest and it suggested that, if the War Office wanted a large order delivered fast, it might be wise to spread production over more than one firm.

On 5 April 1946 Trevaldwyn suggested to Key (the Paymaster-in-Chief) that the tokens could simply be printed with 'British Armed Forces' on one side and the denomination on the other side. He thought they could all be the same colour but that they should be of different sizes. He suggested that the ½d token should be the size of a 6d coin and the 1d tokens the size of a shilling coin. Although Brigadier Golding had specified a requirement of 600 boxes containing 1,600 pieces of each denomination respectively (1,980,000 pieces in all), Trevaldwyn thought it would be wise to order 1,000 boxes so as to cover Austria, as well as having some replacements for Germany. Key did not agree with all Trevaldwyn's proposals. He thought that the suggested sizes would be too small for easy handling and believed that the size of a shilling for the ½d

[5] According to Captain F. Pridmore, these tokens were manufactured by Wollen and Company, Sheffield, England who produced 500.000 of each in March 1946. *The Numismatic Circular*, Spink, London, January 1979, pages 4 and 5.

token and the size of a two-shilling coin for the 1d token would be better. He also felt that the tokens should be round (possibly in order to avoid confusion with the ½ and 1 franc hexagonal tokens). As for the text he felt that, although 'British Armed Forces'could be mentioned on one side only, the denomination should be on both sides of the token. Key did agree, however, to ordering 1,000 boxes containing 3,200,000 tokens in all.

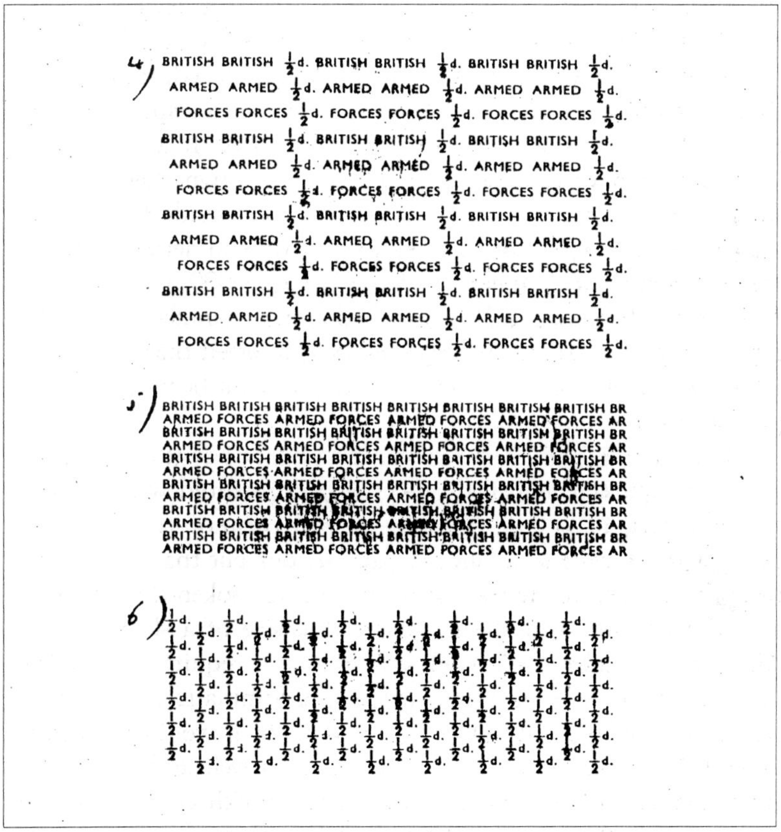

Figure 6. Text sheet used for the production of NAAFI tokens for Germany

On 8 April 1946 Trevaldwyn proceeded to order the round CP3 BAF tokens from the Ministry of Supply, according to Key's specifications, with the final addition that the different denominations should, if possible, '*...be of a different colour.*' . The Ministry did not act on this last recommendation, however, which is strange, since the NAAFI had not been at all happy with the plain brown French laminate tokens produced in 1944 by De La Rue Insulations Ltd. The following comments in a letter to the Chief Controller of Supplies from the Manager of the Overseas Institutes Services aptly express the unsuitability of the brown laminate tokens for normal usage. '*There is no doubt that the new Token is most disappointing in appearance and I anticipate that we shall have difficulty in getting the troops in France to accept it in place of the original token, which was clearly stamped 'Half Franc'. The tiny printing of the new token was agreed with Messrs. De La Rue on the grounds that it could not be forced. As it is impossible to see the printing without a strong magnifying glass, and these Tokens have to be handled during extremely busy periods, it occurs to us that any sheet of* [C]*P3 material with any writing on it at all could not be detected as a forgery under working conditions. .... Owing to the urgency of the demand for Tokens we must accept this 5,000,000 but shall be glad if the matter can be taken up again to try and obtain a really good type bright coloured Token suitably marked, which would be good publicity for the Corporation.*'

When on 6 July 1944, the NAAFI had announced the introduction of the brown French tokens, this had prompted the Sheffield firm, Wollen & Co. Ltd., specialising in the manufacture of tokens and tickets for the distributive trade, to write to the Ministry of Supply stating that they would welcome any share in future contracts for the production of tokens. In February 1946, when the production of a new token for use in Austria became urgent the Ministry of Supply, no doubt with the critical comments of the NAAFI in mind, asked Messrs Wollen to manufacture the colourful Groschen tokens, which were duly produced in March 1946.

It is curious, therefore, that the Ministry of Supply did not suggest to the War Office, when it ordered the unpopular brown tokens in 1946 for BAF use, that the order be changed to the coloured, Groschen-type tokens ordered for the NAAFI. Particularly in view of the fact that the two orders were handled by the Ministry within a month of each other.

Figure 7. $^{1}/_{2}$*d token made of CP3*

Figure 8. 1d token made of CP3

INTRODUCTION OF THE BAFSV

While the design and printing of the notes was in progress, the actual introduction of the BAFSVs to the troops in the various countries that were to use them also needed to be planned. Basically the introduction consisted of the following steps:

- setting a target date for introduction
- dealing with the legal aspects of the BAFSV including the rules and regulations that would govern their use
- instructing the Paymasters in the field
- instructing the troops on the use of BAFSV
- informing the Embassies of the other Allies who were to use the BAFSV of the position
- shipping the notes to the Headquarters of the British Army in the various countries for distribution to the Paymasters

On 25 March 1946, a meeting was held at the War Office attended by Trevaldwyn, Wagstaff, Brigadier Gray (Financial Administrator of the British Army of the Rhine) and Brigadier Golding (Deputy-Paymaster-in-Chief) and chaired by Key (Paymaster-in-Chief). During this meeting a number of technical details relating to the introduction were discussed and a number of decisions were taken.

THE DATE OF INTRODUCTION

Given the scale of the problem it was decided to move as fast as possible and the target date for the introduction of the BAFSV was set at 1 July 1946. Due to the problems encountered with finding the supply of paper, however, this date was eventually moved one month forward so that the actual date of introduction was, in fact, 1 August 1946.

LEGAL ASPECTS

Even a powerful body such as the War Office could not just by-pass the legal and political system when it came to issuing a financial instrument that would involve the Bank of England as well as foreign banks, the Treasury and the British taxpayer in general. So a number of steps had to be taken to ensure that the issued vouchers would have some legal status. In order to achieve this it was necessary to take the issue to Parliament and to secure a Royal Warrant (see Appendix A). The draft Royal Warrant was sent to the Under-Secretary of State on 6 May.

Army Orders (see Appendix B) were also to be issued notifying the troops and officers officially of the legality of the notes. These would have to include the rules and regulations governing the use of the vouchers. Such rules and regulations were published in the form of a so-called General Routine Order (a GRO of the Theatre). The first GRO (no. 2489, Appendix C) was drafted and sent to the War Office for approval on 2 April 1946. This GRO was intended as the preliminary notification of the scheme. During a Series of revisions the text changed considerably, but on 6 May 1946 it was submitted, together with the drafts of the other elements, to the Permanent Under-Secretary of State.

In order to bring the scheme officially into the open, a draft Parliamentary Question and Answer was prepared for a parliamentary discussion. (Appendix D). This would allow the Secretary of State for War to produce the right Answer when prompted with the right Question. Trevaldwyn asked the Permanent Under-Secretary on 6 May 1946 whether the Question could be asked in that same week, because the press had somehow got wind of the story and, eager for details, was asking awkward questions. It was, therefore, essential that the House should debate the question so the scheme could officially be made public. A further reason for urgency was that, on the Friday of that same week, the Control Office for Germany and Austria Estimates were going to be discussed and it was possible that the question of the troops' black-market activities might come up in the debate. It would therefore be better if it could be shown that Parliament had done something about the problem before awkward questions were asked.

Apparently, everything went well and according to schedule because, on 6 June 1946 the newspapers published the scheme with great relish as can be seen from the article in the News Review of 6 June 1946 (Figure 9).

The second GRO (no. 2539, Appendix E) was drawn up by the Pay Services and was sent to the Under-Secretary of State on 31 May 1946. This GRO dealt with all the administrative details of the scheme.

A specially sensitive point was the extent to which troops would be allowed to exchange present holdings of Marks into the new canteen money. It was clear that, if no restrictions were applied, it would be an open invitation to launder all present black-market money and the losses would simply increase. It was therefore decided that the maximum amount that could be exchanged at the initial conversion would be the total of the advances drawn on the last two occasions prior to the general introduction of the vouchers. In practice this meant two months pay drawn. It was also decided that the troops were to have a warning period of at least two months of the new scheme. However, these two steps would make it possible for the troops to draw as much pay as possible in the period of warning and thus launder at least part of their illicit holdings. This danger was, of course, recognised and it was decided to incorporate preventive measures in the GRO. These measures were also to be included specifically in the Unit Orders of the various army units and broadcast on the British Forces Network. At the same time it was clear that individual cases might arise requiring special provisions on a one-off basis.

The official publications all went ahead according to plan. The Royal Warrant (signed by J.J. Lawson, Minister for War, by His

Majesty's Command) was published on 14 July 1946 and the Army Orders (signed by Sir Eric Speed by Command of the Army Council) were published on 10 August 1946.

British troops shopping in Germany will in future have to exchange vouchers for local currency in order to make purchases. But already forecast is a racket in vouchers.

"FLOGGING" RUMBLED

But BAOR Will Find a Way

IN barrack and billet throughout Germany last week there was one general subject of conversation. "Flogging"* had been rumbled and the floggers had until August 1 to make their fortunes.

When War Minister Jack Lawson announced that after that date Rhine Army men would no longer be paid in marks but in vouchers denominated in sterling, and only negotiable in Service establishments, he set the "floggers" a knotty problem. With cigarettes fetching prices between 2s.-4s. each, there was plenty of money to be made. Over one period the Hamburg Army Post Office issued postal orders 15 times the value of pay drawn in that area for the same period.

The illegal sale of NAAFI goods has been well-organised since D plus One, but in Germany it reached a new high. It spread to the sale of coffee and cocoa brought or sent from the UK. To change the marks thus made into postal orders was not so easy. Theoretically a man desiring orders had to draw them across the pay table instead of his pay. But with increasingly lax conditions in some pay offices, the fact that the orders were not always immediately available, difficulties were easily overcome, particularly in small units where "a fiddle could be worked." Postal orders were obtained from APOs on an officer's signature, but in many cases officers rarely checked such chits against records of pay drawn. Some were in on the racket themselves.

There were other ways. The flogger got his mate to draw their pay in postal orders, bought them from them with marks. A soldier would draw no pay until two or three weeks before his leave. The lump sum he then drew he translated into postal orders. No record of this translation was made in his pay book. Arriving at a leave embarkation camp he handed in marks to the amount shown in the book and without question was given sterling. It was dead easy.

Though it will not be easy now, the flogger may still see light through Jack Lawson's proposal. "Arrangements will be made for the exchange of these vouchers for local currency" to enable troops to make purchases in civilian establishments. A trick or two may be worked there after a few week's careful study of procedure. There might even be a racket in vouchers. Furthermore, cigarettes, chocolates and coffee can still be exchanged for jewellery, watches, cameras and clothing which, if the flogger is fly, he can smuggle into the UK and sell for sterling. Many of the silk-stockinged legs now tripping British pavements were clad by the ingenuity of the flogger.

But the new system is going "to hit prices hard." Their mark values will drop, higher quantities of cigarettes and chocolate will be demanded for material goods. Kerbstone black market prices up to now: Cigarettes, 2s.-4s. each; soap, 7s. a bar; chocolate, 7s. 6d.-12s. 6d. a bar; coffee, £3 10s.-£5 a lb.; cocoa, £3 a lb.

Germany has offered the flogger the highest opportunity yet of making his fortune, with the exception of Rotterdam shortly after the liberation, when Canadian soldiers were getting £1 for a cigarette. With Jack Lawson's latest fiat the reaction of the liberated peoples to the Allied soldiers may lose some of its bitter cynicism. But, said Rhine Army men last week, "Flog will find a way!"

* To flog - to sell. In Army parlance it generaly means the illicit sale of food, cigarettes, clothing, etc., for high prices to the occupants of liberated or occupied countries.

Figure 9. Newspaper article from News Review, 6 June 1946

It was recognised quite early on that some of the other Allies, namely the United States, Belgium, Denmark, France, Holland, Luxembourg and Norway, who all had troops stationed in Germany, Austria and Italy (Trieste Free Territory) and used the British Canteen facilities, would need to obtain supplies of BAFSVs. In the case of the Americans it was rather complex because they also operated canteen services in the area used by British troops. Since the latter were only going to be paid in BAFSVs it was imperative that the Americans be persuaded to use BAFSVs as payment in their own canteens. The War Office had been a little uncertain about the willingness of the Americans to do this, but their fears were unfounded. On 27 June 1946 Washington notified the Foreign Office that the Americans would be willing to cooperate and accept the BAFSVs as payment in their canteens as long as the canteen money received in this way would be redeemed in dollars by the British Paymasters (and on condition that the final decision was left to the American theatre commander in the United States Zone). They also agreed to buy a supply of BAFSVs against sterling for use by the American troops in British canteens.

The other allies were notified of the scheme on 4 June 1946 and were asked to provide an estimate of the number of vouchers needed. An initial limit was imposed of £10 per head. A bone of contention in this offer was the insistence by the Treasury that such vouchers would have to be paid for up front in sterling. There was a considerable amount of correspondence with the Dutch in particular since, initially, they were neither prepared nor able to pay in sterling. However, the Treasury, which still had £15 million in worthless Dutch money in its vaults, was unrelenting. In the end the question was settled and the Dutch paid up.

Another difficult case was that of the Danes who seemed willing to buy the vouchers and actually ordered an initial value of £240 and an additional £240 monthly on 1 July 1946, which they raised to £750 monthly on 31 July 1946. However, on 8 August 1946 they wrote to the War Office asking to be excused from the scheme since they no longer had any need to use the British canteen services.

In practically all cases the Governments in question had to be reminded, sometimes more than once, that vouchers would not be delivered before payment in sterling had been received at a London bank.

TRANSPORT OF THE VOUCHERS

Very little is known about the transport and logistics of getting the notes to the HQs of the various army units, but it may be assumed that it will have followed the same pattern as the distribution of subsequent issues, which will be described later.

1 AUGUST 1946

A few days before the actual introduction, on 30 July 1946, it was rumoured that the Germans had already forged BAFSVs to the value of £250,000. An article to that effect appeared in the newspapers, describing the BAFSVs in great detail. Brigadier Golding, the Deputy Paymaster-in Chief of the BAOR, disclaimed these rumours, however, and declared that, in his view, the scare had probably been started by black market forces or by a certain section of the military who wished to discredit the scheme in the hope of delaying its introduction. The War Office did the sensible thing and, ignoring the rumours, started the introduction as planned on 1 August 1946.

FIFTY TONS OF MONEY FOR BAOR

Fifty tons of new money are on their way to BAOR. This represents 50,000,000 pieces of paper - the new official British Armed Forces Special Vouchers (BAFSV).

From 1 August 1946 these vouchers will be BAOR's new money. You will be paid with them. In service canteens, gift shops, post offices, clubs and cinemas, you will hand over not marks, francs, guilders, but BAFSV. It will no longer be marks and pfennigs but shillings and pence, for the BAFSV will be issued in sterling denominations of £1, 10s., 5s., 2s.6d., 1s., 6d., and 3d. For small change there will be plastic tokens of pennies and halfpennies.

As a protection against possible attempts at forgery the paper notes have been skilfully and intricately designed and are printed on special paper. The £1 and 10s. notes have a metal thread running through them like Bank of England notes.

The reason for the introduction of the new currency is to counteract racketeering and "flogging" - the illegal sale of canteen goods, food and cigarettes, for continental money. Racketeers and "floggers" large and small, in the BAOR, Control Commision, and other attached bodies, working their many ingenious rackets have cost Britain many millions of pounds.

Issue of the new currency with the strict regulations attached to it should clean up a lot of the "dirty" money that is araound. Although arrangement have been made for the exchange of BAFSV money into local currency for buying from other than official sources, re-exchange from continental money into sterling or BAFSV will not be permitted except in very special circumstances and then only through Army Cashiers. BAFSV money alone will be exchanged for sterling when men go to the UK from BAOR.

For the Army Paymasters the scheme will mean a lot of extra work. For Britain it will mean a lot of money saved.

Figure 10. Article from The Soldier, the British Army Magazine, July 1946

THE BAFSVs IN PLACE

From 1 August 1946 the BAFSVs became the normal method of paying the British troops who would then use the vouchers to pay for all items purchased in Canteens, as well as for all other goods and services. But, as with any note which carries an intrinsic value, the BAFSV was, by its very nature, prone to counterfeiting, especially so because of the lack of security features. This was acknowledged by the War Office quite soon after the introduction and, in order to assist its Paymasters in the Field to recognise any counterfeits that might turn up, the War Office asked the Bank of England for assistance. First of all it wanted to know the legal position of the Army as well as of the person offering counterfeit BAFSVs in payment and, secondly, how counterfeits were to be recognised as such.

It was on 28 August 1946 that the Bank wrote to Trevaldwyn about the assistance that could be given to the Paymasters in detecting forgeries. This is what it said: '*The thread in the paper of the 10/- and £1 notes requires no explanation but the Paymasters might be told that it may appear in any one of three approximate positions, vist., running from North to South on the Left hand side or Right hand side or in an approximately central position.*' How practical this advice was felt to be at the time we do not know.

SECRET MARKS

The Bank also provided Trevaldwyn with three sets of specimen BAFSVs indicating the secret printing marks[6] which the printer had hidden in the design of the notes. Secret marks are slight imperfections which have been added deliberately by the engraver with a view to foiling the counterfeiters. In the case of the BAFSVs these marks were generally produced by disturbing the balance of a given design, for example by adding a little dot or line in one place and not in a corresponding part of the design. Sometimes a very small part of a line or other design element was removed. Such deliberate

[6] These secret marks can be found on many world banknotes as well. A short sample listing of notes containing these marks is provided in Appendix I.

'mistakes' can normally be discovered by using a strong magnifying glass. However, the Bank stressed the fact that this information was highly confidential and that it should not be relayed to the Paymasters. It was also emphasised that the secret marks were not thought to be infallible because, in cases where photography was employed, they would invariably be recorded on the forgery. The only hope in such cases was that the forger would be under the impression that it was a slight blemish or fault in the print and would erase it from his forgery. Trevaldwyn passed on one of the sets of specimen vouchers with the secret marks indicated to the HQ of the British Army of the Rhine in Hamburg, another set was sent to the British Territorial Army HQ and the third set was kept by the War Office.

SECRET MARKS ON THE FIRST SERIES BAFSVs

On the First Series specimen set of BAFSVs sent to the War Office the secret marks were pointed out by drawing a circle round the area in which the mark was located, with an arrow pointing to the secret mark within the circle. On the vouchers of what has come to be known as 'the First Series' (remember that no Series was mentioned on the vouchers since a 'Second' or 'Third' Series had not yet been thought of) the secret marks were only included on the face of the voucher. In subsequent issues secret marks were included on both the face and the back. The vouchers used by the printer to indicate the secret marks were proper 'specimen' vouchers in that they were fully printed vouchers on which the serial numbers were all zero. It is interesting that these vouchers were not invalidated in any way by overprinting them or otherwise marking them as specimen vouchers. The marks on the First Series can briefly be described as follows.

GROUP 1 *3d, 6d and 1/-*

- a small dot is inserted on the left hand side of the letter 'V' (of the word Voucher)

GROUP 2 *2/6 and 5/-*

- there is a small projection on the right hand (inner) side of the letter 'o' (of the word Voucher)

GROUP 3 *10/- and £1*

- on the 10/- there is a small break in the perimeter of the outer line work of the rosette on the face right hand side.

- on the £1 there is a small break in the perimeter of the outer line work of the rosette on the face right hand side as with the 10/-

- on the £1 there is also a small blemish in the form of a short line (nearly 1/32" long) running at an angle across the printed line work in the second rosette from the right hand side.

The 10/- voucher showed some rather untidy scratches (see Figure 11) which were the result of a slight argument as to whether the mark at the point where the messy scratches appear was indeed a secret mark. The printer decided it wasn't after all, so scratched it out, for which it apologised profusely.

How far this explanation was the entire truth is hard to tell. It may have been that De La Rue decided that it would not give away every single one of the secret marks although it must, of course, not be dismissed out of hand that the printers themselves occasionally lost track of where the engravers had put the secret marks. Whatever the reason in this case, it seems that at least one secret mark on the £1 note was not mentioned at the time. This mark can be found on the face left hand side. It is a vertical line of about 1/32" long at right angles to the double line just underneath the outer rosette. As we will see, the same phenomenon appears with some of the other issues.

Figure 11. First Series 10/- voucher used to indicate the secret marks

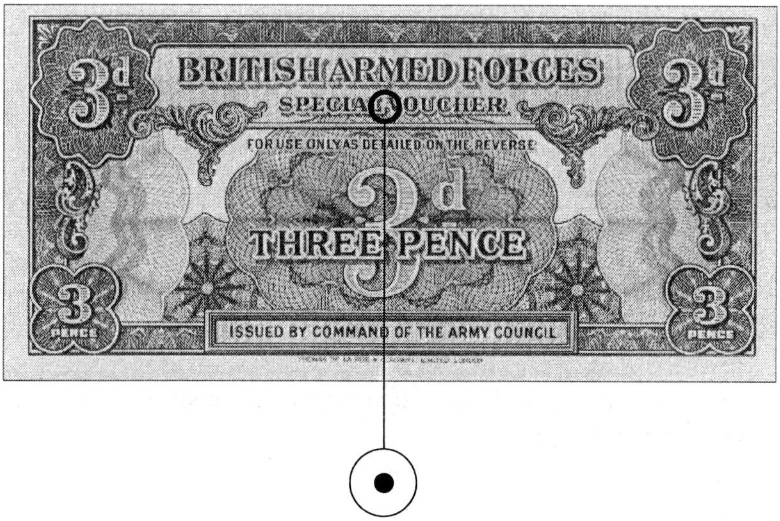

Figure 12. Secret Marks on 3d First Series - face

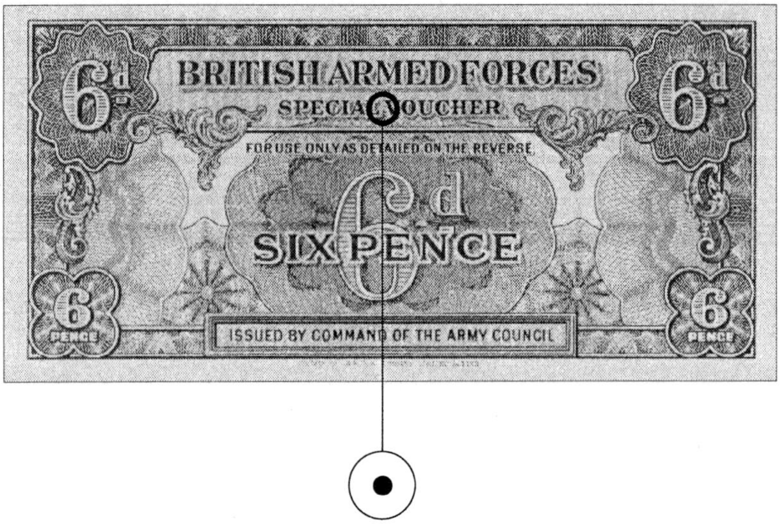

Figure 13. Secret Marks on 6d First Series - face

Figure 14. Secret Marks on 1/- First Series - face

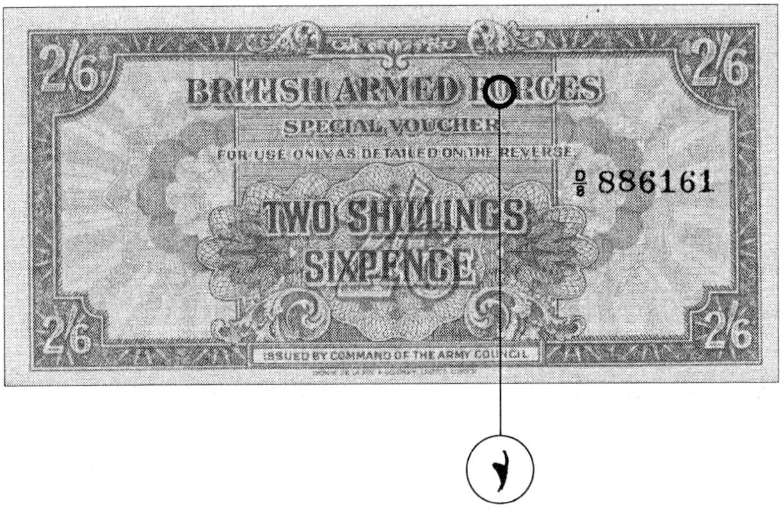

Figure 15. Secret Marks on 2/6 First Series - face

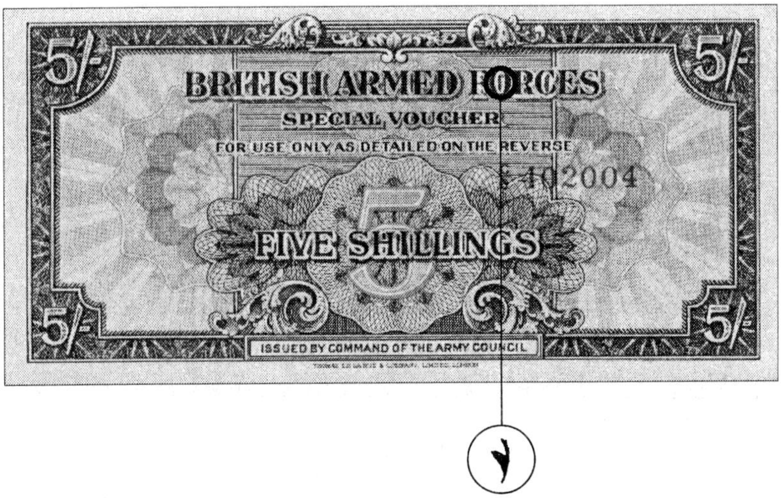

Figure 16. Secret Marks on 5/- First Series - face

Figure 17. Secret Marks on 10/- First Series - face

Figure 18. Secret Marks on £1 First Series - face

Although now able to distinguish between counterfeits and the real thing, officials at the War Office were still not happy about their legal rights to protect 'their' money. The Bank of England could not do much to reassure them. As it stood, both the forgery of banknotes and the possession, without lawful authority or excuse, of a note known to be forged were felonies by the Forgery Act of 1913, *but no statutory authority was given to banks to impound such forgeries.* A Bank manager who was satisfied that a note was a forgery could ask for permission to retain it. Should the presenter insist on its return (which would be the case if he knew it was forged) even after having been informed that the possession of that note would constitute a felony, the only course the manager could take was to notify the police in order to have the 'note' seized for investigation. Of course, the forger would by then have taken to his heels.

Since the BAFSVs were clearly not covered under the sections of the Forgery Act (which deal with *bank*notes) the Army could not instigate any legal procedures regarding forged vouchers. In other words: everybody was entitled to print vouchers. This must have come as a bit of a shock to the War Office but, luckily, the Bank also pointed out that it was probably within the power of the War Office to instruct its cashiers to impound any suspected voucher and call in the Military Police to deal with the presenter who, on the whole, would be easy to trace if not already known to the cashier.

Unhappy with the situation, the War Office was triggered into action by a strong suspicion that the vouchers were being tampered with and by the fact that the Americans had had to replace a Series of Military Payment Certificates which were alleged to have been forged on a large scale[7]. On 5 June 1947 the War Office issued a memorandum to the British Army of the Rhine Paymasters, with copies to all other Paymasters at home and abroad, instructing them as to the action to be taken in case forged BAFSVs should be presented. In short, this action boiled down to: impound the voucher, detain the presenter (if necessary by force) and call in the Military Police.

But it was not only the War Office that was getting worried. The Treasury was also becoming rather nervous and communicated

[7] *The Times*, March 11, 1947.

with the War Office that, if there should be large-scale forgeries of the 'First' Series BAFSVs this could and should be counteracted by utilising an unissued stock of B.M.A. (British Military Authority) notes of which there were still £58,000,000 worth stored in the vaults of the Bank of England. These notes had been used in North Africa and Italy in 1943 but had meanwhile been withdrawn and kept for emergencies.

THE JAPAN CONNECTION

With the First Series of the BAFSVs safely in place in Germany, Austria and Italy (Trieste Free Territory) and with black-market activities diminishing, the objectives seemed to be secured and no more action seemed necessary. However, while all was quiet on the Western front, this was not the case on the Eastern front, notably Japan.

The British element of the Occupation Forces of Japan was constituted by the British Commonwealth Occupation Forces (BCOF). This force was made up of British, Australian, Indian and New Zealand troops, and the canteen services for these troops were provided by the NAAFI.

On 11 October 1946 the Ministry of Defence in Melbourne contacted the Cabinet Office with a problem that had been very familiar to the War Office only a few months earlier.

The Ministry confided the fact that black market yen manipulations had made it necessary to introduce special cash vouchers and tokens for use in the BCOF establishments without delay, in order to avoid loss of public funds occasioned by the redemption of excess yen. A very familiar story.

The problem of introducing a voucher scheme locally was threefold: first of all it appeared not to be possible to produce satisfactory vouchers locally in Japan. Secondly, the use of U.S. vouchers would involve an equivalent dollar debt, something nobody was happy with and, thirdly, to have suitable vouchers produced in Australia would take up to six months. Given the success of the BAFSV scheme in Europe the Ministry in Melbourne thought that perhaps the same vouchers might be used for the BCOF canteen services. If the Cabinet Office could agree to this suggestion then implementation of the scheme could go ahead straight away, provided that vouchers could be made available in sufficient quantities at short notice. The Australian Treasury had already been approached and had expressed its willingness to accept the BAFSVs either in sterling or in Australian face values. Should the latter be chosen then the BAFSVs would have to be overprinted with 'BCOF' to reflect the difference in value. A £1 voucher would be the equivalent of 25 Australian shillings. Having proposed this plan the Ministry of Defence in Melbourne immediately started proceedings by stating the number of notes and tokens it would need for the BCOF, which were as follows:

Table 7. Number of First Series vouchers needed in Japan

denomination	value	no. of notes
£1	£600,000	600,000
10/-	£150,000	300,000
5/-	£80,000	320,000
2/6	£25,000	200,000
1/-	£10,000	200,000
6d	£5,000	200,000
3d	£3,000	240,000
TOTAL	£873,000	2,060,000

Besides the above, a further £1,000 worth of 1d tokens and £200 worth of 1/2d tokens would be required.

The proposal was carefully considered by a number of government bodies, including the Ministry of Defence, the Foreign Office, the Chancellor of the Exchequer and the Secretary of State for the Dominions. By 30 December 1946 the Chiefs of Staff Committee had accepted the need to introduce special vouchers and tokens for use in the BCOF to stop black market yen manipulations. The War Office was asked to prepare the necessary draft paper setting out the terms and conditions.

In this draft paper, completed in January 1947, the War Office advised against the overprint with 'BCOF' on the grounds that it would be a lengthy task. It therefore recommended using BAFSVs on a sterling basis which, since the Australian Treasury had already agreed to that alternative, should pose no problems. The War Office also specified the number of vouchers that could be made available to the BCOF from stock. All denominations could be supplied in sufficient quantities except the £1 voucher. Only 250,000 of these vouchers could be supplied as compared to the 600,000 notes required. However, the difference could be supplied in 10/- vouchers.

The War Office, therefore, proposed sending the following quantities of vouchers to the Chief Paymaster of BCOF and these vouchers were to be held until the face value was reimbursed by the Australian government.

Table 8. Number of First Series vouchers sent to Japan

denomination	value	no. of notes	boxes
£1	£250,000	250,000	5
10/-	£500,000	1,000,000	20
5/-	£87,500	350,000	7
2/6	£25,000	200,000	4
1/-	£10,000	200,000	4
6d	£5,000	200,000	4
3d	£3,125	250,000	5
TOTAL	£880,625	2,450,000	49

On 10 January 1947 the Chiefs of Staff agreed with the War Office's proposals and despatched them to the Ministry of Defence in Melbourne, who acknowledged receipt and started to put the scheme into action. The basis was the same as that used for the GROs when introducing the scheme in Europe.

Meanwhile, the Ministry informed the War Office that the total estimate of losses incurred through black-market activities up to then had been approximately Yen 20,000,000 which, at the appropriate rate of exchange, would amount to £350,000, an estimate which was increased to Yen 40,000,000 or £700,000 on 30 April 1947.

As far as tokens were concerned, the War Office indicated that the UK tokens could not be supplied because they were in very short supply and difficulties in production were anticipated. It suggested therefore that the Australian Government or the Canteen Board had their own tokens made.

In view of this, and anxious to get the scheme into place quickly, the Ministry of Defence in Melbourne decided that, instead of making special tokens, it would use Australian pennies and halfpennies as tokens and their values would be rated as sterling to comply with the BAFSVs. The coins used as tokens were the Australian copper coins which were mostly of one type with the King's head (King George VI) on the face and a kangaroo on the back together with the word 'Australia'. Another type used had the head of King George V on the face and the words 'Commonwealth of Australia' on the back. In total the following numbers of coins were involved:

Pennies	240,000	value	£1,000
Halfpennies	96,000	value	£200

Figure 19. Australian 1/2 d copper coins used as 1/2 d (sterling) tokens

Figure 20. Australian 1d copper coins used as 1d (sterling) tokens

As far as delivery of the vouchers was concerned, there was the ri-t-ual dance about payment before they could be shipped. The Australians refused to pay for the vouchers in sterling, however. According to them it would be unfair if they had to pay for vouchers which were to be used by a force of which they were only a part. After lengthy arguments the War Office, pressed for time, finally decided to finance the BAFSVs itself, (a decision it would come to regret some years later) and shipment could finally go ahead. The vouchers were shipped by a special York aircraft leaving the RAF base at Lynham in Wiltshire at 07.00 hours on 6 March 1947, to arrive at Heneda Airfield (Japan) at 03.15 hours on 14 March 1947. The boxes were marked FC B Z35071(1-49) and it took two three-ton lorries to transport the boxes to Lynham.

During the preparations for introducing vouchers in Japan, the question of the warning time to be given to the troops came up again. It is very interesting to note that the War Office urged the BCOF to keep this warning time to an absolute minimum as introduction in Germany had shown that, during the warning period, balances of illicit currency had accumulated rapidly in the hands of the Paymasters. The BCOF therefore decided to reduce the amount that could be converted upon introduction, to an amount equal to the withdrawal of pay in the last month only, as compared to the two months' pay granted to the troops in Europe.

As all the necessary vouchers and tokens were already available to the BCOF, it was decided to introduce the BAFSVs in Japan on 6 May 1947 and all necessary steps were subsequently taken to publish local Force Routine Orders (FROs) governing the application of the scheme. These FROs were based on the text of those used for the European scheme (Appendix F). A new Royal Warrant still had to be issued, however, and this was published on 6 May 1947.

Although it was possible for the British government to declare that the BAFSVs were the only means of exchange for goods and services within the BCOF, they had no legal power to prohibit the local population from holding BAFSVs. To prevent black market dealings in the vouchers themselves, however, it would be necessary to have the authority to confiscate vouchers held by the local population, and the cooperation of the Japanese government would be needed on this point. So, on 5 May 1947, the Central Liaison Office in

Tokyo contacted the Imperial Japanese Government with a request to enact all necessary legislation to make the possession by the local populace of BAFSVs, as well as Australian 1/2 d and 1d coins, unlawful after 6 May 1947. The Central Liaison Office asked for legislation allowing for the confiscation of the BAFSVs and the coins, as well as for the power to apply punitive measures. In order to enable them to do this, the Japanese government was given a specification of the BAFSVs concerned, as well as a description of the Australian coins that were going to be used. It was probably because of the great hurry that everybody missed the fact that the 6d BAFSV was not included in the specification given to the Japanese Government and, as a result, was not included in the legislation!

The Imperial Japanese Government duly complied with the request and the introduction of BAFSVs in Japan proceeded according to plan on 6 May 1947.

THE NAAFI OVERPRINT VOUCHERS

The most mysterious vouchers in the BAFSV First Series are those that carry the overprint 'ISSUED IN H.M. SHIPS AFLOAT FOR USE IN NAAFI CANTEENS ONLY'. Only a very small number of these notes were produced for exclusive use by a British Naval unit called 'Force T'. This unit was not, at the time, part of the BCOF and as the BAFSVs were introduced to the BCOF troops, the marines serving in 'Force T' would therefore not normally have been supplied with these vouchers. A special request was therefore made to supply these troops with vouchers so that they would be able to use the canteen services when on shore. It was considered necessary, however, to mark these vouchers in such a way that they could be easily distinguished from the regular issue in order to ensure that they could only be changed back for currency by the *Navy* Paymaster. On 7 May 1947 the Chiefs of Staff requested the Commander-in-Chief of the Naval component of BCOF to prepare a small number of vouchers with the necessary overprint and to make them available to 'Force T'. After a local Japanese printer had overprinted these vouchers with the relevant text, these were duly issued to 'Force T'.

Figure 21. The NAAFI overprint on a 1/- voucher for use by 'Force T' marines

THE SECOND SERIES - OPERATION VISTA

DESIGN AND PRODUCTION OF THE SECOND SERIES VOUCHERS

Although the scheme went smoothly enough it was very soon clear that black market practises were not easy to eradicate. The ingenuity of the British troops and of the local population was such that the War Office had already decided at the beginning of 1947 that it would be necessary to take action. A suggestion by the Treasury to substitute BMA notes, of which large numbers were still in stock for BAFSVs, was not received favourably by the War Office and in March 1947 it was decided to replace the BAFSVs with a totally new Series. The purpose of such a move would be to make it possible to 'demonetise' all holdings of BAFSVs by unauthorised personnel. These plans to replace the old issue were, therefore, of the utmost secrecy and the whole operation was given the code-name VISTA. It was decided quite early on that any replacement would only involve the paper vouchers. The tokens issued with the First Series would therefore remain unaffected. This left the War Office with the task of printing another substantial quantity of notes to replace the First Issue.

THE DESIGN OF THE SECOND SERIES

As before, the time available to design and produce the necessary notes was very limited. The printer therefore used the same basic layout when designing the Second Series notes as for the First Series. The size of the notes was also the same so that only the colour scheme and the actual scroll work were to be changed. On the advice of S. B. Chamberlain the General Works Manager of the

Bank of England (St.Luke's) Printing Works[1], a Series denominator was incorporated and the words *Second Series* were added to the notes to avoid confusion in the field.

The prefixes for the Second Series notes were changed from a single to a double prefix-letter, following the pattern of the First Series. Thus the £1, 10/-, 5/- and 2/6 note were given the prefixes AA/x, BB/x, CC/x and DD/x respectively where x was determined by the total number of notes, in millions, that were printed of that denomination. As with the First Series, the lower denominations were not numbered.

By 27 June 1947 all the new designs had been approved by the War Office and the printing was well on the way.

THE PAPER FOR THE SECOND SERIES

The paper needed for the Second Series BAFSVs turned out to be more difficult to obtain than was at first anticipated. One of the requirements was that the paper should contain a metal strip so as to comply with the original request by the War Office for additional security. The only manufacturer capable of making this paper at the time, Portals, advised the printer that it could not produce the required quantities in the given time. It was not until the Bank had exacted considerable pressure that Portals agreed to make the paper as required by De La Rue. It asked for as long a time as possible, however, and was therefore given the go-ahead to make the paper on 25 March 1947, a week before De La Rue was given the order to print.

THE PRINTING OF THE SECOND SERIES

As soon as the designs had been approved by the War Office the printing of the various denominations was started. It took approximately 12 to 14 weeks to engrave and print each of the vouchers and it took about 5 months to complete the whole order and, finally, on 5 September 1947 the whole shipment of 800 boxes, each containing

[1] S.B. Chamberlain was the inventor of the metal thread in the banknote paper of the Bank of England

50,000 notes, was received by the Bank of England and stored in its vaults. These notes were stored in vault B6, together with 24 boxes of BAFSVs which were received from Messrs John Waddington[2] in Leeds on 12 November 1947. These 24 boxes could have been those containing the First Series good-overs, which may suggest that Waddingtons had been involved in the printing of the First Series BAFSVs.

Table 9. First print run of Second Series (metal thread)

denomination	last prefix	no. of notes	value
3d	not used	9,600,000	£120,000
6d	not used	6,400,000	£160,000
1/-	not used	6,400,000	£320,000
2/6	DD/5	4,800,000	£600,000
5/-	CC/5	4,800,000	£1,200,000
10/-	BB/5	4,800,000	£2,400,000
£1	AA/4	3,200,000	£3,200,000
TOTAL		40,000,000	£8,000,000

The reason why fewer notes seemed necessary than for the initial First Series vouchers was that the total number of British troops in the occupied areas was decreasing. Also, it was now possible to assess the requirements of the various denominations more accurately in the light of the experience gained by the actual use of the First Series vouchers.

[2] Waddington was a security printer which sometimes contracted work from the Bank and De La Rue, as for example with the (unissued) Bank of England 2s/6d notes (Pick, 6th Edition, Great Britain number 121) printed by Waddington in November 1940. .

While De La Rue was already busy printing the notes the War Office received the quotation for the work. The costs for printing the notes would be:

Table 10. Quoted printing costs of Second Series per 1,000 vouchers

denomination	costs per 1,000 vouchers
3d, 6d and 1/-	15/-
2/6 and 5/-	21/3d
10/- and £1	29/6d

Based on this quote, the following actual costs for the first print run of the Second Series can be established:

Table 11. Total printing costs of Second Series (first print run)

denomination	total price
3d	£7,200
6d	£4,800
1/-	£4,800
2/6	£5,100
5/-	£5,100
10/-	£7,080
£1	£4,720
TOTAL PRINTING COST	£38,800

This was more expensive than the cost of the First Series vouchers although fewer were involved. The reason for this increase was that the cost of wages and materials had gone up in the meantime, as well as the fact that all of the notes were now printed on threaded paper. Also, as we have seen, the First Series did not include paper charges for several denominations.

THE PACKAGING OF THE SECOND SERIES

Once the vouchers had been printed they were packed in bundles of 1,000 notes each. Each bundle had a piece of cardboard on the top and bottom which were strung together in such a way that it would be impossible to open the bundle without cutting the string. This string was then sealed with a wax seal bearing the printer's inititals 'TdlR' (see Figure 22)

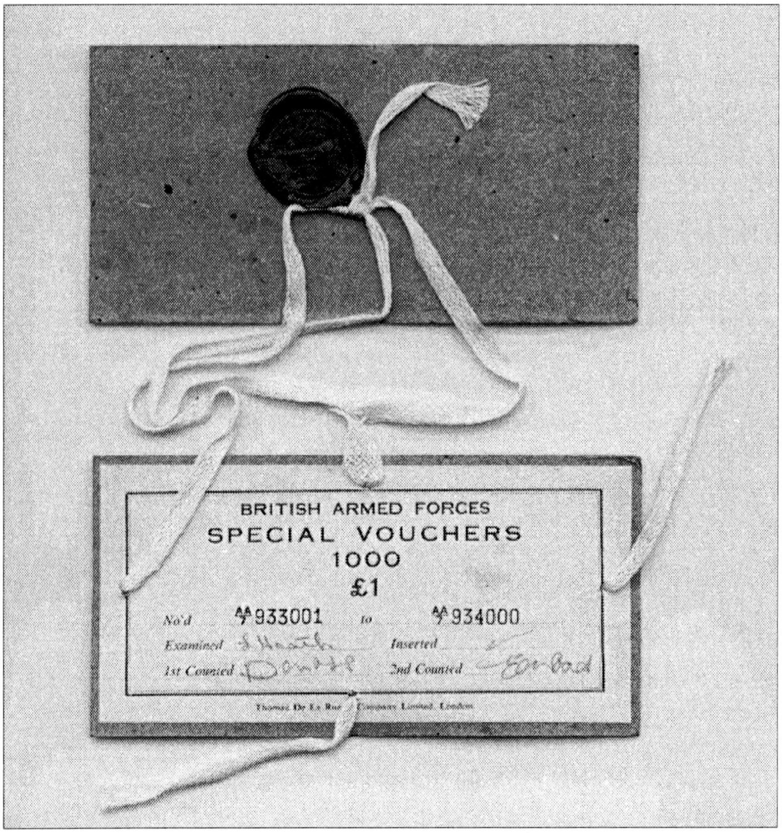

Figure 22. Top cover and wax seal of TdlR bundle of vouchers

On the top piece of cardboard the serial numbers of the notes in the bundle were recorded, as well as the denomination, the number of notes, the Series and the signatures of the officers responsible for packing and checking that particular bundle (see figure 22). The bundles were then stacked, 50 bundles to a box, in wooden boxes lined with heavy tin sheeting. Each box carried a label stating the contents. (see Figure 23)

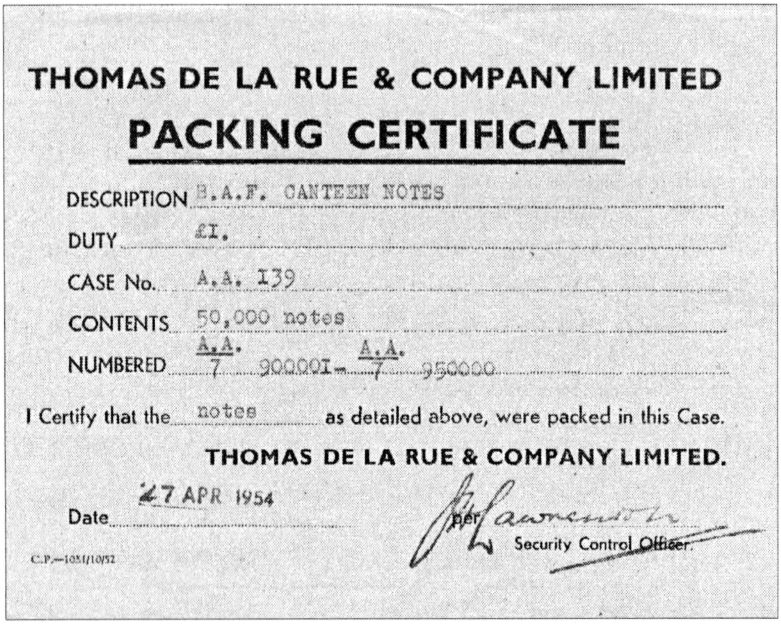

THOMAS DE LA RUE & COMPANY LIMITED

PACKING CERTIFICATE

DESCRIPTION B.A.F. CANTEEN NOTES

DUTY £1.

CASE No. A.A. 139

CONTENTS 50,000 notes

NUMBERED A.A./7 900001 – A.A./7 950000

I Certify that the notes as detailed above, were packed in this Case.

THOMAS DE LA RUE & COMPANY LIMITED.

Date 27 APR 1954

per Security Control Officer.

C.P.—1031/10/52

Figure 23. Packing label Second Series £1 vouchers (second print run) 27 April 1954

Between 1948 and 1958 De La Rue printed at least one more batch of the Second Series notes to replace notes that were taken out of circulation during that period, due to normal wear and tear. As before, these notes were printed on paper containing the metal security strip and there is nothing to distinguish the notes in this batch from the first print run of the Second Series notes, except for the numbering on the four highest values. Since we know where the first print run numbers stopped, we know that any note with a higher number printed on metal strip paper must be from this second print run.

INTRODUCTION OF THE SECOND SERIES

TRANSPORT OF THE SECOND SERIES VOUCHERS

On 8 December 1947 the headquarters, among others, of the British Army of the Rhine was notified by the War Office that conversion of the old BAFSVs into new ones would be unavoidable and was given instructions that everything should be prepared to make conversion possible at a moment's notice, although no firm date was yet given. Meanwhile, the War Office had gone ahead with arrangements to despatch large numbers of the new notes, which were already in storage, to Germany, Austria and Italy.

The HQs of the various armies were notified that, on 11 December 1947, the new notes had been shipped. Guarded by an armed escort of three officers and six other ranks, three railway vans full of vouchers were shipped from Harwich to Zeebrugge during the night of 12 December on the ferry *The Essex*. The vouchers were transported from the Bank of England to Harwich and on the way, one of the vans broke down at Mistley, Essex and had to be towed to the ferry terminus. The three officers escorting the shipment were Captain J.S. Chunchill R.A., Lieutenant K.H. Gill R.A. and Lieutenant T.H. Kelly R.A.. Their job was to accompany the shipment of notes to the various destinations and signal their safe arrival.

GERMANY (BAOR)

The shipment destined for Germany (Hamburg) was under the control of Captain Chunchill and consisted of 294 boxes, each containing 50,000 notes. The total value of this shipment was £3,000,000 and this sum was broken down as follows:

Table 12. Second Series vouchers destined for Hamburg, Germany

denomination.	no. of boxes	box numbers	no. of vouchers
£1	28	AA/1 - AA/28	1,400,000
10/-	34	BB/1 - BB34	1,700,000
5/-	20	CC/1 - CC/20	1,000,000
2/6	42	DD/1 - DD/42	2,100,000
1/-	50	EE/1 - EE/50	2,500,000
6d	60	FF/1 - FF/60	3,000,000
3d	60	GG/1- GG/60	3,000,000
TOTAL	294		14,700,000

The identification details of the vouchers in this Hamburg consignment were:

Table 13. Identification details Second Series Hamburg vouchers

denomination	box numbers	prefix	serial numbers
£1	AA/1-AA/20	AA/1	000001-1000000
	AA/21-AA28	AA/2	000001- 400000
10/-	BB/1-BB/20	BB/1	000001-1000000
	BB/21-BB/34	BB/2	000001 - 700000
5/-	CC/1-CC/20	CC/1	000001-1000000
2/6	DD/1-DD/20	DD/1	000001-1000000
	DD/21-DD/40	DD/2	000001-1000000
	DD/41-DD/42	DD/3	000001- 100000

This shipment reached Hamburg on 16 December 1947. Upon receipt the BAOR felt that the sterling value of £3 million might, after all, prove insufficient to cope with the demand during the early phases of the operation, and an additional £1 million was requested to be shipped by air. Although there is no information with regard to the number of boxes or their contents, we do know that this additional shipment arrived by air between 30 December and 2 January 1948. Assuming that the same breakdown was used, this consignment should have contained about 100 boxes running to another 5,000,000 vouchers. Actually only about 66 boxes can have been involved in this shipment. On 16 July 1948 the Bank of England still held 266 boxes of Second Series vouchers out of the original 800. This means that by that date a total of 534 boxes had been shipped to the various arenas. In total 419 boxes had already been shipped to the BAOR and, assumedly, 49 boxes to Japan for use by the BCOF. This leaves a balance of only 66 additional boxes containing 3,300,000 vouchers which can have been sent to Hamburg by air. This in turn means that this extra consignment must have been mainly made up of high denomination vouchers.

AUSTRIA (BTA)

Another part of the shipment, bound for HQ British Troops in Austria in Klagenfurt, Austria was under the control of Lieutenant Gill and consisted of 95 boxes of 50,000 vouchers each. The total value was £1,315,625 broken down as follows:

Table 14. Second Series vouchers destined for Klagenfurt, Austria

denomination	no. of boxes	box numbers	no. of vouchers
£1	14	AA/29 - AA/42	700,000
10/-	14	BB/35 - BB/48	700,000
5/-	10	CC/21 - CC/30	500,000
2/6	12	DD/43 - DD/54	600,000
1/-	15	EE/51 - EE/65	750,000
6d	15	FF/61 - FF/75	750,000
3d	15	GG/61- GG/75	750,000
TOTAL	95		4,750,000

The identification details of the vouchers in this Klagenfurt consignment were:

Table 15. Identification details Second Series Klagenfurt vouchers

denomination	box numbers	prefix	serial numbers
£1	AA/29-AA/40	AA/2	400001-1000000
	AA/41-AA/42	AA/3	000001- 100000
10/-	BB/35-BB/40	BB/2	700001-1000000
	BB/41-BB/48	BB/3	000001- 400000
5/-	CC/21-CC/30	CC/2	000001- 500000
2/6	DD/45-DD/54	DD/3	100001- 700000

TRIESTE (BETFOR)

The third part of the consignment was heading for Trieste, Italy, under the control of Lieutenant Kelly[3]. The Trieste consignment had a total value of £384,375 and consisted of 30 boxes, again containing 50,000 notes per box broken down as follows:

Table 16. Second Series vouchers destined for Trieste, Italy

denomination	no. of boxes	box numbers	no. of vouchers
£1	4	AA/43 - AA/46	200,000
10/-	4	BB/49 - BB/52	200,000
5/-	3	CC/31 - CC/33	150,000
2/6	4	DD/55 - DD/58	200,000
1/-	5	EE/66 - EE/70	250,000
6d	5	FF/76 - FF/80	250,000
3d	5	GG/76- GG/80	250,000
TOTAL	30		1,500,000

[2] Trieste was the capital of the free Territory of Trieste, in the north-east of Italy. See Appendix J for further background information.

[3] There is some indication that Lieutenants Gill and Kelly accompanied both the Klagenfurt and the Trieste shipments together.

The identification details of the vouchers in the consignment bound for Italy (Trieste) were:

Table 17. Identification details Second Series Trieste vouchers

denomination	box numbers	prefix	serial numbers
£1	AA/43-AA/46	AA/3	100001 - 300000
10/-	BB/49-BB/52	BB/3	400001 - 600000
5/-	CC/31-CC/33	CC/2	500001 - 650000
2/6	DD/55-DD/58	DD/3	100001 - 900000

INTRODUCTION OF THE SECOND SERIES

C-DAY: 6 JANUARY 1948

In the second half of December 1947 the War Office had decided that the date on which the conversion was to take place would be 4 January 1948. On that date all the BAFSVs of the first issue would be demonetised. For reasons unknown, however, this date was later moved to 6 January 1948. On 28 December all Army cashiers were duly briefed and issued with bulk supplies of the new issue. Sealed orders, containing instructions on how to carry out the various types of exchanges, were issued to the Commanding officers, not to be opened before 00.01 hours on 6 January 1948. The orders also drew attention to the British Forces Network broadcasts to be made throughout the day. There is every indication that a high degree of security was maintained and that the British Forces Network announcement would have come as a great surprise had it not been for a U.S. Finance Officer of the European Command at Frankfurt who, without authority and despite the top secret status of which he was fully aware, had divulged the information to the local Forces Radio. On the afternoon of 5 January the information was broadcast and it was consequently relayed by the American Forces Network at 21.00 hours that same day.

U.S. 'LEAK' RUINS NEW MONEY PLAN

An American "leak" robbed currency reorganisation in Bizonia[4] of any real success in catching out black marketeers.

Following large-scale illegal trading in B.A.F.S.V.s (Army currency) it had been decided to call in the existing vouchers and replace them with a new issue as from midnight on Monday night.

But an American official in Frankfurt - who had been officially notified of the impend-ing change by the British - passed on this highly confidential information to a U.S. news agency.

Result was that Hamburg "spivs" were able to get rid of their vast hoard of the old currency at current black market prices, which were ten times as high as the official rate.

Otherwise the transfer was effected smoothly with Army pay offices working overtime to deal with the huge queues which formed.

Figure 24. Article form the Daily Worker 7 January 1948

Although the official reports state that not much material harm was done and that the operation could be considered a success the result was that Hamburg 'spivs' were able to dispose of large quantities of the old BAFSVs at current black market prices ranging from 400 to 500 Reichsmark per £1 BAFSV against an official rate of 40 marks to the pound.

Nevertheless, the operation went ahead fairly smoothly and the whole conversion process was virtually completed by 12.00 hours on 6 January 1948. In total about 100,000 troops and 20,000 civilians were affected by this conversion.

DISPOSAL OF THE OBSOLETE FIRST SERIES BAFSVS

Special measures were taken to collect all the old BAFSVs following conversion to the new, and the assumption was that collection would be completed by 20 January. Due to a number of problems,

[4] Bizonia was the name given to the area in Germany occupied jointly by Great Britain and the US. This area encompassed Schleswig-Holstein, Hamburg, Niedersachsen, Süd Baden, Hessen and Bremen. For a map of this area see Appendix J.

however, of which the largest was the fact that a great number of BAFSVs were in the hands of troops on leave and could only be collected when they were back at their base, the War Office allocated more time to the collection of old notes. On 31 March 1948 the collection was considered to be complete and the old BAFSVs were sent to the Issue Office of the Bank of England in Britain to be pulped.

SECOND SERIES VOUCHERS IN JAPAN

In order to prevent any global trade of First Series BAFSVs the notes that had been in circulation in Japan since 6 May 1947 also had to be converted into notes of the Second Series. Melbourne was first notified of this conversion on 30 December 1947 and, since all arrangements still had to be made, the conversion date for Japan did not align with the European date. We do not know how shipment of the new notes to Japan took place nor what quantities or values were involved but, given the short time span that had passed since the original introduction in Japan, these were probably very much in line with the first issue. Melbourne was given the choice of having the old vouchers returned to Australia to be pulped or having them destroyed locally. We do not know what the outcome of that decision was, but it is likely that they were destroyed locally in view of the high cost of transporting them back to England.

SECOND SERIES VOUCHERS IN SINGAPORE

When the British forces landed in Singapore in August 1945, they faced many of the same tasks as those in Germany and Austria. A large number of Japanese troops had to be disarmed and repatriated and much of the infrastructure on the peninsula had to be rebuilt.

This relatively peaceful period came to an end in 1948 with the Malayan Emergency when 'The People's Anti-British Army' started to carry out acts of intimidation and even went so far as to murder the workers at the plantations and the tin mines. This emergency came to an end in January 1949 in Singapore itself but lasted considerably longer in Malaya where it kept the British Army busy until July 1960. One of the results of this was that the base at Singapore was considerably extended in a slow but steady buildup.

In December 1962 the base became involved once more in jungle warfare when the Brunei Rebellion broke out. This rebellion was later to grow into the Borneo Operation. During this operation vouchers of the Second Series appear to have been used in the area. We do not know how many vouchers were shipped to Singapore for this purpose or when, but we do know that on 11 April 1967, after the hostilities had ended in 1966, a total of 41 boxes of Second Series vouchers were shipped back to Britain. This consignment held 28 unopened boxes of an unknown value and 13 boxes containing mixed denominations with a value of £301,000.

On 11 April 1961, 3 boxes of British Armed Forces Tokens were shipped to Singapore by air, presumably to be used in conjunction with the Second Series vouchers. Whether they were actually used is not clear, but it appears that these tokens were shipped back to Britain in 1967 also.

SECRET MARKS ON SECOND SERIES VOUCHERS

On 8 January 1948 the Bank of England sent five specimen sets of the Second Series notes, indicating the secret printer's marks, to Trevaldwyn. As with the First Series, these marks were indicated on proper specimen notes, this time marked as such and with the serial number 000000, preceded by the double-prefix letters over a number indicating the million last printed for that print run. In contrast with the First Series vouchers, the secret marks were now indicated by writing a description of them in the margin of the vouchers by hand. In the Second Series the secret marks were inserted not only on the face of the notes but also on the back. Instead of secret marks per group of notes, as with the First Series, this time every single note had its own different secret marks. Two of the sets were sent on to the HQ of the British Army of the Rhine, one set was sent to the British Territorial Army HQ, at Salisbury (UK) and two sets were retained in the War Office files. The secret marks on the Second Series can be described as follows:

Figure 25. Second Series 3d voucher used to indicate secret marks

GROUP 1 *3d, 6d and 1/-*

3d face:

- on the top left hand side a curly line, present on the right, has been omitted in the artwork just under the box containing the denominationon
- at the bottom right a very small line has been omitted on the outside just above the box containing the denomination

3d back:

- on the far left in the centre of the note a small line has been omitted in the filling scroll work just under the acanthus leaf

6d face:

- in the left bottom corner the shading is omitted from the berry in the centre of the bundle of leaves projecting from the box containing the denomination
- a small line is omitted just on the left hand top corner of the box containing the denomination on the right hand bottom corner of the note

6d back:

- the berry on the far left in the top bar of the note contains only one line of shading instead of two. The berry is next to the box on the left containing the denomination

1/- face:

- a very small vertical, dangling, line in the artwork just above the 'B' for British is missing
- a very small horizontal line is missing in the artwork just above the right hand top corner of the box containing the denomination in the right hand bottom corner of the note

1/- back:

- on the left hand side of the box containing the text, the centre of the loop is missing

GROUP 2 *2/6 and 5/-*

2/6 face:

- there is a break in one of the lines of the motif underneath the '2' of the series denominator
- there is a break in the horizontal line inside the right hand horizontal edge underneath the denomination panel on the bottom right

2/6 back:

- the centre of the diamond shape is omitted inside the scroll work left of the box containing the text

5/- face:

- a vertical line is omitted in the right top corner of the frame surrounding the text 'BRITISH ARMED FORCES'
- a small circle is omitted in one of the border elements to the left of the large figure '5' on the left

5/- back:

- the centre of the diamond on the top left hand of the design has been omitted

GROUP 3 *10/- and £1*

10/- face:
- the inside curve of the small left hand curl on top of the box containing the prefix and serial number in the lower left corner is broken
- a small horizontal line is omitted in the decoration inside the right hand border design just above the left top corner of the lower right hand denomination panel

10/- back:
- a small dot has been omitted in the lower part of the frame surrounding the left hand text 'TEN SHILLINGS'

£1 face:
- there is a break in the small horizontal line inside the left bottom frame surrounding the box containing the prefix and serial number in the lower left corner
- the shading in the (tiny) left hand berry on top of the design just underneath the downstroke of the 'N' in 'POUND' has been omitted

£1 back:
- there is a break in one of the horizontal lines directly underneath the bottom of the frame surrounding the top left text 'ONE POUND'

Figure 26. Secret marks on 3d Second Series with metal thread - face

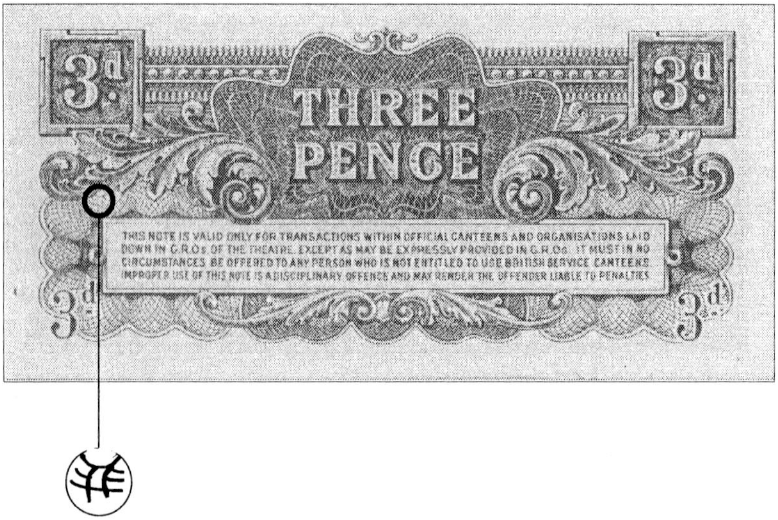

Figure 27. Secret marks on 3d Second Series with metal thread - back

Figure 28. Secret marks on 6d Second Series with metal thread - face

Figure 29. Secret marks on 6d Second Series with metal thread - back

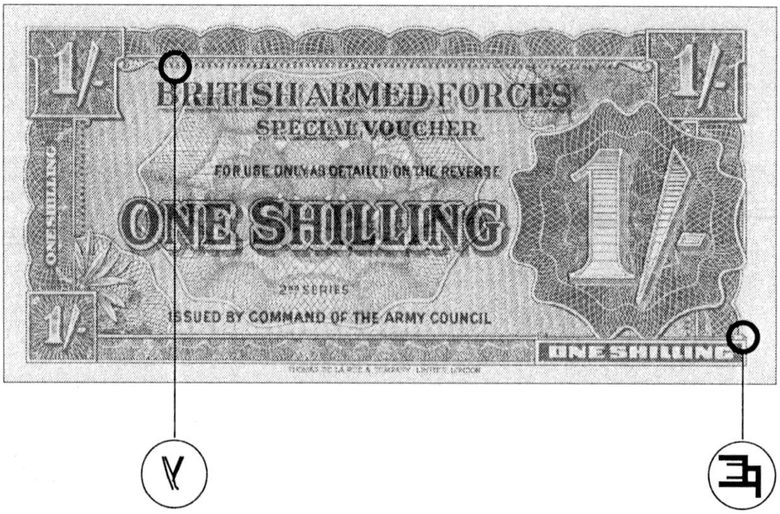

Figure 30. Secret marks on 1/- Second Series with metal thread - face

Figure 31. Secret marks on 1/- Second Series with metal thread - back

Figure 32. Secret marks on 2/6 Second Series with metal thread - face

Figure 33. Secret marks on 2/6 Second Series with metal thread - back

Figure 34. Secret marks on 5/- Second Series with metal thread - face

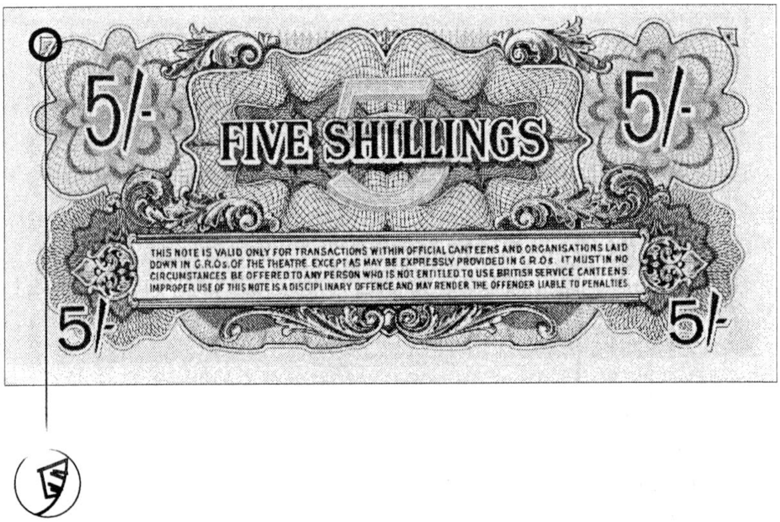

Figure 35. Secret marks on 5/- Second Series with metal thread - back

Figure 36. Secret marks on 10/- Second Series with metal thread - face

Figure 37. Secret marks on 10/- Second Series with metal thread - back

Figure 38. Secret marks on £1 Second Series with metal thread · face

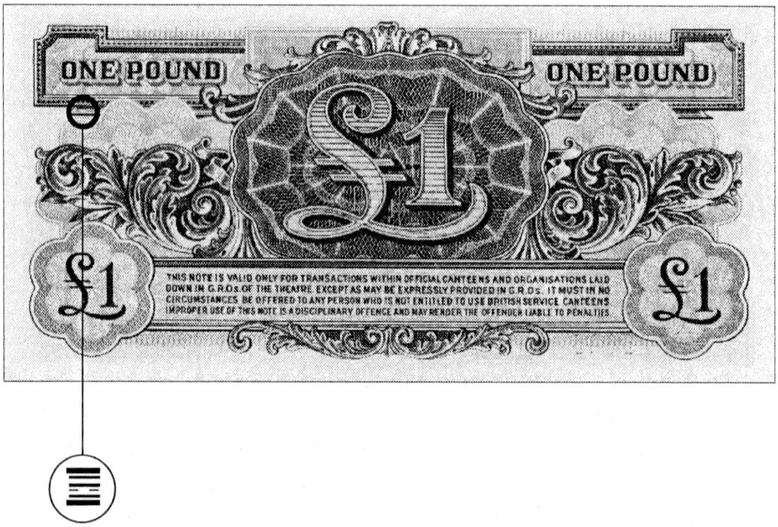

Figure 39. Secret marks on £1 Second Series with metal thread · back

SECOND SERIES VOUCHERS ON WATERMARKED PAPER

In 1958 the War Office came into action again on the Second Series BAFSVs front. It was then that the £5 note on watermarked paper was added to the Second Series which was still in circulation. On 15 October 1961 the War Office received, again via the Bank of England, five sets of black pulls of the face and back of the £5 note again showing the secret marks.

At the same time, the other denominations (except for the £1 note) were replaced by Second Series vouchers printed on watermarked paper instead of on paper with the metal thread which had been used up to that time in the Second Series.

The £5 note was, of necessity, of a completely new design, and the numbering was kept broadly in line with the rest of the Second Series. In order to be exactly in line with the prefix system the £5 note should have had the AA prefix denoting the highest value, but because the AA prefix had already been used for the Second Series £1 note, the £5 note was given the prefix EE. Since no £5 vouchers have been reported with a prefix higher than EE/1 we may safely assume that not more than 1,000,000 of those were printed in all, although we do not know the exact date of printing.

The watermarked 5/- voucher of the Second Series has often been taken to be just a reprint of the old voucher but on watermarked paper instead of on metal thread paper. However, this note was either newly engraved or the old engraving had been altered, because the secret marks used on the 'old' Second Series 5/- voucher differ from those on the watermarked 5/- note in that Series. The difference was also visible in a new prefix. Whereas the old 5/- voucher had the prefix CC the new one was given the prefix CD. Here, the maximum print run seems to have been no more than 2,000,000 as no prefix higher than CD/2 has been reported.

One of the reasons for introducing these two new notes was the withdrawal of all BAFSVs from all areas on 1 November 1959, except from the West Berlin arena, where Second Series Vouchers remained in use until the introduction of the Sixth Series in 1972, necessitated by the decimalisation of British currency.

Although the 5/- voucher with metal thread was still in stock in August 1960 it was not in circulation at that time and appears to have been withdrawn between November 1959 and August 1960. The reason for this is not clear, but the fact that a new 5/- was commissioned and printed at about the same time might indicate that some form of emergency was encountered, forcing the Army to change this denomination to a watermarked variety with a clearly different prefix. This may also explain why the other denominations were changed to a watermarked variety. The emergency may even have been serious enough to be the real reason behind the commissioning of the Fourth as well as a Fifth Series in 1961. (see The Fourth Series.)

PAPER USED FOR THE SECOND SERIES WATERMARKED VOUCHERS

The reprints and the additional vouchers of the Second Series were printed on paper with a simple watermark. This mark consisted of horizontal bands of wavy lines connected by vertical lines.

PACKAGING OF THE SECOND SERIES WATERMARKED VOUCHERS

As the additions and watermarked replacements to the Second Series were once again printed by Thomas De La Rue, the packaging remained very much the same as it had been for the previous vouchers. Packaging was still in bundles of 1,000 notes, tied together with string with cardboard on both the top and bottom and with a wax seal with the TdlR initials. There were still 50 bundles to a wooden box making 50,000 notes per box.

STORAGE OF THE SECOND SERIES

Originally all Second Series notes (800 boxes) had been transferred from De La Rue directly to the Bank of England where they arrived on 5 September 1947. Also stored at the Bank of England were 24 boxes of what must have been First Series BAFSVs and which may possibly have been the good-overs described earlier. By 6 July 1948 a total of 268 boxes were still kept at the Issue Office of the Bank of England.

A little later on the Issue Office apparently received a request to store an unknown number of boxes of First Series BAFSVs which had been returned from the BAOR in Germany. As we know, these were the notes returned to be pulped. At this time the Issue Office was already unhappy about storing all the Second Series notes, which it felt were '*...taking up valuable vault space...*' and was certainly not prepared to take the First Series vouchers as well, as it (the Issue Office) '*....might be faced with another destruction job...*'.

So, with the Third Series vouchers already being printed and shortly to require storage at the Bank, the situation became a rather uneasy one for the War Office. For this reason they asked Wagstaff to do his utmost either to change the Bank's attitude toward storing the vouchers or to find alternative storage facilities.

Wagstaff apparently felt that the second option would prove the easier one and a number of possible locations were inspected, among which were a hotel, and Thames House. For the latter location plans were even drawn up to adapt the building in order to accommodate the storage of the vouchers. All these options were either too lengthy a task or too expensive, however, and in November 1948 plans were made to store all the vouchers, including the Third Series which had meanwhile been printed, in the vaults of the Bank Deutsche Länder in Germany. But this option was felt to be unsound because, if the voucher were ever to be stolen, they would be available at the only place they could be used.

Having explored every avenue to try and store the vouchers elsewhere it was finally decided to store the vouchers in the basement of Lansdowne House in Berkeley Square. This was a Ministry of Defence building and the seat of the War Office in the centre of London. Wagstaff could now go back to the Bank of England to ask for their assistance only until the new storage capacity had been freed and made suitable for storing the vouchers. Given the urgency of the situation, the Bank decided to help out once more and agreed to store the boxes, but this time not before the War Office had promised to have the alternative accommodation ready by September of 1948. Apparently all went according to plan and in September 1948 all the vouchers stored at the Bank were transported to their new housing.

As far as Second Series vouchers were concerned 268 boxes of vouchers were taken to Lansdowne House containing the vouchers shown in Table 18.

Table 18. Second Series vouchers in storage at the Bank of England in September 1949

denomination	no. of boxes	box numbers	no. of vouchers
£1	2	AA 66-67	100,000
10/-	30	BB 69-98	1,500,000
5/-	58	CC 44-101	2,900,000
2/6	25	DD 77-101	1,250,000
1/-	41	EE 93-133	2,050,000
6d	25	FF 108-132	1,250,000
3d	87	GG 106-192	4,350,000
TOTAL	268		13,400,000

From 1950 onwards, Second Series vouchers were distributed to the BAOR and to Singapore from Lansdowne House and, by 20 November 1969, during a surprise stock-taking, a total value of £3,498,500 was found to be still in storage, broken down as follows:

Table 19. Second Series vouchers still in storage on 20 November 1969

denomination	no. of boxes	no. of vouchers	value
£5	5	250,000	£1,250,000
£1	24	1,180,000	£1,180,000
£10/-	10	500,000	£250,000
5/-	18	900,000	£225,000
2/6	24	1,200,000	£150,000
1/-	32	1,600,000	£80,000
6d	33	1,625,000	£40,625
3d	35	1,750,000	£21,875
mixed (ex-Singapore)	13	650,000	£301,000
TOTAL	194	9,655,000	£3,498,500

These tables show that, in just over 20 years, a total of at least 4,000,000 Second Series vouchers had been used, but this does not include the extra Second Series vouchers printed in the additional print runs both on paper with metal strips and on watermarked paper. Also, in November 1948, the BAOR still had a stock of 199 boxes of vouchers which, presumably, was also used during this twenty-year period.

During the stock-taking it further transpired that, over a period of nearly two years from 19 December 1967 to 20 December 1969 a total of 650,000 vouchers with a total value of £106,875 had been shipped to the only area still using the vouchers of the Second Series, West Berlin, Germany.

Table 20. Second Series vouchers shipped to Germany during 1968 and 1969

denomination	no. of boxes	no. of vouchers	value
£1	1	50,000	£50,000
10/-	1	50,000	£25,000
5/-	1	50,000	£12,500
2/6	1	50,000	£6,250
1/-	3	150,000	£7,500
6d	3	150,000	£3,750
3d	3	150,000	£1,875
TOTAL	13	650,000	£106,875

This gives us a clear indication of the relatively small number of vouchers used in the Berlin area during the later years of the BAOR.

Figure 40. Secret marks on £5 Second Series with watermark - face

Figure 41. Secret marks on £5 Second Series with watermark - back

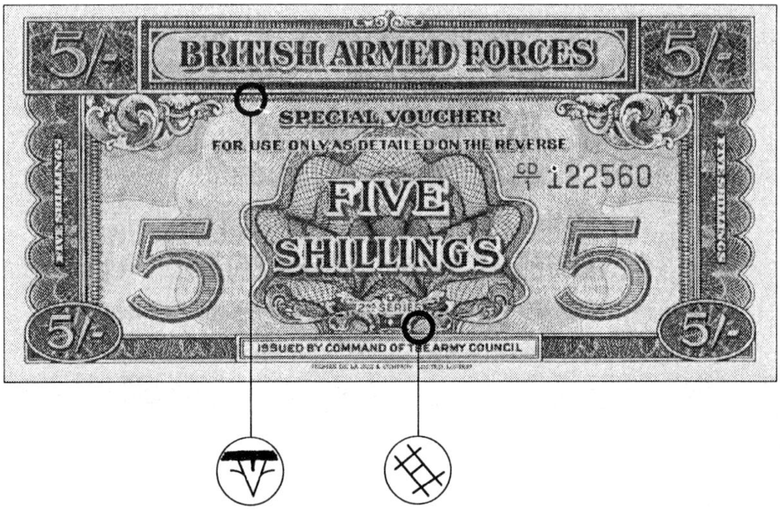

Figure 42. Secret marks on new issue 5/- Second Series with watermark - face

Figure 43. Secret marks on new issue 5/- Second Series with watermark - back

THE THIRD SERIES

As soon as the Second Series had been placed in circulation, the War Office, once again left without a reserve Series and worried in case there might suddenly be a need for one, asked the Bank to intervene once again with De La Rue on its behalf. The request was for the production of a Third Series, different in design and colour from the First and Second Series and marked with the words 'Third Series'. On 10 March 1948 the printer replied that it was becoming rather difficult to comply with the request for increasingly complex colour schemes. So far they had produced 14 different colour schemes and they found it progressively difficult to come up with colours which did not cause some sort of confusion with colours on the earlier vouchers. To resolve this problem De La Rue proposed a drastically new design which would get away from '*...the squiggles of one sort or another...*'.

The Bank, after consulting with Wagstaff, was under the impression that there would be no objection to a 'Lion' and/or a 'Crown' appearing as an emblem, provided these did not resemble the B.M.A. notes and advised the printer accordingly. De La Rue started the design work on a rough sketch of the £1 denomination for approval before proceeding any further. This sketch, containing a lion's head as the main feature, was sent to the Bank who passed it on to the War Office on 19 April 1948.

On 2 May 1948 the War Office replied that it liked the new design very much, '*except for the lion's head...which has not met with full approval here...*'. The War Office instructed the printer to substitute the lion's head with the combined medallion/lion's head emblem as used on the BMA notes! It further instructed the printer to keep the various denominations the same size as those of the First and Second Series.

Possibly because of the emergency caused by the Russians closing off all land and rail links to Berlin in May 1948 and the ensuing airlift. there appears to have been considerable time pressure again and the new design was only in part used on the backs of the 10/- and £1 vouchers of the Third Series.

Probably pressured by events in Berlin and/or by the Malayan operations in June 1948, the War Office decided it had to move fast and by 5 July 1948 had given orders to prepare a Third Series along the old lines. On that same date the War Office received two proofs of the £1 and the 10/- vouchers respectively of the Third Series as we know them. When sending the proofs to the War Office, the Bank of England included the suggestion that, in order to stay in line with the prefixes on the First and Second Series, the prefix-letters as in Table 21 should be used for the Third Series.

Two days later, however, the Bank wrote that it had had second thoughts about this suggestion and, as '*...second thoughts were often better..*' suggested that the prefixes instead run as shown in Table 22. The reason for these '*...second thoughts..*' was that the Bank itself apparently never used the letter F in a prefix because it could so easily be 'adapted' to an E and it decided to give the War Office the benefit of this experience. As we know, the suggestion not to use the letter F was acted on by the War Office and the prefixes for the Third Series were thus established as in Table 22.

Table 21. Suggested prefixes for Third Series vouchers

denomination	prefix
£1	E
10/-	F
5/-	G
2/6	H

Table 22. Selected prefixes for Third Series vouchers

denomination	prefix
£1	E
10/-	G
5/-	H
2/6	J

NUMBER OF THIRD SERIES VOUCHERS ORDERED

The War Office spent a lot of time working out exactly how many vouchers would be needed in case of an emergency. To do this it based its calculations on the number of First and Second Series vouchers actually used and the total numbers destroyed. After some complicated mathematics it was finally decided that, since £5,321,875 worth of Second Series vouchers had been used up to 27 July 1948, a similar value for the Third Series would not be far wrong.

On 9 August 1948 the War Office ordered the following number of vouchers from the printer via the Bank of England:

Table 23. Total number of Third Series vouchers ordered initially

denomination	value	no. of boxes	no. of vouchers
£1	£2,400,000	48	2,400,000
10/-	£1,400,000	56	2,800,000
5/-	£750,000	60	3,000,000
2/6	£400,000	64	3,200,000
1/-	£200,000	80	4,000,000
6d	£120,000	96	4,800,000
3d	£60,000	96	4,800,000
TOTAL	£5,330,000	800	25,000,000

On the same date that this order was given, two proofs of each denomination were sent to the War Office for approval and these were duly returned with suggestions for some minor alterations on some of the notes.

THE PRINTING OF THE THIRD SERIES

Although the vouchers of the Third Series had been commissioned from De La Rue by the Bank of England Printing Works and De La Rue had even put its name on the vouchers, the actual printing was apparently done by John Waddington Ltd., a security printer in Leeds with whom De La Rue seemed to have had a close working relationship. The reason for this subcontracting was probably the fact that, as before, a large number of vouchers were needed in a great hurry. The fact that the vouchers could hardly be described as first class security printing might also have played a role. This would make it all the more likely that the assumption referred to earlier, that Waddington had also printed the Second Series vouchers, was not without grounds1. The fact that De La Rue's name appears on the vouchers, however, makes it likely that the actual design and engraving of the plates was done by De La Rue.

The printing of the vouchers was finished by 30 September 1948 and De La Rue advised the Bank of England that the vouchers were ready for collection in Leeds. However, the problem was that the Bank of England was very short of vault space at that time and there had been a considerable amount of correspondence between the Bank and the War Office already about the 268 boxes of Second Series vouchers still in storage, as well as an undisclosed number of boxes of used First Series vouchers just returned from Germany for pulping. At the insistence of the Bank the War Office was exploring every avenue in an effort to find extra space to store the ever-increasing stocks of vouchers. The problem was exacerbated by the fact that the BAOR meanwhile wanted to return an additional 199 boxes of new Second Series vouchers to the MoD as these were surplus to requirements. Wagstaff had the difficult task of either making the Bank relax its attitude or find some other location where the vouchers could be stored. Not surprisingly Wagstaff tried the second option first and in November 1948 he even went so far as to suggest to the Treasury that space might be found in the Bank Deutsche Länder in Germany which would have the added advantage of '..having the vouchers where they would be needed..'. This last remark underlines the fact that, originally, the Third Series was indeed destined as a back-up Series for use in Germany.

[1] Waddington had a history of contracting work from the Bank of England as is shown by the fact that they printed some of the 2/6 notes for the BoE in November 1940. See the article on Fractional Bank of England Notes by A.M.M. van Laere, Banknote News no. 41, Token Publishing Ltd. Honiton UK.

But space was hard to find and in the end Wagstaff succeeded once more in getting the Bank of England to help out . The Bank once again came to the rescue of the War Office and agreed to store the vouchers in its vaults, but not before having very clearly underlined the temporary nature of such an arrangement.

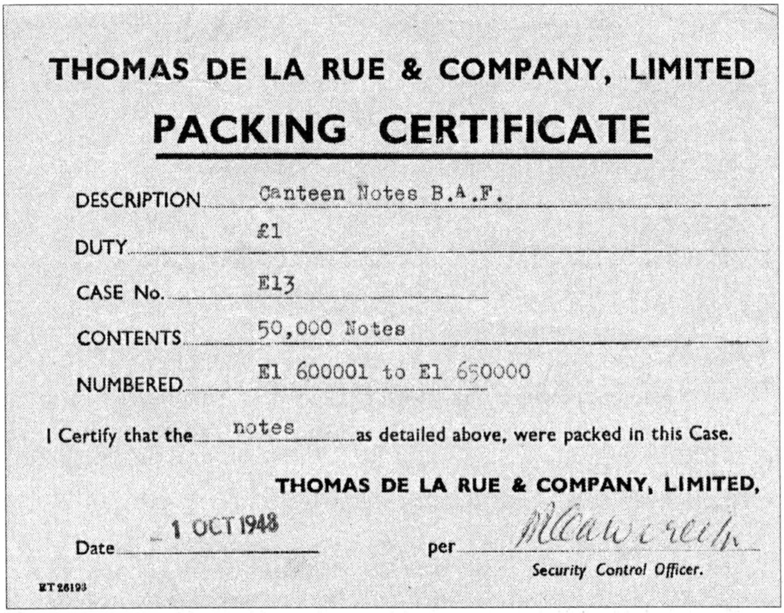

THOMAS DE LA RUE & COMPANY, LIMITED

PACKING CERTIFICATE

DESCRIPTION Canteen Notes B.A.F.

DUTY £1

CASE No. E13

CONTENTS 50,000 Notes

NUMBERED E1 600001 to E1 650000

I Certify that the notes as detailed above, were packed in this Case.

THOMAS DE LA RUE & COMPANY, LIMITED,

Date 1 OCT 1948 per

Security Control Officer.

ET 26193

Figure 44. Packing label of Third Series £1 vouchers (prefix E1) dated 1 October 1948

THE PRINTING COSTS OF THE THIRD SERIES VOUCHERS

On 11 January 1949 De La Rue invoiced the Bank for the amount of £28,816.6s being the total printing costs for the Third Series vouchers. This invoice covered the 25,000,000 vouchers ordered on 9 August 1948 including the costs for engraving and designing the vouchers.

Table 24. Printing costs of Third Series vouchers ordered initially

denomination	no. of vouchers	cost per 1000	amount
£1	2,400,000	33/-	£3,960
10/-	2,800,000	33/-	£4,620
5/-	3,000,000	24/-	£3,600
2/6	3,200,000	24/-	£3,840
1/-	4,000,000	17/5	£3,483 6s 8d
6d	4,800,000	17/5	£4,180
3d	4,800,000	17/5	£4,180
sketching and engraving			£950
TOTAL	25,000,000		£28,813 6s 8d

THE THIRD SERIES GOOD-OVERS

As with the First Series the printer discovered that, when printing was completed, an excess number of vouchers had been produced. On 8 February 1949 these good-overs were offered to the War Office at half price. This time the following numbers were involved:

Table 25. Number of good-overs of Third Series vouchers

denomination	no. of vouchers	prefix	serial number	no.of boxes
£1	90,000	E/3	400,000-490,000	2
10/-	45,000	G/3	800,000-845,000	1
5/-	40,000	H/4	000,001-040,000	1
2/6	110,000	J/4	200,000-310,000	3
1/-	70,000	none	none	2
6d	140,000	none	none	3
3d	180,000	none	none	4
TOTAL	675,000			16

The War Office replied immediately that it would be happy to take all the good-over vouchers on offer as long as the prefixes and numbering would follow the original pattern. The printer duly complied and a total of 16 boxes of good-overs was added to the 800 boxes still waiting to be collected at Waddingtons.

TOTAL NUMBER OF THIRD SERIES VOUCHERS PRINTED

Given the original order for 25,000,000 vouchers and the additional order for the good-overs the following total number of Third Series vouchers were available for circulation:

Table 26. Total number of Third Series vouchers available for circulation

denomination	box numbers	prefix/serial numbers	number of vouchers
£1	E1-E50	E/1 000,001 to E/3 490,000	2,490,000
10/-	G1-G57	G/1 000,001 to G/3 845,000	2,845,000
5/-	H1-H61	H/1 000,001 to H/4 040,000	3,040,000
2/6	J1-J67	J/1 000,001 to J/4 310,000	3,310,000
1/-	1-82	none	4,070,000
6d	1-99	none	4,940,000
3d	1-100	none	4,980.000
TOTAL			25,675,000

It was not until 30 May 1949 that the consignment of Third Series vouchers was actually shipped from Leeds to the Bank of England. The reason for this delay was the time involved in pulping the First Series vouchers already in storage at the Bank. As we know, the Bank was extremely short of vault space and, although willing, simply had to make space first.

But on 30 May 1949, at the request of Wagstaff, Movement Control Northern Command sent ten three-ton lorries to Leeds and delivered the 516 boxes of Third Series vouchers the next day to the Bullion Yard of the Bank of England. This time, however, the

Bank made absolutely certain that there could be no misunderstanding about their commitment. On 2 June the Bank wrote to the War Office confirming that it had received 516 boxes of vouchers '...*to be held temporarily on behalf of the WO*...' making it very clear that this was only until other accommodation could be found.

Although the War Office looked at various locations it finally decided that the best thing might be to store all the boxes in the basement of Lansdowne House. This was one of the buildings occupied by the Ministry of Defence and was in Berkeley Square, in the middle of London.

Given the constant reminders by the Bank of England that the boxes '...*were taking up valuable vault space*...' and'...*these boxes were only temporarily stored*...' the War Office acted with considerable speed once the decision to house the boxes at Lansdowne House was taken. On 2 September 1949 Wagstaff arranged for a working party to move the 268 boxes of Second Series vouchers and the 516 boxes of Third Series vouchers to Lansdowne House. The whole shipment weighed about 39 tons and, given the large number of boxes involved, it was decided to move them over a number of days. The following schedule was kept:

Table 27. First shipment from BoE to MoD on 5 September 1949

denomination	no. of boxes	box numbers	series
£1	2	AA 66-67	2
10/-	30	BB 69-98	2
5/-	58	CC 44-101	2
2/6	25	DD 77-101	2
1/-	19	EE 93-111	2
TOTAL	134		

Table 28. Second shipment from BoE to MoD on 6 September 1949

denomination	no. of boxes	box numbers	series
1/-	22	EE 112-133	2
6d	25	FF 108-132	2
3d	87	GG 106-192	2
TOTAL	134		

Table 29. Third shipment from BoE to MoD on 7 September 1949

denomination	no. of boxes	box numbers	series
£1	50	E1-50	3
10/-	57	G1-57	3
5/-	61	H1-61	3
2/6	32	J1-32	3
TOTAL	200		

Table 30. Fourth shipment from BoE to MoD on 8 September 1949

denomination	no. of boxes	box numbers	series
2/6	35	J33-67	3
1/-	82	1-82	3
6d	83	1-83	3
TOTAL	200		

Table 31. Fifth shipment from BoE to MoD on 9 September 1949

denomination	no. of boxes	box numbers	series
6d	16	84-99	3
3d	100	1-100	3
TOTAL	116		

This schedule not only tells us the exact dates of transfer of the vouchers to the MoD, but it also gives us a detailed insight into the stock position of Second Series vouchers still available on 9 September 1949.

PACKAGING OF THE THIRD SERIES VOUCHERS

The method of packing the vouchers was the same as that of the First and Second Series. This time, however, under instructions from the War Office, the lower denominations (1/-, 6d and 3d) were wrapped in paper bands per 100 before being wrapped in bundles of 1,000 notes, an instruction that was to apply to all subsequent deliveries of vouchers.

As before, the bundles of 1,000 vouchers were wrapped by covering top and bottom with a piece of cardboard, threaded and tied by a piece of cotton tape and sealed by a wax seal bearing De La Rue's logo. The top piece of cardboard carried a label stating the denomination, the serial numbers of the vouchers in the bundle and the inspector's name and initials. These bundles were packed in tin-lined packing cases, 50,000 vouchers (50 bundles) to a case.

THE USE OF THIRD SERIES VOUCHERS

With all available vouchers safely stored at Lansdowne House, a period of relative quiet set in. Apparently there was no reason to use the Third Series vouchers and the Second Series proved sufficient and reliable enough to be used in the BAOR arena as well as in Singapore during the Borneo Operation up to 1966.

But the sudden crisis in the Middle East brought on by the nationalisation of the Suez canal in June 1956, and the resulting British and French airborne landings at Port Said (Operation Musketeer) on 5 November 1956 in order to secure the Suez canal, changed all this.

Cyprus and Malta were heavily involved in the preparation and execution of Operation Musketeer and would also play a role as 'clearing stations' for the BAFSVs used during this operation. The British Army had had trouble in Cyprus for some time, stemming from the Cyprus Emergency in 1955 in which the highly trained Greek EOKA[2] guerrillas were fighting a Turkish minority (and the British) on the island. Despite this, using Third Series vouchers had not been felt to be necessary. But with the problems in Egypt coming to a head, preparations were made to use the Third Series in Egypt following Operation Musketeer. In August 1956 a number of emergency shipments were made to various arenas in the Middle East and at Home. These shipments were:

Table 32. Shipment of Third Series vouchers to the District Paymaster, Nicosia, Cyprus on 10 August 1956

denomination	no. of vouchers	no. of boxes	value
£1	500,000	10	£500,000
10/-	500,000	10	£250,000
5/-	300,000	6	£75,000
2/6	700,000	14	£87,500
1/-	1,000,000	20	£50,000
6d	1,000,000	20	£25,000
3d	1,000,000	20	£12,500
TOTAL	5,000,000	100	£1,000,000

[2] *Ethniki Organosis Kuprion Agoniston* or National Organisation of Cypriot Fighters

Table 33. Shipment of Third Series vouchers to the District Paymaster, Southern Command, Salisbury, UK on 20 August 1956

denomination	no. of vouchers	no. of boxes	value
£1	100,000	2	£100,000
10/-	150,000	3	£75,000
5/-	100,000	2	£25,000
2/6	200,000	4	£25,000
1/-	300,000	6	£15,000
6d	250,000	5	£6,250
3d	300,000	6	£3,750
TOTAL	1,400,000	28	£250,000

Table 34. Shipment of Third Series vouchers to the District Paymaster, Tripolitania, Libya on 22 August 1956

denomination	no. of vouchers	no. of boxes	value
£1	50,000	1	£50,000
10/-	50,000	1	£25,000
5/-	50,000	1	£12,500
1/-	150,000	3	£7,500
6d	150,000	3	£3,750
3d	100,000	2	£1,250
TOTAL	550,000	11	£100,000

Table 35. Shipment of Third Series vouchers to the Command Paymaster, Eastern Command, Hounslow, UK on 27 August 1956

denomination	no. of vouchers	no. of boxes	value
£1	50,000	1	£50,000
10/-	50,000	1	£25,000
5/-	50,000	1	£12,500
2/6	50,000	1	£6,250
1/-	150,000	3	£3,750
6d	200,000	4	£2,500
TOTAL	550,000	11	£100,000

Table 36. Shipment of Third Series vouchers to the Command Paymaster, Malta on 22 August 1956

denomination	no. of vouchers	no. of boxes	value
£1	50,000	1	£50,000
10/-	50,000	1	£25,000
5/-	50,000	1	£12,500
1/-	150,000	3	£7,500
6d	150,000	3	£3,750
3d	100,000	2	£1,250
TOTAL	550,000	11	£100,000

Table 37. Shipment of Third Series vouchers to the Royal Army Pay Corps, Devizes, UK on 22 August 1956

denomination	no. of vouchers	no. of boxes	value
£1	1,000,000	20	£1,000,000
10/-	1,000,000	20	£500,000
5/-	600,000	12	£150,000
2/6	1,400,000	28	£175,000
1/-	2,000,000	40	£100,000
6d	2,000,000	40	£50,000
3d	2,000,000	40	£25,000
TOTAL	10,000,000	200	£2,000,000

Table 38. Shipment of Third Series vouchers to the Staff Paymaster, 41 Garrison, Hook of Holland on 27 August 1956

denomination	no. of vouchers	no. of boxes	value
£1	200,000	4	£200,000
10/-	200,000	4	£100,000
5/-	100,000	2	£25,000
2/6	300,000	6	£37,500
1/-	400,000	8	£20,000
6d	500,000	10	£12,500
3d	400,000	8	£5,000
TOTAL	2,100,000	42	£400,000

Table 39. Shipment of Third Series vouchers to the Command Paymaster, Western Command, Chester, UK on 27 August 1956

denomination	no. of vouchers	no. of boxes	value
£1	50,000	1	£50,000
10/-	50,000	1	£25,000
5/-	50,000	1	£12,500
2/6	50,000	1	£6,250
6d	150,000	3	£3,750
3d	200,000	4	£2,500
TOTAL	550,000	11	£100,000

After all these shipments of Third Series vouchers had been made to the various arenas the total stock of vouchers had dwindled from the original 516 boxes to 102 boxes.

Although a consignment of 5,000,000 of Third Series vouchers was sent to Cyprus to stop black market practices from developing in Egypt, it was felt that, should things really start to move, it might be prudent to have a sufficient stock of invasion[3] money on hand to be used in the occupied territory. The War Office therefore ordered 22,000,000 British Military Authority notes to be shipped to Cyprus for this purpose. These notes had been printed in 1942 for use in North Africa and 2,633 boxes of these notes with a value of £25,721,250[4] were still stored in the vaults of the Bank of England. In August 1956, 150 boxes of these BMA notes were sent to the Rear General Headquarters in Nicosia, Cyprus, containing the following notes:

[3] Invasion money is used to replace national currencies in times of war in order to control the economy. This is distinctly different from canteen money, such as the BAFSV, which was exclusively for internal use by the military.

[4] In April 1948 the total value of BMA notes stored at the Bank was still £58,556,033.2s.6d. However, in July 1948 115,648,856 used BMA notes with a total value of £32,834,758.2s.6d. were destroyed leaving a stock with a value of £25,721,250 as backup in case of emergency.

Table 40. Breakdown of BMA notes shipped to Cyprus

denomination	no. of notes	no. of boxes	value
£1	1,000,000	20	£1,000,000
10/-	1,000,000	20	£500,000
5/-	500,000	10	£162,500
2/6	1,000,000	20	£162,500
1/-	1,500,000	30	£97,500
6d	2,500,000	50	£75,000
TOTAL	22,000,000	150	£1,997,500

The Anglo-French Suez adventure only lasted until 21 November 1956 when a hastily assembled United Nations Force arrived - a party of Norwegians wearing helmets painted a bright pale blue. They were met by a crowd of civilians who gave them such an enthusiastic reception that the British had to rescue them from the mob. With more contingents of UN troops arriving, the British troops began to leave and the last British troops embarked on 22 December 1956. Thus it was only for a period of about two months that the Third Series vouchers were used and on a very limited scale at that.

DEFECTIVE THIRD SERIES VOUCHERS

Although the period of use of Third Series vouchers was very short indeed it was long enough to find that some of the vouchers were defective in that the paper would split at the point where the metal thread was inserted. This made it possible to split the vouchers in half and/or remove the metal thread. This was felt to be rather undesirable, especially since a split note could possibly be passed off as two notes.

The War Office asked the Bank of England to look into this phenomenon and after consultation with the paper maker it transpired that this defect was mainly confined to some of the 2/6 vouchers which were printed on paper cut with the wrong machine settings. This did nothing to alleviate the concern of the War Office, but it at least localised the problem. No further action seems to have been taken except for the destruction of a small batch of 2/6 vouchers.

RETURNING THE THIRD SERIES VOUCHERS

Most of the boxes sent to the various arenas for use in Operation Musketeer were shipped back to Lansdowne House unopened. Used vouchers were only returned from Cyprus and Malta, which were used as clearing stations for the vouchers used in Egypt, underlining the fact that Third Series vouchers were not used locally at the other locations. The following shipments were returned:

Table 41. Total number of vouchers returned to the MoD up to 16-4-1957

date	returned from	no. of boxes	status	value
30-1-57	Salisbury, UK	28	unopened	£250,000
5-2-57	Chester, UK	11	unopened	£100,000
1-2-57	Hounslow, UK	11	unopened	£100,000
14-3-57	Malta	18[5]	some used	£151,875
13-2-57	41 Garrison, Hook	42	unopened	£400,000
22-2-57	Cyprus	137	unopened	£1,245,625
7-2-57	Cyprus	13	used	£312,500
16-4-57	Cyprus	19	used	£246,873.15s
7-3-57	Cyprus	17	used	£215,625
30-1-57	RAPC Devizes UK	25	not used[6]	£336,250
TOTAL RETURNED		321		£3.358,748.15s

[5] There must have been some inter-arena traffic of Third Series vouchers since only 11 boxes were shipped directly to Malta. Perhaps the Tripolitania vouchers were shipped to Malta and/or Cyprus, as there is no record of them being shipped back to Britain.

[6] These boxes had been opened in readiness for use, but were closed again without the vouchers actually having been unpacked.

Apart from these known shipments of vouchers a total number of 91 boxes of unknown composition were received prior to 30 January 1957. When a final account was produced on 16 April 1957 the following number of vouchers were still outstanding, all other vouchers having been accounted for and stored at Lansdowne House once more.

Table 42. Outstanding vouchers of the Third Series per 16 April 1957

denomination	no. of vouchers	value
£1	389	£389
10/-	283	£14 10s
5/-	530	£132 10s
2/6	989	£122 7s 6d
1/-	3,293	£164 13s
6d	4,779	£119 9s 6d
3d	7,290	£91 2s 6d
TOTAL	17,535	£1,160 12s 6d

Most of these vouchers, especially the lower values, will have been kept by the troops as memorabilia, but a substantial number of the high value vouchers (notably the £1 and 10/-ones) were presented in due course to the War Office for reimbursement.

The B.M.A. notes shipped to Cyprus in August 1956 were also returned unopened in February 1957 and were stored once more in the vaults of the Bank of England. It later transpired that these vouchers had to be re-packed since the original boxes were in the words of a Bank official '*...in doubtful condition after having been sent abroad...*'.

There is no clear indication that the Third Series vouchers were used again after they were consigned to the basement of Lansdowne House in 1957.

However, on 20 November 1969, a surprise check on the stocks of vouchers revealed that only the following numbers of Third Series were still in store with the MoD at Lansdowne House:

Table 43. Stock of Third Series vouchers on 20 November 1969

denomination	no. of vouchers	no. of boxes	value
£1	499,600	10	£499,600
10/-	449,700	9	£224,850
5/-	649,400	12	£162,350
2/6	348,606	7	£43,575 15s
1/-	766,700	16	£38,335
6d	785,200	16	£19,630
3d	872,640	17	£10,908
TOTAL	4,371,846	87	£999,248 15s

It is not quite clear what happened to the Third Series vouchers between 1957 and 1969 but perhaps Lansdowne House, too, had encountered problems with the storage of such a large number of boxes and that over time some of the vouchers had been pulped. On the other hand, some of the vouchers may have been moved to Malta as a result of the new 'major user principle' which the Ministry of Defence adopted in 1959 as part of the Mountbatten reforms and which, among other things, meant that all stores and supplies were handled and stored at the location where they might be needed most.

In 1980, the 10/- and 1/- vouchers of this stock were offered for sale by the MoD but only one dealer bought 100,000 vouchers of each denomination. All the other vouchers of these denominations were destroyed (see A Very Private Deal in Chapter 8). All the £1 vouchers were kept at least until 1991, when they were included in a total clearout sale by auction. (see Chapter 12). What happened to the denominations of 3d, 6d, 2/6 and 5/- is anybody's guess. They were probably destroyed before 1980 when the 10/- and 1/- were offered, otherwise they would most probably have been included in the private sale by the MoD.

On 10 September 1948, the Bank of England sent one proof each of the Third Series main printings (i.e. the main colours only) to the War Office showing the secret marks of the 3d, 6d, 1/-, 2/6, 5/-, 10/-, and the £1 denominations, stating that that was the only set De La Rue had supplied. As we know, the War Office was by now in the habit of sending these sets to their various HQs so Wagstaff asked the Bank to arrange for another four sets, which duly arrived on 22 September 1948.

The secret marks on the 3rd Series notes can be described as follows:

GROUP 1 *3d, 6d and 1/-*

3d face:
- on the top right hand side a small line has been inserted in the the border surrounding the denomination.
- a small line has been inserted within the border of the denomination area just where this border joins the outside vertical left hand edge

3d back:
- on the acanthus leaf to the left of the centre of the note a small sign shaped like ' ~ ' has been inserted.

6d face:
- on the right hand side a small line has been inserted within the inner vertical border just above the bottom right denomination area
- a small line has been inserted inside the border of the bottom left hand denomination area just where this border joins the lower horizontal border of the design

6d back:
- in the top of the acanthus leaf to the left of the centre, beneath the text, a small sign shaped like ' / ' has been inserted.

1/- face:

- a very small crooked line has been inserted in the middle of the letter 'O' of 'ONE'
- a very small vertical line has been inserted in the space between the letters 'L' and 'I' of the word 'SHILLING'

1/- back:

- the centre of the curled tip on the right hand curl of the acanthus leaf below the text contains an extra line shaped like '/ '.

GROUP 2 *2/6 and 5/-*

2/6 face:

- the lattice work in the very top left hand corner contains a dot in one of the lattice work triangles
- the rosette in the border on the right hand side with the words 'TWO SHILLINGS SIXPENCE' contains a small mark shaped like an 'L' on its side in one of the lattice work diamond shapes

2/6d back:

- a small slanted line with a small circle on top has been inserted near the middle of the right hand leaf supporting the box containing the text

5/- face:

- the rosette in the border on the left hand side with the words 'FIVE SHILLINGS contains a small horizontal line on the left edge in one of the lattice work diamond shapes
- a small circle has been inserted to the left of the inner border of the right hand rosette, between the border and the top of the corner motif

5/- back:

- an extra curved line and a dot have been inserted within the bottom of the 'scroll' which decorates the tip of the border to the left of the 5/- at the top right

GROUP 3 *10/- and £1*

10/- face:

- under the top left denomination, a small dash has been added to the design against the bottom curl of the acanthus leaf where the right hand curl of the acanthus leaf to the left of the right hand bottom denomination actually touches the leaf itself, a small circle (°) has been added.

10/- back:

- in the gap to the right of where the curl of the acanthus leaf under the left hand text 'TEN SHILLINGS' touches the box with the text, a small curved dash has been added to the design.

£1 face:

- the space formed by the curl of the acanthus leaf on the bottom left side a small, almost vertical dash has been added to the design
- in the space between the curl of the acanthus leaf on the bottom right and the border of the £1 denomination, a small dash has been added

£1 back:

- in the far left tip of the tentacle of the acanthus leaf just under the left hand text 'ONE POUND', a small circle (°) has been added between the lines of this tentacle.

In contrast to the former 'secret mark' specimen notes, this time De La Rue had not used original notes with a 000000 number but black pulls of the main printings of the notes. On these prints, the secret marks had been shown as before by encircling the area in which the marks were to be found and showing the mark itself in the margin without describing it in words.

Figure 45. Secret marks on Third Series 3d - face

101

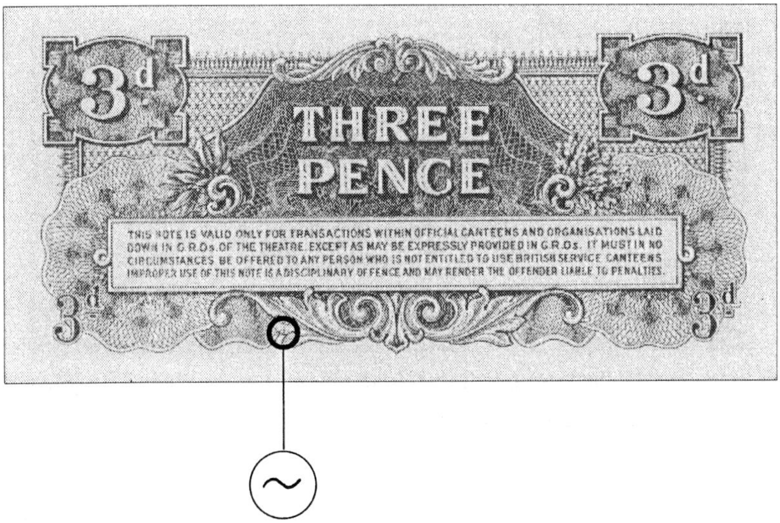

Figure 46. Secret marks on Third Series 3d - back

102

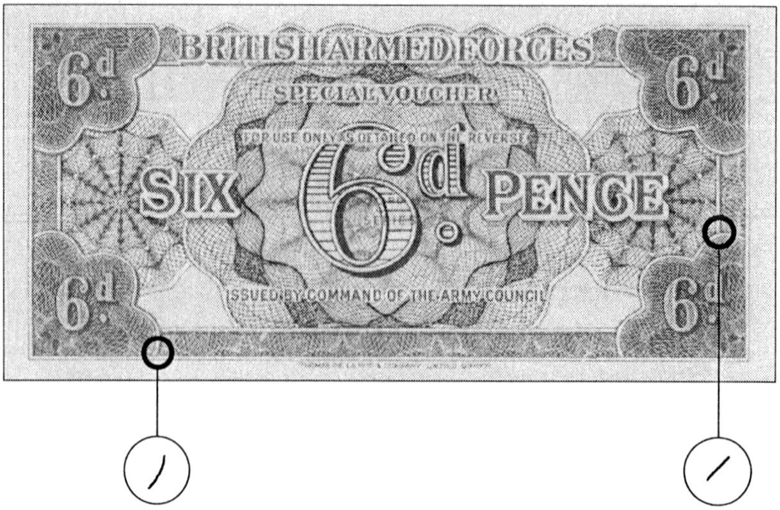

Figure 47. Secret marks on Third Series 6d - face

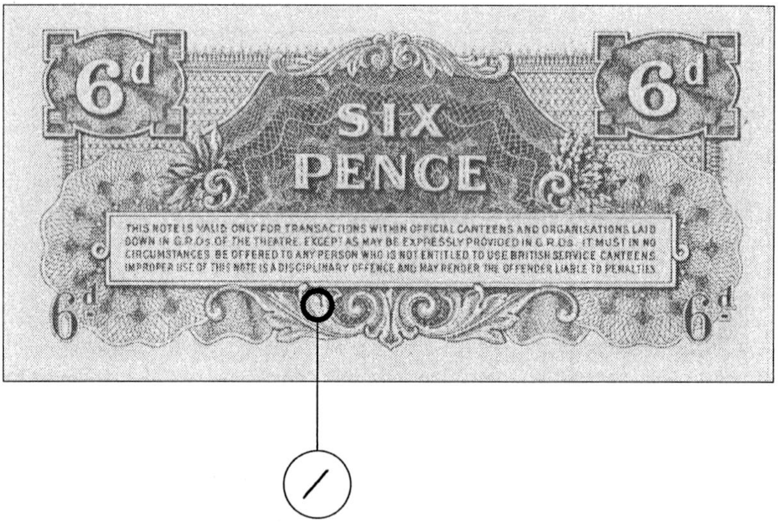

Figure 48. Secret marks on Third Series 6d - back

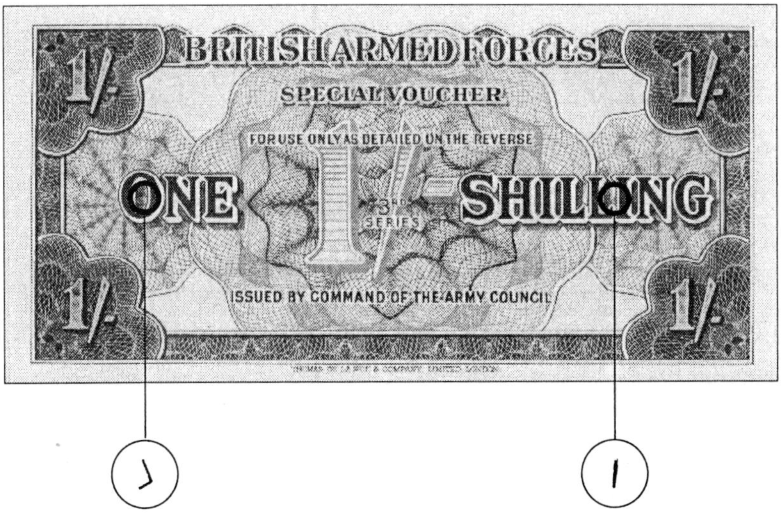

Figure 49. Secret marks on Third Series 1/- - face

Figure 50. Secret marks on Third Series 1/- - back

Figure 51. Secret marks on Third Series 2/6 - face

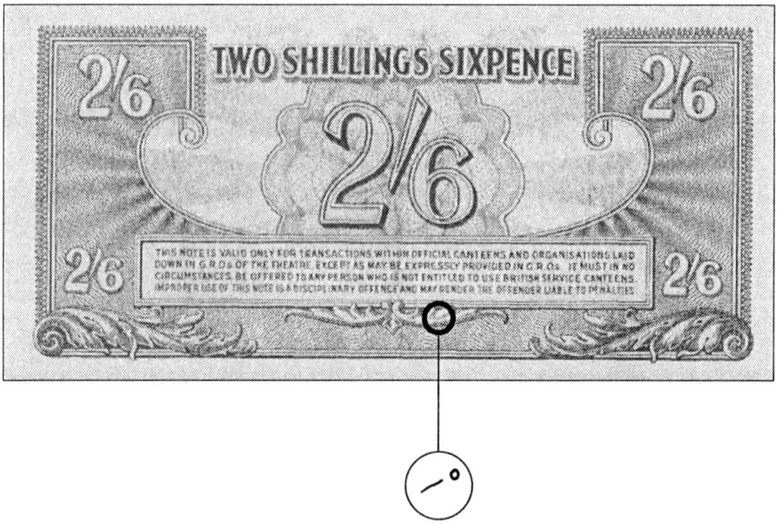

Figure 52. Secret marks on Third Series 2/6 - back

Figure 53. Secret marks on Third Series 5/- - face

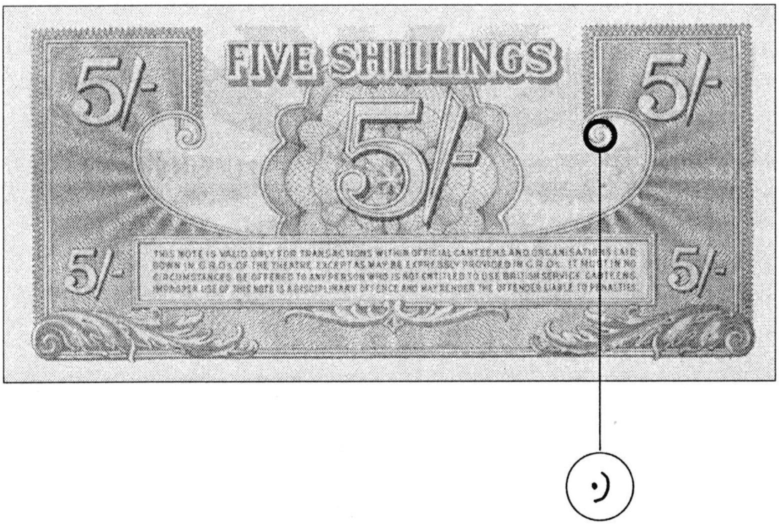

Figure 54. Secret marks on Third Series 5/- - back

Figure 55. Secret marks on Third Series 10/- - face

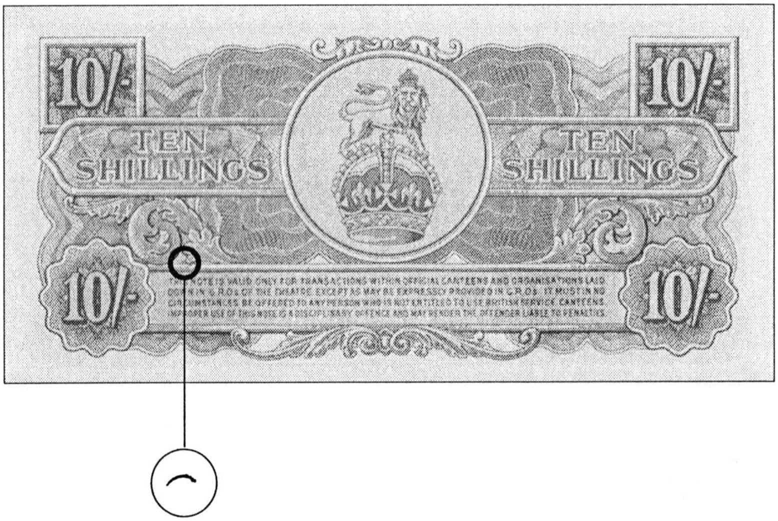

Figure 56. Secret marks on Third Series 10/- - back

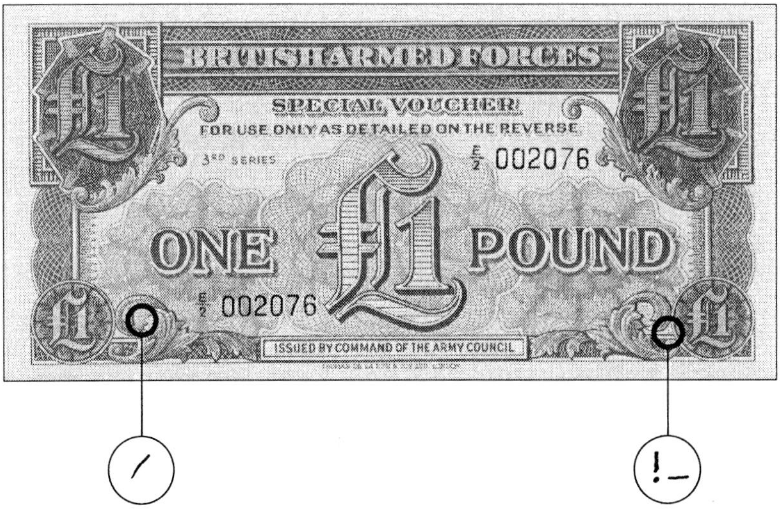

Figure 57. Secret marks on Third Series £1 · face

Figure 58. Secret marks on Third Series £1 · back

BACK IN JAPAN

When the BAFSVs were introduced in Japan for use by the British Commonwealth Occupation Forces the War Office was more or less obliged to finance these vouchers itself, after a wrangle with the Australian Government. At the time, the Australians felt that it was unfair for them to have to back the vouchers in sterling since the BCOF included a number of other nationalities besides the Australians.

In September 1949, however, the BCOF had dwindled down to an Australian contingent of about 3,000 troops and no other British or foreign forces were any longer involved. On 15 September 1949 the War Office contacted the Treasury to point out that it, the War Office, was still financing the vouchers in use in Japan. It felt that it should no longer be backing the £250,000 worth of vouchers still carried on its books since these vouchers were used for the sole benefit of the Australians. It therefore proposed withdrawing the vouchers from the arena altogether and letting the Australians work out their own arrangements. Although the Prime Minister's Office, which was also informed, did not object to this plan, the Treasury was less co-operative. While understanding the problem the Treasury wanted to avoid angering the Australians and, after a long delay, proposed solving the problem by cutting down the stock of unused vouchers. But this, as Wagstaff pointed out, '*...would not solve the problem one iota since the books still could not be closed...*'. The Treasury did not relent, however. It suggested a meeting between the various parties involved and put forward the argument that, since the Americans had to be paid in dollars, the Australians should be paid in BAFSVs. But by March 1950 they still had not agreed to the withdrawal of the BAFSVs. By this time the War Office had run out of patience and was insisting that the Australians be contacted to secure the withdrawal of BAFSVs as soon as possible. In June 1950 informal contacts with the Australian government revealed that the Australian contingent, and thus the BCOF, would soon be withdrawn and, if that were the case, the need for BAFSVs would cease automatically. In view of this the War Office, Downing Street and the Treasury agreed to exercise further patience. In the end, however, the War Office gave up all hope of ever resolving this problem and when, in December 1950, the Foreign Office asked for assurances that all would be settled the War Office replied that it would no longer attempt to resolve the matter of '*...getting control over our own BAFSVs, since it was made clear to us that the Australian Government would take strong objection to any interference from here. The fact is that BAFSVs in Japan are under the control of the Commander of the BCOF and he is an Australian General who will not....be influenced by what we may say...... but if you want any assurances ... you will have to go to the Australian Government, who alone are, I think, responsible...*'.

THE BRITISH ARMED FORCES UNIT TOKENS

In November 1951, with only the Second and Third Series available, the War Office made a number of proposals to the Treasury for the provision of special currency in case war should break out in the Middle East. Part of these provisions concerned the matter of small change. When buying their cups of tea and buns the troops were owed change from the smallest denomination of BAFSV which was the 3d note, This voucher was the most unpopular with the Pay Services because of the administrative work it entailed as compared to the value of the note. When the BAFSVs were first introduced in 1946, plastic tokens of 1d and ½d were issued to be used as small change, but these tokens were very quickly absorbed and there had been repeated request for their re-issue. Up to November 1951 these requests had been resisted because of the high cost of manufacture and improvisation at the local level had meant that re-issue could be avoided. In certain cases the NAAFI had used tokens of its own, while in the BAOR a certain amount of British copper had been used. In places like Korea and Japan, Australian coins had been used. It was now felt, however, that, should there be a war in the Middle East, the minor inconvenience of the shortage of small change would become a major problem, and that immediate steps should be taken.

When discussing the various options it was soon decided that plastic or bakelite tokens would be too expensive and too bulky since the 3.2 million tokens produced in 1946 were said to have cost £4,650[1] and filled 1,000 wooden packing cases. It therefore seemed

[1] This is strange since the original quote by De La Rue in March 1946 for 2 million pieces had been for 7/- per 1,000. This means that the final order for 3,200,000 CP3 tokens should not have cost more than £1,120.

logical to ask the Royal Mint for advice in the matter and, although it was recognised that metal alloy would probably be in very short supply, the War Office nevertheless asked the Royal Mint for a quote on a total of 6 million coins, 3 million each of 1d and ½d respectively[2]. Should this quote be favourable it was thought that a certain number of these 'coins' could also be made available for peace-time use in the existing BAFSV areas to alleviate the shortage of tokens in circulation.

The Treasury responded positively to the proposals and gave permission for the Royal Mint to be approached but warned that the Mint might not be too happy with the extra work just then since it was apparently under very heavy pressure due to demand for coins from the colonies. As it turned out, the Mint foresaw very few problems when contacted by the War Office in March 1952, and put forward its proposal for the new 'coins' in May. It suggested making the tokens in the shape of round coins consisting of brass weighing 60 grains for the 1d tokens and 30 grains for the ½d tokens. Both types were to have a 7mm perforation in the centre. Two specimen blanks of the suggested tokens were also submitted.

Table 44. Quoted manufacturing costs of BAF tokens in 1952

denomination	weight each	Ø mm	manufacturing costs per 1,000[4]	metal costs per 1,000
one unit	60 grains	25	26/-	24/-
half unit	30 grains	20	18/-	12/-

The cost of the 6 million tokens would come to £12,400[3] with a total face value of £18,750. The total weight of such a number of coins was expected to be 16 ½ tons and an estimated 400 boxes would be required for their storage, well under the estimated 2000

[2] The real reason for the preference to order from the Royal Mint turned out to be that in this way tendering could be avoided.

[3] Originally a milled edge instead of a perforation was discussed but this would cost an extra 10%, which was felt to be prohibitive.

[4] This included the costs of the striking dies.

boxes that would have been needed for an equivalent number of plastic tokens of the types already in use. The War Office had no

Table 45. Total costs of BAF tokens quoted in 1952

denomination	no. of spieces	production costs	original dies	total cost
one unit	3,000,000	£7,500	£225	£7,725
half unit	3,000,000	£4,500	£175	£4,675
TOTAL	6,000,000	£12,000	£400	£12,400

comparable quote for plastic tokens but had discovered that those recently supplied to the NAAFI had cost ½d each and so the current requirements would probably cost £12,000 also if these, in the War Office's view not such nicely finished, tokens were chosen. The Mint was therefore asked to prepare a trial order of 500,000 pieces of each value. At the same time it was decided that, rather than making tokens of a penny and a halfpenny value they would be of one unit and a half unit. This would enable the War Office to make them represent any value that might be necessary in a particular area. The trial tokens were to bear the inscription 'British Armed Forces - ONE UNIT' and 'ONE HALF UNIT'. The cost for this trial order was estimated at between £2,000 and £3,000.

In the months following these discussions the Mint agreed to manufacture the tokens and also suggested that it perhaps might be desirable to have a design on one side of the coins. This could, for example, be a replica of the Royal Coat of Arms or a special War Office design. This suggestion was taken up by the War Office but '*..an innoxious floral design..*' was chosen. The material to be used for the tokens was to be the usual nickel-brass also used for the three-penny bits, consisting of 79% copper, 1% nickel and 20% zinc. The total cost would be £2,400, well within the cost estimate.

Table 46. Actual costs of trial order of 1,000,000 BAF tokens in 1953

denomination	number ordered	production costs	original dies	total costs
one unit	500,000	£1,250	£225	£1,475
half unit	500,000	£750	£175	£925
TOTAL	1,000,000	£2,000	£400	£2,400

It was not until March 1953 that production of the tokens actually began and it was June 1953 when the tokens were finally delivered to the War Office, packed in 75 boxes, 50 boxes containing 10,000 one unit tokens each and numbered T1-1 to 50 and 25 boxes containing 20,000 half unit tokens each numbered T½-1 to 25, each box weighing approximately 100 lbs.

Figure 59. Front and back of British Armed Forces Token of One Unit

Although these tokens could hardly be described as having strategic significance they were important enough for the War Office to refuse permission for the Royal Mint to mention the production of these tokens in its Annual Report for 1953.

A number of boxes containing the one unit tokens from this batch were actually transported to Cyprus, presumably to be used during the Suez crisis in 1956.

In September 1960 the War Office placed a second order for BAF Tokens. This time the quantities ordered were 1 million of each at a cost of £4,337.10s, As before, they were to be packed in boxes containing 10,000 tokens of one unit and 20,000 tokens of one half unit respectively and measuring 22" x 8" x 8" with each box weighing approximately 100 lbs.

Table 47. Actual costs of final order for 2,000,000 BAF tokens in 1960

denomination	number of pieces	production costs per 1,000[5]	total costs
one unit	1,000,000	£2.12s.5d.	£2,620.16s.8d.
half unit	1,000,000	£1.14s.4d.	£1,716.13s.4d.
TOTAL	2,000,000		£4,337.10s.0d.

The box numbering was to follow the former pattern and was T1-51 to 150 for the one unit tokens and T½-26 to 75 for the half unit tokens. As the numbering was consecutive with that on the boxes of the first batch, we can be fairly certain that no tokens were produced in the meantime. The tokens from this second batch were collected by the military on 27 March 1961 from the Royal Mint and transported to Lansdowne House in London where the Ministry of Defence had its offices.

They did not stay there for long, however, because on 11 April 1961 120 boxes of tokens were on their way to the Headquarters of the British Army of the Rhine in Mönchen Gladbach and 3 boxes of the tokens were shipped to Singapore. The shipment to the BAOR consisted of 80 boxes of one unit tokens (boxes T1-51 to 130) and 40 boxes of half unit tokens (box numbers T½-26 to 65). Their safe arrival at the BAOR was acknowledged on 3 May 1961 by the Command Paymaster. The composition of the Singapore shipment is not known, but we may assume that this was made up of 2 boxes of one unit tokens and 1 box of half unit tokens.

[5] no original die costs were involved in this order since these dies were already available from the trial order.

There is no concrete evidence of any of the tokens ever having been used except for an obscure note in a War Office file. It was not even generally known that they existed until 1971, when 6 boxes of one unit tokens were sunk off the coast of Cyprus[6].

In 1987 the Command Pay Office of the BAOR still held the 120 boxes of tokens shipped there in 1961, and the Command Pay Office of the UK Land Forces in Salisbury (UK) held a grand total of 646,052 one unit tokens (65 boxes) and 675,422 half unit tokens (34 boxes), which were shipped to the MoD at Lansdowne House in 1969.

The total stock of tokens in 1987 was therefore

one unit tokens 1,475,422 pieces
half unit tokens 1,446,052 pieces

As a total of 1,500,000 of each were produced this leaves 53,948 one unit tokens and 24,578 half unit tokens still unaccounted for. A number of these are known to have been dumped off the coast of Cyprus and the figures would make it likely that the batch dumped at sea consisted of 5 boxes of one unit tokens (50,000 tokens) and 1 box of half unit tokens (20,000 tokens). This would leave 3,948 one unit tokens and 4,578 half unit tokens out 'in the field' and this may well point to their actually having been used in Egypt during Operation Musketeer in 1956 or during the Borneo Operation in Singapore from 1962 to 1966. Only a few of these tokens have found their way into numismatics collections and must be among the most scarce types of NAAFI-tokens.

All this is, of course, assuming that the Singapore shipment of 3 boxes finally found its way back to Lansdown House and became part of the inventory held there in 1987. Otherwise we must conclude that the six boxes dumped at sea were only partly filled with BAF tokens.

[6] For the story of this event see the article *Burial at Sea* by Michael Santamas in Spink Numismatic Circular, 1971, page 321

THE FOURTH SERIES

Whether it was because the War Office was concerned about the fact that it had no backup Series (as had become apparent in the case of the Middle East crisis) or because the British Government was already contemplating stationing British Troops in Aden permanently, by 1961 the War Office had actually given orders for the design not only of a Fourth Series, which had already been discussed in 1952 but also a Fifth Series of vouchers. The proofs of the Fourth Series vouchers were sent to the War Office on 7 December 1961 while the proofs of the Fifth Series followed one week later on 14 December 1961. In contrast to the older notes no printer was mentioned on the vouchers of the Fourth Series and, as it turned out later, the printing of these vouchers was not done by Thomas De La Rue, but by Bradbury Wilkinson.

The reason why the Ministry of Defence changed to another printer is understandable if we think back to the post-war years when the Bank of England had been asked to order the vouchers so as to circumvent the need for alternative tenders. During the 1960s the Ministry could not use the same mechanism since it could hardly claim that it was pressed for time and it was therefore obliged to ask for tenders from different printers. It was apparently Messrs Bradbury who won the order for the Fourth as well as the Fifth Series vouchers.

THE PRINTING OF THE FOURTH SERIES

The Fourth Series vouchers were printed during the first half of 1962 and were shipped straight to Malta, probably as part of the 'major user principle' established by the Ministry of Defence in 1959. Basically this meant that in the Far East, Cyprus, Malta and

Gibraltar the Army handled and stored all the necessary fuel, provisions and stores for all Services, while in Aden this became the responsibility of the RAF. Although we do not know the exact number of Fourth Series vouchers printed, a fairly accurate estimation can be made from various sources.

Table 48. Estimated number of Fourth Series vouchers printed

denomination	value	no. of notes	prefixes
£1	£3,000,000	3,000,000	K/1-K/3
10/-	£2,250,000	4,500,000	L/1-L/5
5/-	£1,125,000	4,500,000	M/1-M/5
2/6	£562,500	4,500,000	N/1-N/5
1/-	£450,000	9,000,000	none
6d	£225,000	9,000,000	none
3d	£112,500	9,000,000	none
TOTAL	£7,075,000	43,500,000	

The Fourth Series vouchers were never released for circulation, although a number of vouchers were shipped to Aden, presumably via Malta, to be ready for use. Most of the vouchers seem to have been destroyed locally, probably to avoid the transportation costs of shipping them back to Britain. A number of boxes, however, found their way back to Britain in December 1967 as a result of the withdrawal from Aden. In total 42 boxes of vouchers with a total value of £500,000 were received from Aden as well as a return shipment of 59 boxes from Malta with a value of £575,000. Together with 32 boxes of Fourth Series vouchers already in store on that date a total of 143 boxes, containing 7,150,000 Fourth Series vouchers with a total value of £1,575,000 were stored at Lansdowne House.

Table 49 *Fourth Series vouchers in store on 20 November 1969*

denomination	no. of boxes	no. of vouchers	value
£1	13	650,000	£650,000
10/-	8	400,000	£200,000
5/-	32	1,600,000	£400,000
2/6	40	2,000,000	£250,000
1/-	18	900,000	£45,000
6d	16	800,000	£20,000
3d	16	800,000	£10,000
TOTAL	143	7,150,000	£1,575,000

From this stock 100,000 1/- vouchers and 100,000 10/- vouchers (both of these batches cancelled by two 6 mm perforations) were sold in 1980. The remainder of these denominations were destroyed by the MoD. It must be assumed that the other shillings-and-pence denominations had been destroyed earlier for lack of space, otherwise they would no doubt have been offered for sale as well. The £1 denomination was still usable, even in a decimalised system and it was not until 1991 that 2,350,000 £1 vouchers were sold by public auction. This last figure shows that more of the £1 vouchers must have been returned from Malta to Lansdown House between 1969 and 1980 because on 20 November 1969 £1 vouchers with a total value of only £650,000 were in stock (see Table 49). The other values had probably already been destroyed locally in order to avoid the transportation costs of bringing them back to Britain.

PACKAGING OF THE FOURTH SERIES NOTES

With the change of printer we also see a different method of packing the vouchers. Instead of the painstaking care and precision of De La Rue's wrapping technique, Bradbury packed the vouchers in bundles of 100 notes wrapped in a small paper band only. These bundles were then stacked into heavy tin-lined wooden boxes, 500 bundles to a box, with each box again containing 50,000 notes. The boxes were secured with wire which was sealed on the edges of the box with a tin seal bearing the Bradbury Wilkinson logo.

Figure 60. Tin seal (right) used to secure Bradbury Wilkinson packing cases (top)

A VERY PRIVATE DEAL

In 1980, in a private offer to certain major London banknote dealers, the Ministry of Defence put its stock of vouchers in the old pence and shillings denominations up for sale. It had no further use for these vouchers in a decimalised system, of course. The 'shilling' denominations included in this offer were the Second Series 5/- voucher on watermarked paper, the Third Series 1/- and 10/- vouchers, and the 1/- and 10/- vouchers of the Fourth Series. It seems logical that, had there been any other shilling or pence denominations available, these would have been included in the offer as well. It can therefore be assumed that these other denominations had been destroyed prior to 1980.

In total 100,000 vouchers of each denomination were bought by only one of the dealers and the remainder was destroyed by the Ministry of Defence, a fact they duly acknowledged. Sadly for collectors the Treasury required that all vouchers included in this deal be cancelled. Initially the vouchers were to be overprinted with the word 'cancelled', but the Treasury later agreed it would be satisfactory to have two 6 mm perforations drilled through them. This was carried out and notes from this lot are still freely available to collectors. A very small number of these vouchers seem to have inadvertently escaped the perforation.

The £1 vouchers from the Second, Third and Fourth Series which were still in stock at the time were obviously not included in this deal as these could still be used even in a decimalised system.

Table 50. Vouchers sold privately by the MoD in 1980

Series	denomination	no. of vouchers
2nd (wm)	5/-	100,000
3rd	1/-	100,000
	10/-	100,000
4th	1/-	100,000
	10/-	100,000
TOTAL		500,000

SECRET MARKS ON THE FOURTH SERIES

As before, the Ministry of Defence was issued with black pulls of the main printings with the secret marks indicated on them. Since the printing was now done by Bradbury Wilkinson we may assume that these pulls, too, were prepared by Bradbury. This time, instead of numbered copies of the pulls, unnumbered copies were presented with only the marks themselves being indicated. Besides the fact that Bradbury Wilkinson had incorporated more secret marks in the designs of the Fourth Series than had been included in earlier series, the marks themselves are slightly more obscure compared to De La Rue's marks. The pulls had been trimmed to note size in contrast to the pulls from De La Rue, which were on rough-sized paper. Another difference is that the Bradbury pulls of the Fourth Series are proper, plate printed, specimens of the main plates. The special pulls supplied by De La Rue indicating the secret marks on the Second and the Third Series were either lithographs or photographic reproductions.

The secret marks on the Fourth Series are:

GROUP 1 *3d, 6d and 1/-*

3d face:

- there is a break in the semi-circle pattern in the top of the left vertical border
- there is a break in one of the lattice-work squares to the right of the semi-circle pattern on the lower right side of the large '3d' denomination on the left of the voucher
- there is a small extra line within the border design in the right hand vertical border 1/2" above the '3d' denomination in the lower right hand corner of the voucher

3d back:

- there is a slight extension of one of the lines forming the pattern just above the box containing the text, about 1/4" below the 'C' of 'PENCE' in the top denomination description
- there is a small break where one of the pattern lines should touch the line surrounding the word 'PENCE' in the lower right half of the voucher. This break appears just to the right of the bottom horizontal stroke of the final letter 'E'

6d face:

- an extra line has been added inside the diamond shaped pattern just to the left of the 'D' of the bottom left denomination

- the converging lines of the diamond pattern are fragmented in the top border of the box containing the diamond motif just below the top right denomination, just below where the border comes down into a tip
- a small hook-like feature has been inserted in the pattern of the toorder just above and, to the left of letter 'R' of 'BRITISH'

6d back:
- a small horizontal line has been added to the neck of the bottle-shaped design element in the top left corner border of the box containing the text
- one of the lines in the design just under the bottom left border of the box containing the denomination on the right of the voucher protrudes into the border

1/- face:
- one of the twin vertical lines in the border design of the box containing the text 'ISSUED BY COMMAND OF THE ARMY COUNCIL' just underneath the 'A' in 'ARMY' is slightly shorter than the other
- a thin drop-like feature has been inserted just above the bottom tip of the heart-like shape in the top of the vertical design element on the left of the voucher. This *does not* appear, however, in the equivalent design on the right
- a small horizontal line has been inserted in the top of the semi-circle design right of the top left '1/-' denomination

1/- back:
- a slight dot-like protrusion has been added to the left top of the right vertical stroke of the 'N' in 'ONE'
- just below the top right-hand pointed tip of the border of the oval design containing the word 'ONE SHILLING', the line of the lattice design hooks down to the right

GROUP 2 *2/6 and 5/-*

2/6 face:
- a small slanted line has been added parallel to the inner line of the border of the lower point of the motif on the left vertical edge of the voucher just above the 'W' of 'TWO' in the bottom left corner

- the diamond pattern in the horizontal border design just above the shilling stroke in the top right corner is irregular
- at the centre of the motif on the right vertical edge two (mirrored) designs are present depicting a small triangle over a circle surrounded by a hoop. The upper design has a break at the top of the hoop

2/6 back:
- a small line has been added in the second roof-like design element from the left in the top border of the box containing the text
- a small line has been added to the scroll work joining the border of the box containing the text above the letter 'C' of 'CANTEENS'

5/- face:
- the design in the top border above the letter 'R' in 'FORCES' has been made irregular
- the design in the vertical right border just to the right of the lower tip of the acanthus leaf has been made irregular
- there is a small line break in the design of the lower horizontal border underneath the 'NG' of 'SHILLING' on the bottom right

5/- back:
- a small horizontal line has been added in the right-hand circle at the centre of the design in the large oval on the left of the centre
- a very small line has been added in the scroll work of the right vertical border of the box containing the text, just to the right of the word 'IMPROPER'

GROUP 3 *10/- and £1*

10/- face:
- the design in the lower right corner of the box containing the 10/- denomination on the top left has been made irregular
- the design just above the dash in the box containing the 10/- denomination on the lower left has been made irregular
- one of the design elements in the lower horizontal border to the right of the denomination box in the lower left corner has an extra small vertical line, which is missing in the equivalent element on the left of the lower right hand denomination box

10/- back:
- the design just under the 'I' in 'SHILLING' on the left has been made irregular
- there is a break in one of the diagonal lines in the design work about 1/2" above the top of the '0' in the centre '10/-'

£1 face:
- one of the tiny diamond shaped design elements in the lower horizontal border just underneath the 'O' in 'POUND' in the right bottom corner of the voucher has not been inked in
- the scroll work in the design to the left of the '£' symbol in the right hand denomination box has been made irregular
- there is a small break in one of the open lines of the scroll work above the box containing the text 'ISSUED BY COMMAND OF THE ARMY COUNCIL' just above the 'U' in 'COUNCIL'

£1 back:
- there is a small break in the pattern just to the right of the upper tip of the acanthus leaf which decorates the main design
- a very small vertical line has been added within the top ray projecting vertically from the right hand upper tip of the box containing

As already mentioned, not all secret marks were disclosed by the printer, which would appear to be the case on the back of the Fourth Series 1/- voucher. No mention has been made by the printer of a small protrusion, added to the line which ends up just above the top left hand tip of the border design to the left of the oval containing the words 'ONE SHILLING'. In the case of the Fourth Series £1 the secret mark indicated at the bottom right of the face is repeated about 1/2 " to the right of the indicated mark, this time without being mentioned. Again, it could be that the printers themselves lost track, or that they deliberately held back some of the information.

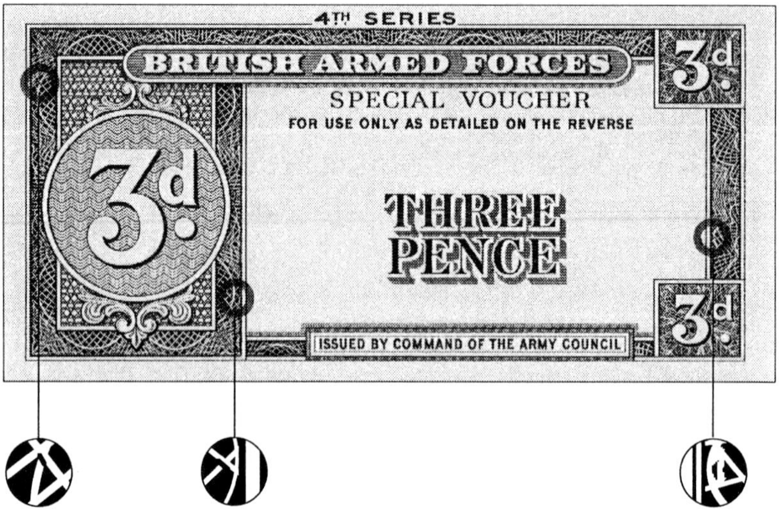

Figure 61. Secret marks on 3d Fourth Series - face

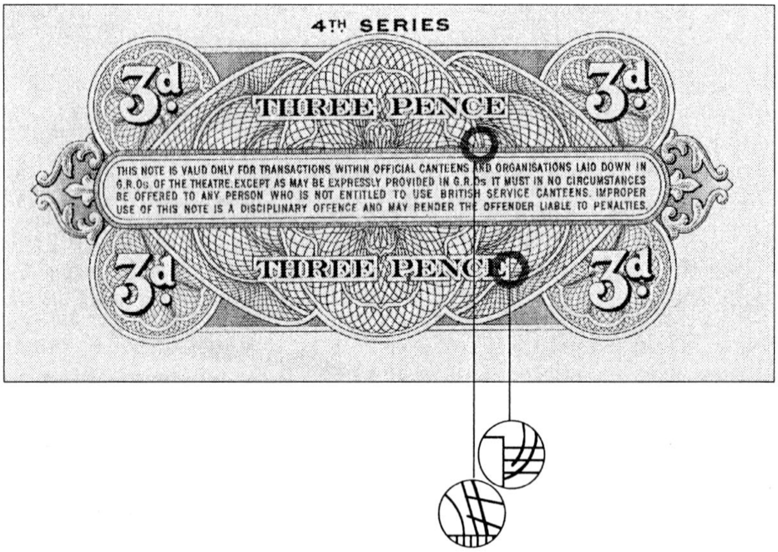

Figure 62. Secret marks on 3d Fourth Series - back

Figure 63. Secret marks on 6d Fourth Series - face

Figure 64. Secret marks on 6d Fourth Series - back

Figure 65. Secret marks on 1/- Fourth Series - face

Figure 66. Secret marks on 1/- Fourth Series - back

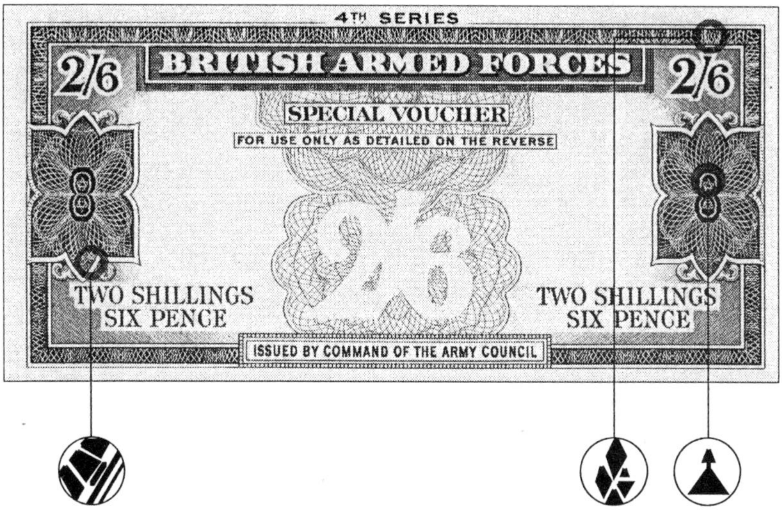

Figure 67. Secret marks on 2/6 Fourth Series - face

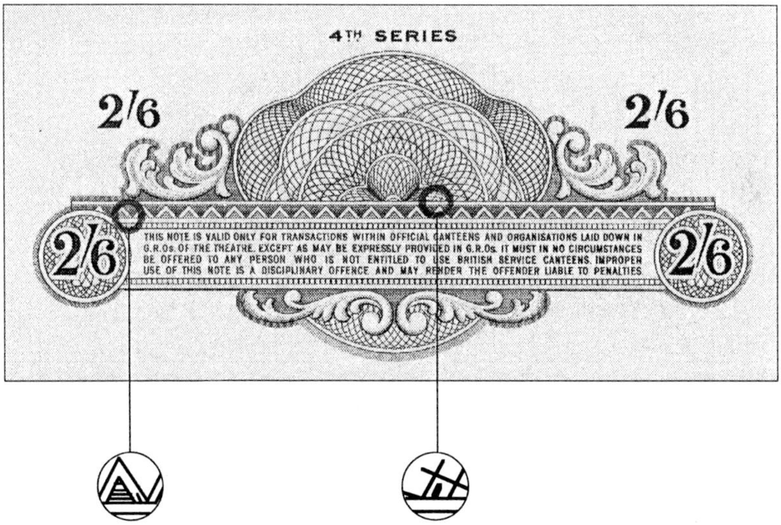

Figure 68. Secret marks on 2/6 Fourth Series - back

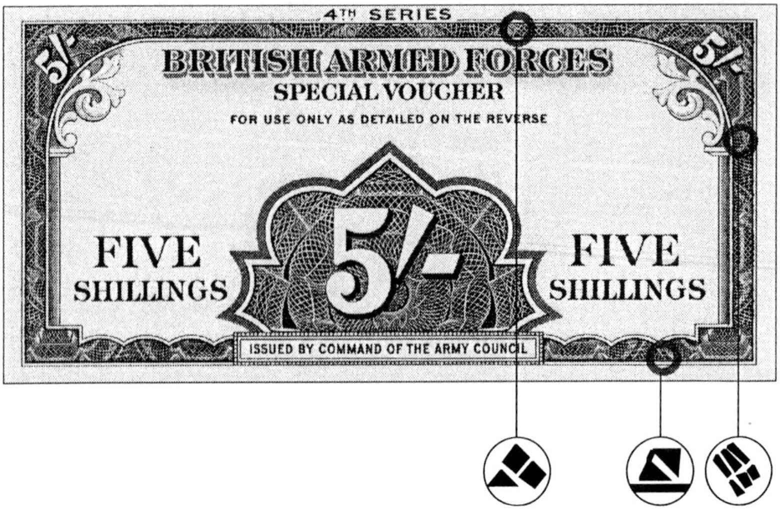

Figure 69. Secret marks on 5/- Fourth Series - face

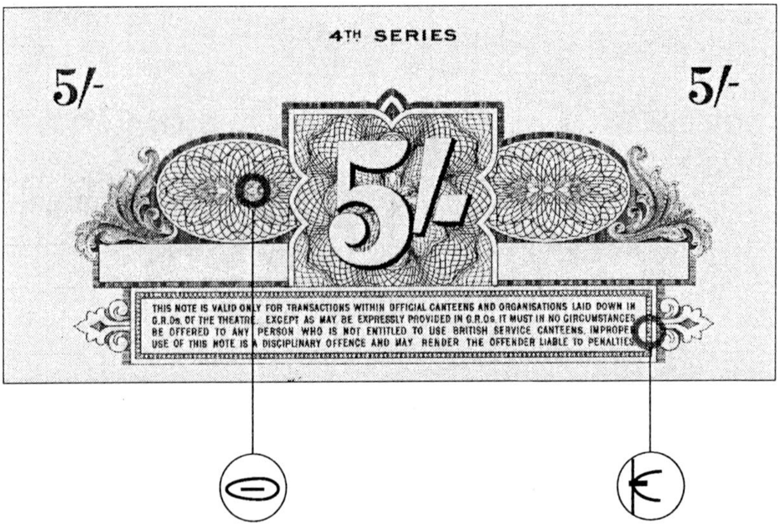

Figure 70. Secret marks on 5/- Fourth Series - back

Figure 71. Secret marks on 10/- Fourth Series - face

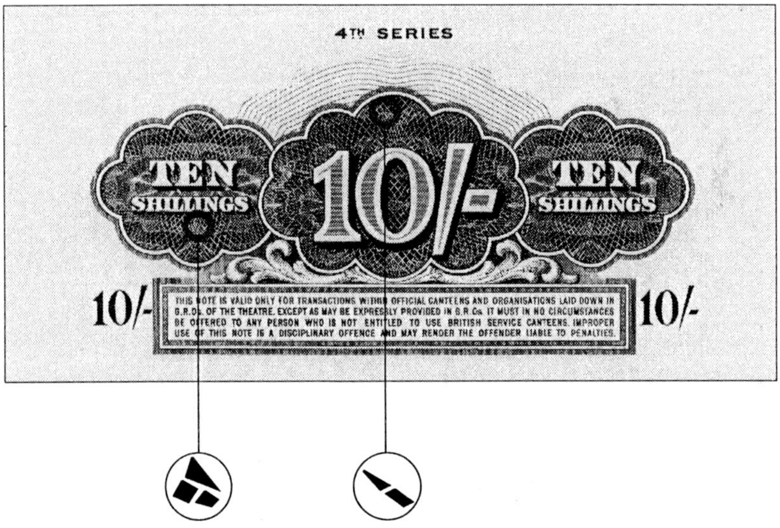

Figure 72. Secret marks on 10/- Fourth Series - back

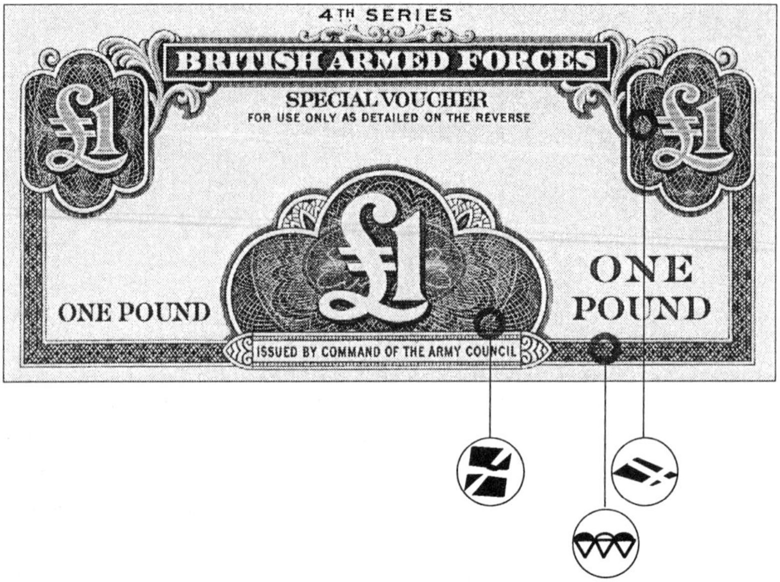

Figure 73. Secret marks on £1 Fourth Series - face

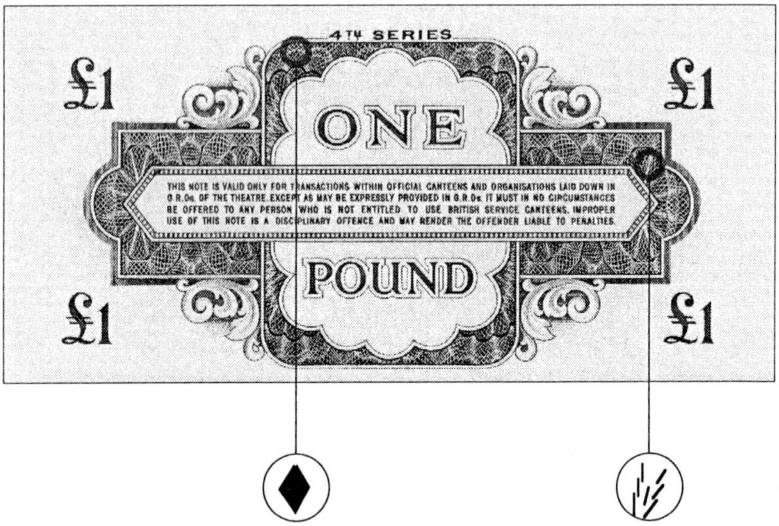

Figure 74. Secret marks on £1 Fourth Series - back

THE FIFTH SERIES

The Fifth Series vouchers are known in essay form only and, as far as we can tell, no print run of any size has been produced. Essay BAFSVs, in this as well as other Series, were cancelled by the printer using a *one* or two 4-mm hole punch cancellation. These vouchers are extremely rare and should not be confused with the vouchers cancelled by 6-mm holes which are fairly common and are all from the batch sold by the MoD in 1980

Although we do not have the actual Fifth Series vouchers, we do have the secret marks that they would have contained. The fact that the black pulls of the 2/6, the 10/- and the £1 of this Series were still incomplete when they were sent to the War Office also suggests that they were never actually put into production. The fact that the pulls were of the same type as the pulls for the Fourth Series indicates that the Fifth Series notes were also prepared by Bradbury Wilkinson and would have been printed by them if it should have come to that.

The secret marks on the Fifth Series can be described as follows:

GROUP 1 *3d, 6d and 1/-*

3d face:
- a small break has been inserted in the design of the top horizontal border above the right branch of the acanthus leaf over the '3d' denomination on the left
- small irregularities have been introduced in part of the design within the border surrounding the '3d' denomination on the right just underneath the left branch of the acanthus leaf

- a very small vertical line has been added within the bottom horizontal border just below the middle of the acanthus leaves underneath the '3d' denomination on the right

3d back:
- an extra line has been added dividing one of the diamond shaped designs within the scroll work of the horizontal edge just below the 'T' of '5TH SERIES'
- one of the lines of the scroll work just under the 'N' of 'PENCE' on the right of the voucher has been slightly extended

6d face:
- a small irregularity has been inserted within the design work of the top border just above the first 'I' in 'BRITISH'
- a small break has been introduced into one of the open lines in the design of the vertical right border just right of the centre of the lower acanthus leaf joining this border
- a small break has been introduced into one of the open lines in the lower horizontal border under the 'I' in 'ISSUED'

6d back:
- the lower curves of two of the wavy lines have been connected by a very small vertical line, below the word 'NOTE', right against the lower edge of the border
- a small vertical line has been inserted in the design above the final 'N' of the word 'ORGANISATIONS'

1/- face:
- a small break across an open line has been inserted in the design of the left hand vertical border at the same level as the top of the word 'SHILLING'
- a small ink triangle has been inserted near the bottom of the lower horizontal border just under the 'MM' in 'COMMAND

1/- back:
- a small horizontal line has been inserted in one of the diamond shaped design elements under the lower left corner of the figure '1' in the left top denomination

- a very small horizontal line has been inserted in one of the design elements immediately above the top right hand corner of the box containing the text

GROUP 2 *2/6 and 5/-*

2/6 face:
- one of the open lines in the centre of the design within the top horizontal border just under the figure '5' in '5TH SERIES' has been interrupted
- a small horizontal mark has been added just above the branching point of the tree-like shape within the top horizontal border just above the 'CE' in 'FORCES'
- a very small open line has been omitted near the top of the design in the lower horizontal border just under the right hand tip of the acanthus leaf on the lower left of the voucher

2/6 back:
- a small extension has been added to one of the lines inside the scroll work within the quarter circle on the top left of the main circle
- a very small line has been added inside one of the petals of the small rosette in the lower right corner of the voucher

5/- face:
- an extra slanting vertical mark has been added to the design of the top horizontal border design just under the left vertical stroke of the 'R' in 'SERIES'
- a small vertical mark has been added to the design between the figure '5' and the shilling stroke of the denomination on the left of the voucher
- there is a small line irregularity in the lower horizontal border design just under the 'ND' of 'COMMAND'

5/- back:
- there is a small extension to one of the lines within the scroll work just under the second 'L' in 'SHILLING' on the left of the voucher

- a small vertical line has been added to the border design on the top of the right corner of the box containing the text

GROUP 3 *10/- and £1*

10/- face:

- there is a small line break in the design on the left of the lower horizontal border just under the small lower left acanthus leaf
- there are some irregularities in the design just above the figure '1' in the central '10/-' denomination
- a small design element is missing in the design of the top horizontal border above the 'S' in 'FORCES'

10/- back:

- a small vertical line has been added in the vertical left border design just above the clover shaped corner element in the lower left corner
- there is a break in one of the lines in the scroll work of the central rosette above the text box just right of the centre under the final 'S' of 'SERIES'

£1 face:

- a small circle in the tip of the design element of the lower horizontal border is missing below the 'O' in 'POUND' on the left of the voucher
- a small ink line has been added to the design of the right vertical border of the voucher just to the right of the 'D' in 'POUND'
- there is a break in an open line in the design of the top horizontal border just above the right half of the 'R' in 'BRITISH'

£1 back:

- a small line has been added in the scroll work of the border design in the left half of the central rosette above the tip of the left acanthus leaf on the same level as the cross strokes of the '£' signs
- a small ink line is missing from the design in the top horizontal border just over the '1' in the large '£1' denomination on the right of the voucher

Figure 75. Secret marks on 3d Fifth Series - face

Figure 76. Secret marks on 3d Fifth Series - back

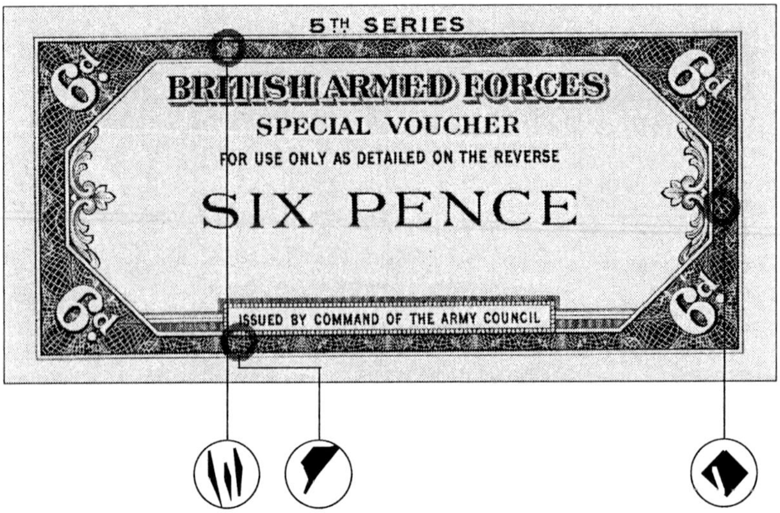

Figure 77. Secret marks on 6d Fifth Series - face

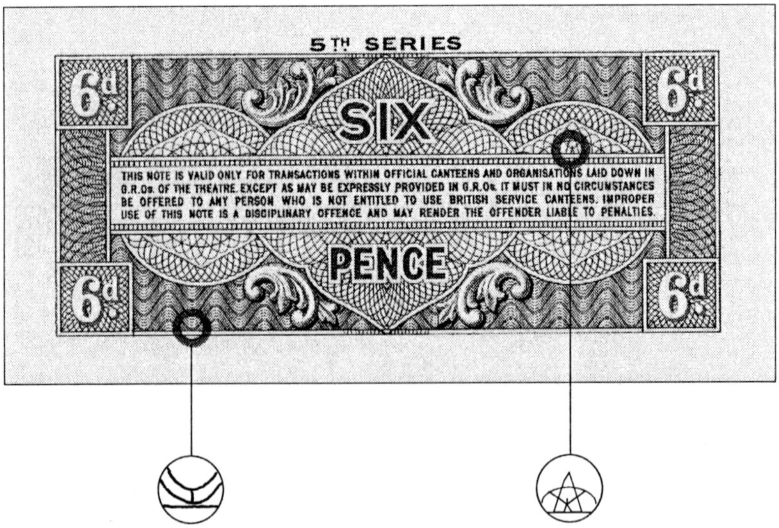

Figure 78. Secret marks on 6d Fifth Series - back

Figure 79. Secret marks on 1/- Fifth Series - face

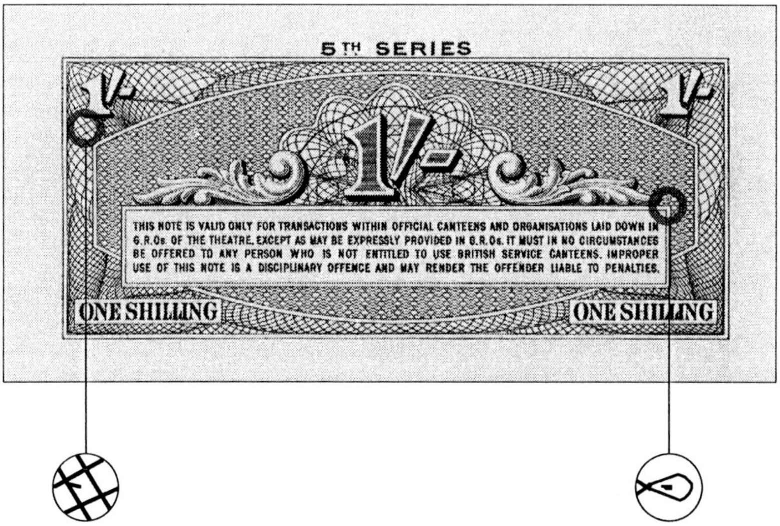

Figure 80. Secret marks on 1/- Fifth Series - back

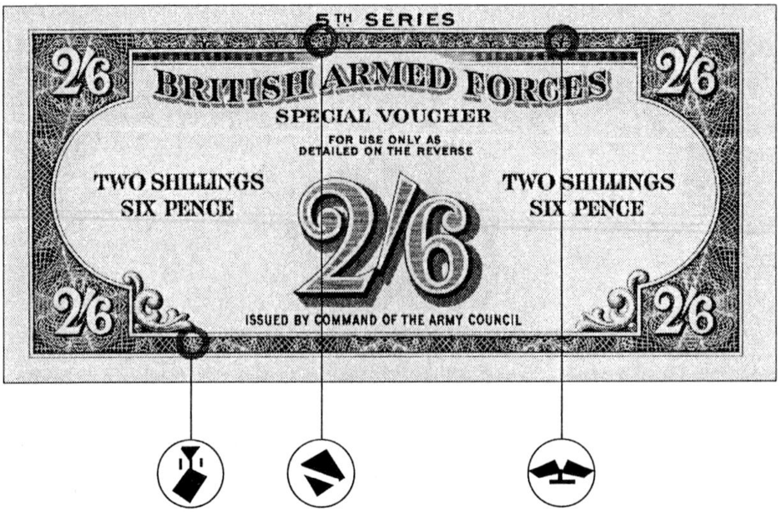

Figure 81. Secret marks on 2/6 Fifth Series - face

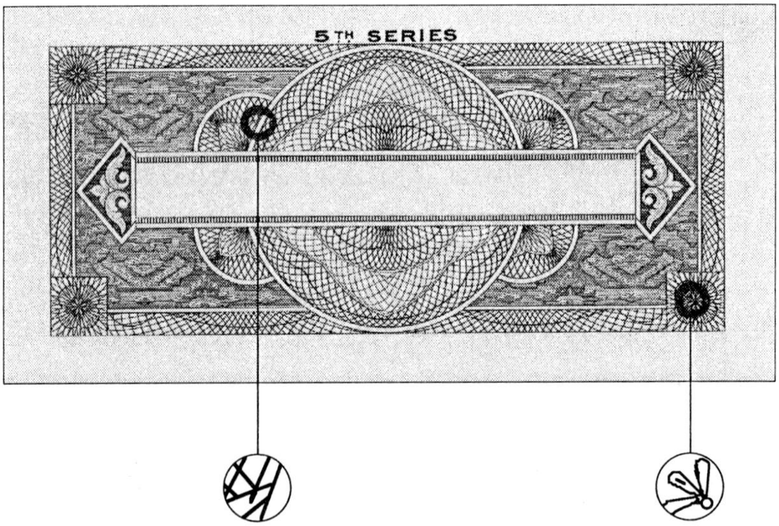

Figure 82. Secret marks on 2/6 Fifth Series - back

Figure 83. Secret marks on 5/- Fifth Series - face

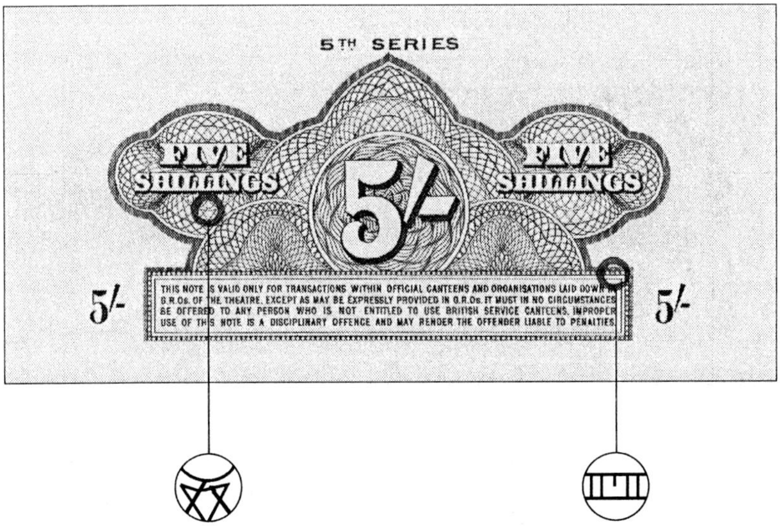

Figure 84. Secret marks on 5/- Fifth Series - back

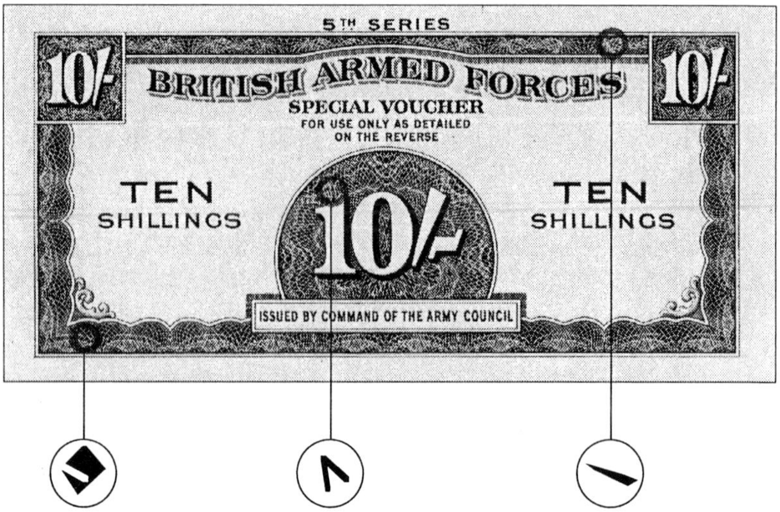

Figure 85. Secret marks on 10/- Fifth Series - face

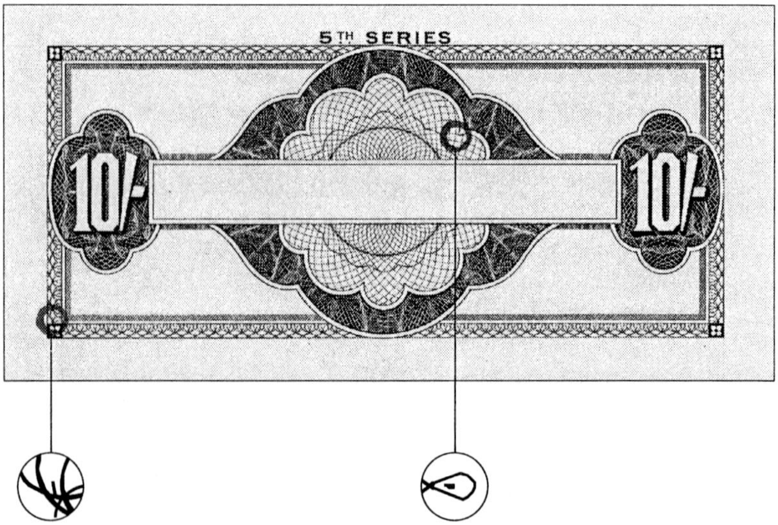

Figure 86. Secret marks on 10/- Fifth Series - back

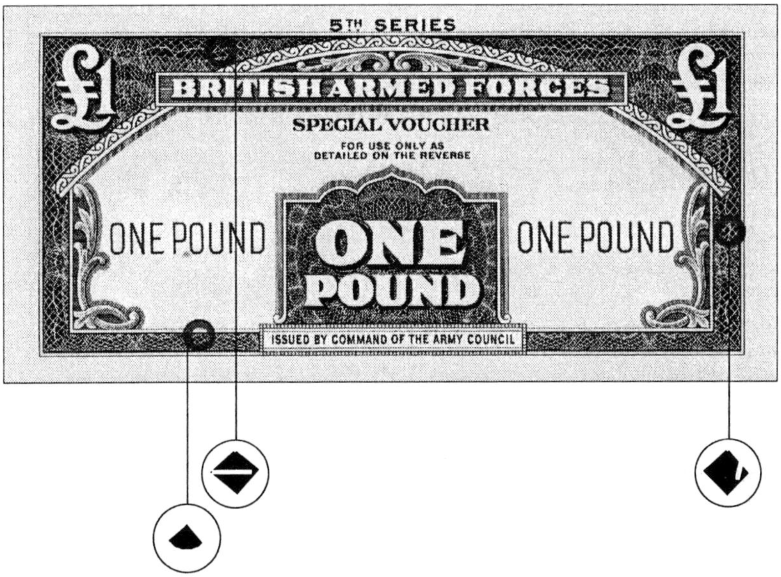

Figure 87. Secret marks on £1 Fifth Series - face

Figure 88. Secret marks on £1 Fifth Series - back

THE SIXTH SERIES

With the Sixth Series we have arrived at the last Series of BAFSVs. In
contrast to the Fourth and Fifth Series the notes of the Sixth Series really circulated. The Sixth Series was necessary when Britain went decimal in 1972 and, as a consequence, the shillings-and-pence notes could no longer be used. Because the £1 and £5 notes of the Second Series were not affected by this decimalisation they did not have to be replaced and the Second Series notes for £1 and £5 remained in circulation. The Sixth Series, together with the Second Series £1 and £5 were used in Berlin up to 31 December 1979, when BAFSVs were withdrawn altogether.

The notes used during this period were printed by Thomas De La Rue, long considered to be the only printer of Sixth Series notes. However, as it turned out, another order was placed by the Ministry of Defence for Sixth Series notes with Bradbury Wilkinson. In contrast to the Fourth and the Fifth Series notes Bradbury now put its name on the notes. The Bradbury notes were actually printed, but as far as we know, never circulated. At first glance, the notes printed by De La Rue and those printed by Bradbury Wilkinson look identical. However, the notes are distinctly different in that the underprint pattern is different as well as the design used to fill in the letters. The secret marks on the notes are also different with both printers and the quality of engraving on the De La Rue notes is infinitely more crisp and precise than on the Bradbury notes.

Also, the prefixes on the two different runs are different. Whereas the De La Rue issue has a double letter prefix over a digit, the Bradbury issue has a single digit of a bolder type over a single digit. From the digits reported and from the actual numbers offered for sale by the MoD in 1991 (see Chapter 12) it can be deduced that the following (maximum) number of Sixth Series vouchers were printed over the years by each of the printers involved.

Table 51. Estimated number of Sixth Series vouchers printed

denomination	printer	prefix	number printed
5 p	De La Rue	not used	?
10 p	De La Rue	DD/10[1]	1,000,000
50 p	De La Rue	BB/10	1,000,000
5 p	Bradbury	not used	5,000,000
10 p	Bradbury	A/1-A/6	6,000,000
50 p	Bradbury	B/1	1,000,000

One change incorporated in the Sixth Series which both printers had to deal with was the change in issuing authority. In 1971, when the Sixth Series came into existence, the Army Council had ceased to exist and was replaced by the Defence Council, following the reorganisation of the Ministry of Defence in 1963/1964 (see Appendix G for more details). The duties of the Army Council were taken over by the Defence Council and it was the latter body which now became the issuing authority for BAFSVs. The vouchers of the Sixth Series, conceived in 1970, therefore carry the text 'ISSUED BY THE DEFENCE COUNCIL'.

PAPER USED FOR THE SIXTH SERIES

The paper used for the Sixth Series vouchers contains a very simple watermark of vertical bands of wavy lines. This paper was used for both the De La Rue and the Bradbury vouchers and was the same as that used for the Second Series watermarked vouchers, although in the latter the bands of wavy lines run horizontally.

[1] The lower digits with the double-letter prefix DD were used for the 2nd series 2/6 voucher

DESIGN OF THE SIXTH SERIES

Although there was clearly one overall design agreed between the two printers, probably under the auspices of the Bank of England, the details of the design differ sufficiently to recognise the printer. The main difference between the two sub-designs lies in the geometrical underprint patterns.

On top of these differences the secret marks on the notes as well as some other small design elements are clearly distinct for the two printers

PACKAGING OF THE SIXTH SERIES VOUCHERS

De La Rue's method of wrapping and packing the notes had not changed much over the years. The vouchers were again packed 1,000 to a bundle with a cardboard top and bottom but this time held together with thin string rather than a cotton tape. Again this was secured by a wax seal bearing their company logo. These bundles were than stacked in heavy tin-lined tea chest type boxes at 50,000 vouchers per box.

In contrast to the De La Rue method, Bradbury Wilkinson basically shrink-wrapped their bundles of vouchers in plastic foil bearing the Bradbury Wilkinson company logo. These bundles also contained 1,000 vouchers. The bundles of 10p and 50p vouchers were subdivided into 10 packs by wrapping a plain paper band around every 100 vouchers before being shrink-wrapped. This pattern was not followed with the bundles of 5p Bradbury vouchers. This can be regarded as fairly strange, since, in contrast to the 10p and 50p notes, the 5p note has no serial number, so there is no way of easily subdividing a pack of 5p notes, except by actually counting them. De La Rue, however, also subdivided its 5p vouchers into packs of 100 before making up a bundle of 1,000. This followed the original instruction by the War Office from July 1948 when the Third Series was ordered with De La Rue.

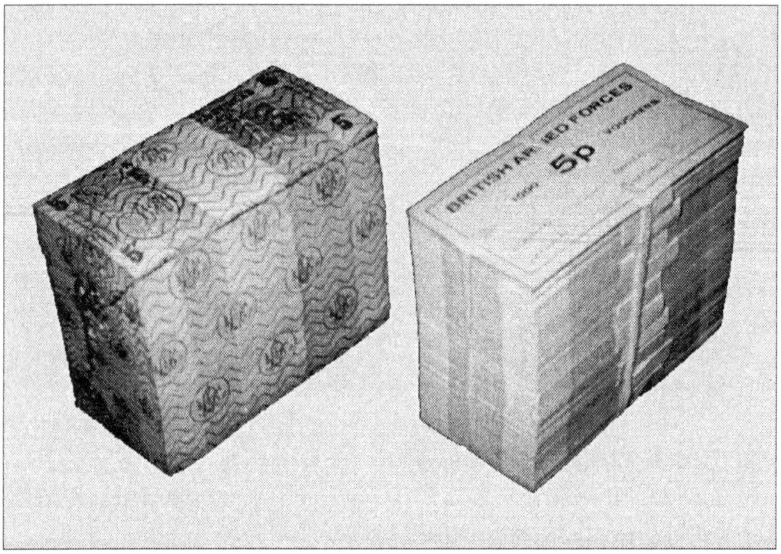

Figure 89. Bundles of 1,000 Sixth Series vouchers wrapped by TdlR (right) and BW (left)

SECRET MARKS ON THE SIXTH SERIES 'DE LA RUE' VOUCHERS

With the introduction of the Sixth Series the relative importance of secret marks as a means of deterring counterfeiters had deminished considerably. Photographic and printing techniques had developed tremendously between the early 1950s and the period of the printing of the Sixth Series. Although still present in the Sixth Series, the secret marks were probably put in by the printer to establish an easy way of recognising the actual plates and print runs that a certain voucher was produced with. This would also account for the fact that the two printers used different secret marks. The total number of secret marks on the vouchers printed by De La Rue had been reduced to the bare minimum of one mark per side.

The secret marks on the De La Rue set of Sixth Series notes can be described as follows:

5p face:

- an extra line has been added connecting the two right hand curves of the scroll work throught the right side of the large '5' of the main '5P' denomination

5p back:

- a small break has been made in one of the lines in the scroll work just under the tip of the large '5' of the '5P' denomination in the top right

10p face:

- a small '+' has been added right in the centre of the scroll work on top of the large '1' of the main '10P' denomination

10p back:

- a very small line has been added connecting two of the curls in the top of the scroll work between the 'P' in the top left '10P' and the'T' in 'TEN' on the centre top of the voucher

50p face:

- a small extra line has been added connecting two of the scroll work lines in the lower tip of the large '5' in the main '50P' denomination

50p back:

- a small line has been added connecting three of the scroll work lines right in the middle of the extreme right border

Figure 90. Secret marks on 5p Sixth Series De La Rue printing - face

Figure 91. Secret marks on 5p Sixth Series De La Rue printing - back

Figure 92. Secret marks on 10p Sixth Series De La Rue printing - face

Figure 93. Secret marks on 10p Sixth Series De La Rue printing - back

152

Figure 94. Secret marks on 50p Sixth Series De La Rue printing - face

Figure 95. Secret marks on 50p Sixth Series De La Rue printing - back

The secret marks used by Bradbury Wilkinson are very obscure. Some of the marks are hardly visible even under strong magnification. This is in line with the secret marks found on the Fourth and Fifth Series vouchers which also tended to be more obscure than the marks used by De La Rue. Also, in contrast to the De La Rue's Sixth Series secret marks, there are more of them hidden in the design and not always the same number on each denomination.

The secret marks on the Bradbury Sixth Series issue are:

5p face:
- there is a small break in the brown scroll work lines extending toward the left of the voucher nearly touching the vertical text 'for use only as detailed on the reverse'

5p back:
- a small solid dot has been incorporated in the scroll work just above the right hand corner of the large '5' in the lower left corner of the voucher
- a small extra line has been added to the scroll work just above the previous mark

10p face:
- a small vertical forked line has been added to the centre of the whirl just above the large '1' on the left of the voucher
- there is a break in one of the scroll work loops going up to and just below the letter 'S' in 'FORCES'

10p back:
- there is a break in one of the outer scroll work loops on the far left and centre of the voucher

50p face:
- a small extra line has been added connecting the bottom two lines of the scroll work just under the 'F' in 'FORCES' on the top of the voucher

- there is a small whirl added to one of the scroll work loops just to the lower right of the last digit of the serial number on the lower left
- there is a small break in one of the scroll work lines just right of the last letter 'E' in 'PENCE'

50p back:

- none, which is strange given the fact that more secret marks were hidden on the lower denominations than seemed warranted by the value of these vouchers

Figure 96. Secret marks on 5p Sixth Series Bradbury Wilkinson printing - face

Figure 97. Secret marks on 5p Sixth Series Bradbury Wilkinson printing - back

Figure 98. Secret marks on 10p Sixth Series Bradbury Wilkinson printing - face

Figure 99. Secret marks on 10p Sixth Series Bradbury Wilkinson printing - back

Figure 100. Secret marks on 50p Sixth Series Bradbury Wilkinson printing - face

BRITISH ARMED FORCES SPECIAL VOUCHERS

DESTRUCTION OF USED BAFSVS

During the period in which the BAFSVs were used, the Army was confronted with all aspects of banknote circulation, most notably the need to replace worn and dirty notes and provide for their destruction. Apart from the actual replacement of the notes and their physical destruction this also involved proper procedures in terms of accountability, administration and so on.

This was not an easy task. In May 1952, four years after their introduction, some £4,000,000 worth of vouchers of the Second Series had been destroyed, half of the value of the initial print run of 1947! The following figures, relating only to the British Army of the Rhine arena, speak for themselves:

Table 52. Second Series vouchers destroyed by BAOR to April 1952

up to	value	
30.06.1950	£559,000	
30.09.1950	£444,000	
31.12.1950	£479,000	
31.03.1951	£360,000	
30.06.1951	£458,000	
30.09.1951	£455,000	
31.12.1951	£354,000	
31.03.1952	£400,000	approx.
30.04.1952	£200,000	approx.
TOTAL DESTROYED	£3,709,000	

Taking into account the true net circulation in BAOR, excluding special reserves and the stocks in the hands of cashiers, it was getting to a stage where complete replacement would take place every 15 months.
Worried about the cost that would be incurred, the War Office urged the Deputy Paymaster-in-Chief to look into the matter and perhaps impose lower standards and only take out of circulation those notes which had clearly become sub-standard, (the War Office was apparently unaware that the average circulation period of the Bank of England's 10/- notes was 6 to 7 months at that time!)

The procedure of counting and destroying unserviceable notes was simple. The BAFSVs which were considered unfit for further use were taken out of circulation by the army cashiers and sent to their respective Headquarters. There, a so-called Currency Destruction Board would convene each month to examine, count and physically destroy the accumulated unserviceable BAFSVs.

A Currency Destruction Board would typically consist of three officers, assisted by two Warrant Officers or Senior NCOs and would be employed for four or five days examining and counting every note and, finally, in burning those approved for destruction.

The number of notes destroyed frequently exceeded 300,000 of which about half would be notes of small denominations i.e. 3d, 6d and 1/-. The notes concerned would be delivered to the Board in bundles of 100 notes and double banded with brown paper tape, each bundle bearing the stamp of the originating cash office and signed by two of its members. The notes themselves, when unwrapped, were very soiled and crumpled and could only be counted at a very slow rate. However, guidelines insisted that every note had to be accounted for, so this laborious routine was followed faithfully and apparently without much opposition with regard to the actual necessity of such a stringent procedure.

To get an idea of the actual work done we could look more closely at the details of a Currency Destruction Board sitting in June 1958, when an accumulation of two months was offered to the Board for destruction. At this sitting the Board consisted of a Captain RE, a Lieutenant RACP, a Command Secretariat Representative, a Warrant Officer and two Sergeants.

The following number of notes were involved on that occasion:

Table 53. Second Series vouchers destroyed in sample sitting 1958

denomination	no. of vouchers	value
£1	127,700	£127,700
10/-	69,900	£34,950
5/-	96,400	£24,100
2/6	93,100	£11,637.10
1/-	144,100	£7,205
6d	125,300	£3,132.10
3d	145,200	£1,815
TOTAL	801,700	£210,540

After sitting for a week the Board had counted and destroyed about 350,000 of the vouchers offered, after which they had to stop due to other duties and a general shortage of staff in all units concerned. This meant that the next sitting would start with a backlog of some 450,000 notes.

Judging from the actual numbers involved it is clear that more than half the vouchers were of the low denominations and represented a value of just over 5 % of the total value If it were to be permitted to destroy the lower denominations without physically checking every single note this would dramatically lighten the burden of the Currency Destruction Boards.

On this assumption the Deputy Paymaster-in-Chief called in the Organisation & Methods department of the War Office to try and help him find a way of minimising the workload. O&M complied and worked out that, if a 10 % check were to be made on the bundles of low denomination notes, this would prove adequate to find any discrepancy. Should discrepancies be found then the Board would have to increase the numbers checked to ensure that no significant variants existed. Applied to the numbers of the example mentioned above this would mean that, in total, only 328,560 notes would have to be counted which in turn would mean that the Currency Destruction Board could have completed the work in one week and could have dealt with *all* the notes. The War Office accountants did not like the idea, however,. By comparing the data of various Currency Destruction Boards they felt that some boards seemed to cope better than others and therefore those 'other' boards should work harder. To substantiate this they quoted two boards which destroyed 481,000 and 294,744 notes respectively in one-week sittings. They therefore felt that the President of the Boards ought to set a daily target at which to aim. However, they were not altogether certain that their approach would work and they offered to allow a further one or two officers to be involved in the work of the CDBs, at the same time aware that this might make the Boards unwieldy.

The suggestion that some Boards (and thus probably *their* Boards) did not work as hard as others was not taken very kindly by the Command Secretary of the BAOR. The proposal to increase the number of staff on the Boards was dismissed out of hand, as was the setting of daily targets. In his view this could only lead to careless counting and his response to the War Office was to leave it to the Deputy Paymaster-in-Chief and to the Command Secretary to introduce such measures as were necessary. After lengthy correspondence between various War Office departments in September 1958 the War Office finally wrote to all concerned that the existing procedure was to remain in place. The whole fight became rather academic shortly after that, because, in 1959, all BAFSVs were withdrawn except those for use in West Berlin. But, sure enough, in 1967 the Command Secretariat of the BAOR approached the Ministry of Defence about the work involved in collecting, counting and destroying the unserviceable BAFSVs circulating in West Berlin. Although by now Currency Destruction Boards only met every six months in Berlin it was estimated that, at each sitting, some 65,000 notes still had to be counted by hand and destroyed. Apparently this took a Board comprising twelve members about 6 hours. As the Assistant Command Secretary, J. Meyers, pointed out at the time: '*The notes are filthy, and so are the members* [of the Board] *after emptying the grill to ensure that no voucher has escaped destruction.*' To solve this problem it was proposed to count only the notes of 2/6, 5/-, 10/- and £1 denominations and take a 10% check on the notes of lower values, since this would cut in half the time needed to process the notes concerned and, as before, this suggestion was put to the Ministry of Defence. But this time, instead of being dismissed out of hand as had happened in 1958, the Ministry of Defence suggested that the whole procedure could be made much more efficient if the cashier counted not only the notes in bundles of 100, but also applied some indelible means of cancellation such as punching holes or cutting off a corner of each bundle. The Boards would then only have to check whether this had been done on the lower denominations, take a 10% check and proceed with the destruction unless they felt there was a particular need to count the bundles after all. Besides making the work easier for the Boards it would have the added advantage that bundles in transit from the cashier to the Boards would be worthless if stolen or lost. Subject to this the War Office agreed to relaxing the procedure and even went so far as to say that it '*...did not wish to stick slavishly to the earlier* [guide]*line...*' and suggested that the Deputy Paymaster-in-Chief looked into the practicability of invalidating the vouchers concerned. But the War Office remained every bit as suspicious and carried on to suggest that the Boards should definitely check each and every bundle by flicking through them in order to make sure that they did contain BAFSVs and not '*...bits of paper as make-weights...*'. However, when the War Office transmitted these proposals to the Command Secretariat of the BAOR the latter was not at all pleased and saw no need to go to such lengths. As for the added security these measures would bring, the BAOR pointed out that the Board in fact assembled in the same building as, and actually near to the cashier's strong room with the burning taking place within the same compound. This seemed to them an adequate security procedure. The Assistant-Command Secretary suggested that the War Office accountants should get in touch with the Bank of England to find out what procedure was followed there, apparently in the hope that this would settle the matter in his favour. As it turned out, he was mistaken. The Bank of England appeared to apply the same procedure as that proposed by the War Office and suggested that the old procedure be kept in place and in addition, that pre-cancellation of all notes and a 100 % check of the contents of all bundles be introduced. However, the War Office pointed out that it would not insist on such a rigorous procedure since the purchasing power of the notes involved was very circumscribed. But nothing changed. The procedure remained in place and the Boards became as grubby when counting and destroying as always. That is, until April 1968, when a special note counting machine was demonstrated to the War Office Organisation & Methods Department by Pitney-Bowes, an office machine supplier. Among a number of apparently amazing things it could do was to cancel and/or mutilate notes which were unserviceable while counting them at a speed of 600 notes per minute. This machine, the Totomaster, which included a fixed imprinter to overprint notes, would cost £700 and, as the Paymaster-in-Chief pointed out when suggesting its purchase, this amount would be paid out of the Berlin budget. The Command Secretariat was delighted that something was happening at last, but not for long. The WO Accountants thought that the machine was too expensive and '*.... possibly not able to cope with marmalade coated 3d notes...*' and they felt that even an alternative British machine costing £90 was too expensive for the purpose. Instead, on 8 August 1968 they proposed buying a simple punch costing £20 and finally agreed that, subject to this being used to make holes in the old vouchers, the rule about counting each and every low-denomination note could be relaxed.

Instead of pursuing the previous line of argument and counter-argument the Command Secretariat now adopted a new tactic. It wrote to the accountants of the War Office it was were delighted with the relaxation of the procedure and understood that this was subject to the notes being previously cancelled by a suitable machine. The Command Secretariat went ahead and bought the Pernuma 2180 which was an electric machine, foot operated, of German manufacture and which could drive a hole of about 15 mm (over 1/2 ") diameter through a large bundle of notes. (The cost to the Berlin budget was DM 3,180, about £334 at the time). At last, the matter was resolved.

HOW IT ALL ENDED

THE SALE OF THE CENTURY

In a final grand clearance in 1991, the Ministry of Defence disposed of all the BAFSVs it still had in store. Whereas previously it had only sold off the shilling and pence denominations, this time it sold the decimalised vouchers and all the pound vouchers from the Second, Third and Fourth Series as well as the £5 vouchers, in other words all vouchers that may still have been put to use. Obviously this was triggered by the fact that the last potential black market area where the British were involved had disappeared with the reunification of Germany and consequently of West and East Berlin in 1990. Since the British troops could go home and the likelihood of their immediate involvement in other war arenas looked slim at the time, there appeared to be no more immediate need for canteen money.

Most of the Sixth Series vouchers in this lot had been printed by Bradbury Wilkinson (and had never been released for circulation). Fewer than 50,000 vouchers of each Sixth Series denomination in this sale were of the type printed by De La Rue and these were left over from the Sixth Series vouchers actually in circulation.

In the numbers mentioned as 'uncirculated' a small number of vouchers are included which had been repacked into bundles of 100 vouchers, which was usually done when an original bundle of 1,000 vouchers was 'broken into'. The circulated vouchers had seen considerable use and it is reported that the used £5 examples were ultimately destroyed by one of the buyers.

The following vouchers, most of them uncirculated but some used, were included in this grand clearance sale:

Table 54. Vouchers sold by the MoD in 1991 auction[1]

Series	denomination	printer	uncirculated vouchers	circulated vouchers
2nd	£1	TdlR	1,772,000	67,000
	£5	TdlR	184,000	54,000
3rd	£1	BW	499,600	
4th	£1	BW	2,350,000	
6th	5p	BW	5,019,000	
	5p	TdlR	< 50,000	
	10p	BW	5,642,000	
	10p	TdlR	< 50,000	
	50p	BW	1,302,000	
	50p	TdlR	< 50,000	
TOTAL			< 16,918,600	121,000

In contrast to the private deal in 1980 the sale of this bulk lot of BAFSVs was conducted by public auction at Phillips of London on 14 February 1991. The result was remarkable. Not only was a record number of over 17,000,000 vouchers packed in 352 boxes put on sale in one lot, but this lot also weighed a massive 14 tons (15,000 kilo) and was therefore easily the heaviest lot ever put up for sale. To top it all, the price, estimated in the auction catalogue at £25,000 to £30,000 proved to break a third record when the lot was sold for £129,000, the highest sum ever paid for one lot of vouchers. The buyer of this lot was a consortium of British note dealers who were intent on keeping the vouchers in Britain and available to the collecting community. In contrast to the sale of vouchers in 1980 the vouchers sold by auction were not cancelled nor was cancellation required which, of course, greatly enhances their desirability for collectors.

[1] These figures are based on an actual count of the vouchers in this batch. The official figures quoted in various publications are slightly lower with a total of 17,029,000 vouchers.

Although this appears to be the end of the phenomenon of British Armed Forces Canteen Money the idea must not be dismissed out of hand that the Government may have a completely new Series of vouchers printed and stored, ready to be put into action should this ever prove to be necessary.

CATALOGUE

reference number : E-01

denomination : 3 pence
series : 1 (no series designator)
paper : plain
size : 11.4 x 5.7 cm
dominant colours : purple/orange
date printed : June 1946
printed by : Thomas De La Rue
number printed : 8,000,000
prefixes : none

remarks
- Used in Germany (BAOR), Austria (BTA), Japan (BCOF) and Trieste (BETFOR, Italy)

reference number : E-02

denomination	: 6 pence
series	: 1 (no series designator)
paper	: plain
size	: 11.4 x 5.7 cm
dominant colours	: brown/red
date printed	: June 1946
printed by	: Thomas De La Rue
number printed	: 10,000,000
prefixes	: none

remarks

- Used in Germany (BAOR), Austria (BTA), Japan (BCOF) and Trieste (BETFOR, Italy)

reference number : E-03

denomination	: 1 shilling
series	: 1 (no series designator)
paper	: plain
size	: 11.4 x 5.7 cm
dominant colours	: blue/green
date printed	: June 1946
printed by	: Thomas De La Rue
number printed	: 8,000,000
prefixes	: none

remarks

- Used in Germany (BAOR), Austria (BTA), Japan (BCOF) and Trieste (BETFOR, Italy)

reference number : E-04

denomination	: 2 shillings and 6 pence
series	: 1 (no series denominator)
paper	: plain with vertical metal thread
size	: 12.6 x 6.3 cm
dominant colours	: red/green
date printed	: July 1947
printed by	: Thomas De La Rue
number printed	: 8,000,000
prefixes	: D/1 to D/8 inclusive

remarks

- Used in Germany (BAOR), Austria (BTA), Japan (BCOF) and Trieste (BETFOR, Italy)

reference number : E-05

denomination	: 5 shillings
series	: 1 (no series designator)
paper	: plain
size	: 12.6 x 6.3 cm
dominant colours	: green/purple
date printed	: June 1946
printed by	: Thomas De La Rue
number printed	: 8,000,000
prefixes	: C/1 to C/8 inclusive

remarks

- Used in Germany (BAOR), Austria (BTA), Japan (BCOF) and Trieste (BETFOR, Italy)

reference number : E-06

denomination : 10 shillings
series : 1 (no series designator)
paper : plain with vertical metal thread
size : 14 x 6.9 cm
dominant colours : purple/orange
date printed : June 1946
printed by : Thomas De La Rue
number printed : 8,050,000
prefixes : B/1 to B/9 inclusive

remarks
- Used in Germany (BAOR), Austria (BTA), Japan (BCOF) and Trieste (BETFOR, Italy)

reference number : E-07

denomination	: 1 pound
series	: 1 (no series designator)
paper	: plain with vertical metal thread
size	: 14 x 6.9 cm
dominant colours	: blue/red
date printed	: June 1946
printed by	: Thomas De La Rue
number printed	: 2,350,000
prefixes	: A/1 to A/3 inclusive

remarks

- Used in Germany (BAOR), Austria (BTA), Japan (BCOF) and Trieste (BETFOR, Italy)

reference number : E-08

denomination : 3 pence
series : 1 (no series designator)
paper : plain
size : 11.4 x 5.7 cm
dominant colours : purple/orange
date printed : June 1946
printed by : Thomas De La Rue
number printed : ?
prefixes : none

remarks
- A very small number of E-01 vouchers was overprinted in Japan with the text 'ISSUED IN HM SHIPS AFLOAT FOR USE IN NAAFI CANTEENS ONLY'.
- These vouchers were for the exclusive use of marines serving in a British Naval unit called 'Force T' when on shore leave in Japan.

reference number : E-09

denomination : 6 pence
series : 1 (no series designator)
paper : plain
size : 11.4 x 5.7 cm
dominant colours : brown/red
date printed : June 1946
printed by : Thomas De La Rue
number printed : ?
prefixes : none

remarks

- A very small number of E-02 vouchers was overprinted in Japan with the text 'ISSUED IN HM SHIPS AFLOAT FOR USE IN NAAFI CANTEENS ONLY'.
- These vouchers were for the exclusive use of marines serving in a British Naval unit called 'Force T' when on shore leave in Japan.

reference number : E-10

denomination : 1 shilling
series : 1 (no series designator)
paper : plain
size : 11.4 x 5.7 cm
dominant colours : blue/green
date printed : June 1946
printed by : Thomas De La Rue
number printed : ?
prefixes : none

remarks
- Avery small number of E-03 vouchers was overprinted in Japan with the text 'ISSUED IN HM SHIPS AFLOAT FOR USE IN NAAFI CANTEENS ONLY'.
- These vouchers were for the exclusive use of marines serving in a British Naval unit called 'Force T' when on shore leave in Japan.

reference number : E-11

denomination : 2 shillings and 6 pence
series : 1 (no series denominator)
paper : plain with vertical metal thread
size : 12.6 x 6.3 cm
dominant colours : red/green
date printed : July 1947
printed by : Thomas De La Rue
number printed : ?
prefixes : D/1 to D/8 inclusive

remarks

- A very small number of E-04 vouchers was overprinted in Japan with the text 'ISSUED IN HM SHIPS AFLOAT FOR USE IN NAAFI CANTEENS ONLY'.
- These vouchers were for the exclusive use of marines serving in a British Naval unit called 'Force T' when on shore leave in Japan.

reference number : E-12

denomination : 5 shillings
series : 1 (no series designator)
paper : plain
size : 12.6 x 6.3 cm
dominant colours : green/purple
date printed : June 1946
printed by : Thomas De La Rue
number printed : ?
prefixes : C/1 to C/8 inclusive

remarks
- A very small number of E-05 vouchers was overprinted in Japan with the text 'ISSUED IN HM SHIPS AFLOAT FOR USE IN NAAFI CANTEENS ONLY'.
- These vouchers were for the exclusive use of marines serving in a British Naval unit called 'Force T' when on shore leave in Japan.

reference number : E-13

denomination : 10 shillings
series : 1 (no series designator)
paper : plain with vertical metal thread
size : 14 x 6.9 cm
dominant colours : purple/orange
date printed : June 1946
printed by : Thomas De La Rue
number printed : ?
prefixes : B/1 to B/9 inclusive

remarks

- A very small number of E-06 vouchers was overprinted in Japan with the text 'ISSUED IN HM SHIPS AFLOAT FOR USE IN NAAFI CANTEENS ONLY'.
- These vouchers were for the exclusive use of marines serving in a British Naval unit called 'Force T' when on shore leave in Japan.

reference number : E-14

denomination	: 1 pound
series	: 1 (no series designator)
paper	: plain with vertical metal thread
size	: 14 x 6.9 cm
dominant colours	: blue/red
date printed	: June 1946
printed by	: Thomas De La Rue
number printed	: ?
prefixes	: A/1 to A/3 inclusive

remarks

- A very small number of E-07 vouchers was overprinted in Japan with the text 'ISSUED IN HM SHIPS AFLOAT FOR USE IN NAAFI CANTEENS ONLY'.
- These vouchers were for the exclusive use of marines serving in a British Naval unit called 'Force T' when on shore leave in Japan.

reference number : E-15

denomination	: 3 pence
series	: 2
paper	: plain with vertical metal thread
size	: 11.4 x 5.7 cm
dominant colours	: brown/green
date printed	: August 1947
printed by	: Thomas De La Rue
number printed	: 9,600,000 in first print run
prefixes	: none

remarks
- An unknown number of vouchers was printed in subsequent print runs
- Used in Germany (BAOR), Austria (BTA), Trieste (BETFOR, Italy), Japan (BCOF) and Singapore

reference number : E-16

denomination	: 6 pence
series	: 2
paper	: plain with vertical metal thread
size	: 11.4 x 5.7 cm
dominant colours	: green/orange
date printed	: August 1947
printed by	: Thomas De La Rue
number printed	: 6,400,000 in first print run
prefixes	: none

remarks

- An unknown number of vouchers was printed in subsequent print runs
- Used in Germany (BAOR), Austria (BTA), Trieste (BETFOR, Italy), Japan (BCOF) and Singapore

reference number : E-17

denomination : 1 shilling
series : 2
paper : plain with vertical metal thread
size : 11.4 x 5.7 cm
dominant colours : brownish red/purple
date printed : August 1947
printed by : Thomas De La Rue
number printed : 6,400,000 in first print run
prefixes : none

remarks
- An unknown number of vouchers was printed in subsequent print runs
- Used in Germany (BAOR), Austria (BTA), Trieste (BETFOR, Italy), Japan (BCOF) and Singapore

reference number : E-18

denomination : 2 shillings and 6 pence
series : 2
paper : plain with vertical metal thread
size : 12.6 x 6.3 cm
dominant colours : purple/green
date printed : August 1947
printed by : Thomas De La Rue
number printed : 4,800,000 in first print run
prefixes : DD/1 to DD/5 inclusive

remarks
- 1,700,000 vouchers were printed in subsequent print runs (up to DD/7 500,000)
- Used in Germany (BAOR), Austria (BTA), Trieste (BETFOR, Italy), Japan (BCOF) and Singapore

reference number : E-19

denomination : 5 shillings
series : 2
paper : plain with vertical metal thread
size : 12.6 x 6.3 cm
dominant colours : blue/orange
date printed : August 1947
printed by : Thomas De La Rue
number printed : 4,800,000 in first print run
prefixes : CC/1 to CC/5 inclusive

remarks
- Between 2,000,000 and 5,000,000 vouchers were printed in subsequent print runs
- Used in Germany (BAOR), Austria (BTA), Trieste (BETFOR, Italy), Japan (BCOF) and Singapore

reference number : E-20

denomination : 10 shillings
series : 2
paper : plain with vertical metal thread
size : 14 x 6.9 cm
dominant colours : green/orange
date printed : August 1947
printed by : Thomas De La Rue
number printed : 4,800,000 in first print run
prefixes : BB/1 to BB/5 inclusive

remarks
- 1,200,000 vouchers were printed in subsequent print runs.
- The last prefix for this variety is BB/6
- Used in Germany (BAOR), Austria (BTA), Trieste (BETFOR, Italy), Japan (BCOF) and Singapore

reference number : E-21

denomination : 1 pound
series : 2
paper : plain with vertical metal thread
size : 14 x 6.9 cm
dominant colours : brown/purple
date printed : July 1947
printed by : Thomas De La Rue
number printed : 3,200,000 in first print run
prefixes : AA/1 to AA/4 inclusive

remarks
- 6,800,000 vouchers were printed in subsequent print runs (last prefix AA/10)
- 1,772,000 new and 67,000 used vouchers of this type were sold by the MoD by public auction in February 1991
- Used in Germany (BAOR), Austria (BTA), Trieste (BETFOR, Italy), Japan (BCOF) and Singapore

reference number : E-22

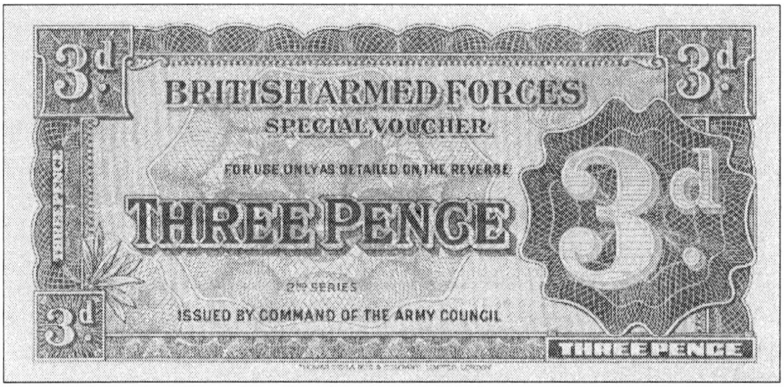

denomination	: 3 pence
series	: 2
paper	: watermarked (vertical)
size	: 11.4 x 5.7 cm
dominant colours	: brown/green
date printed	: 1961
printed by	: Thomas De La Rue
number printed	: ?
prefixes	: none

remarks
- Used in Germany (BAOR)

reference number : E-23

denomination	: 6 pence
series	: 2
paper	: watermarked (vertical)
size	: 11.4 x 5.7 cm
dominant colours	: green/orange
date printed	: 1961
printed by	: Thomas De La Rue
number printed	: ?
prefixes	: none

remarks
– Used in Germany (BAOR)

reference number : E-24

denomination	: 1 shilling
series	: 2
paper	: watermarked (vertical)
size	: 11.4 x 5.7 cm
dominant colours	: brownish red/purple
date printed	: 1961
printed by	: Thomas De La Rue
number printed	: ?
prefixes	: none

remarks
- Used in Germany (BAOR)

reference number : E-25

denomination	: 2 shillings and 6 pence
series	: 2
paper	: watermarked (vertical)
size	: 12.6 x 6.3 cm
dominant colours	: purple/green
date printed	: 1961
printed by	: Thomas De La Rue
number printed	: 2,500,000
prefixes	: DD/7 to DD/9 inclusive

remark
- The numbering of these vouchers carried on from the metal thread variety in mid-prefix!
- Used in Germany (BAOR)

reference number : E-26

denomination	: 5 shillings
series	: 2
paper	: watermark (vertical)
size	: 12.6 x 6.3 cm
dominant colours	: blue/orange
date printed	: 1961
printed by	: Thomas De La Rue
number printed	: 2,000,000 in first print run
prefixes	: CD/1 to CD/2 inclusive

remarks

- Vouchers numbered CD/1 950,001 to 1,000,000 and CD/2 000,001 to 050,000 were cancelled by two 6mm perforations and were sold by the MoD in 1980 to a London dealer. A small number of notes in this lot inadvertently escaped the hole cancellation. The remaining vouchers were destroyed by the MoD in 1981.
- Used in Germany (BAOR)

reference number : E-27

denomination : 10 shillings
series : 2
paper : watermarked (vertical)
size : 14 x 6.9 cm
dominant colours : green/orange
date printed : 1961
printed by : Thomas De La Rue
number printed : 3,000,000
prefixes : BB/7 to BB/9 inclusive

remarks
– Used in Germany (BAOR)

reference number : E-28

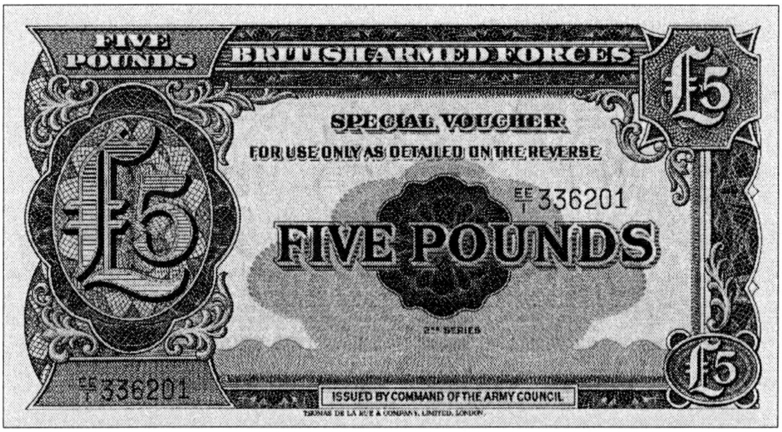

denomination	: 5 pound
series	: 2
paper	: watermarked (vertical)
size	: 14.8 x 8.1 cm
dominant colours	: blue/green
date printed	: 1961
printed by	: Thomas De La Rue
number printed	: 1,000,000
prefixes	: EE/1

remarks
- Used in Germany (BAOR)
- 184,000 new and 54,000 used vouchers of this type were sold by the MoD by public auction in February 1991. The 54,000 used ones are believed to have been destroyed.

reference number : E-29

denomination : 3 pence
series : 3
paper : plain with vertical metal thread
size : 11.4 x 5.7 cm
dominant colours : green/orange red
date printed : September 1948
printed by : Thomas De La Rue (John Waddington)
number printed : 4,980,000
prefixes : none

remarks
- Only 7,920 vouchers of those which actually circulated are unaccounted for. All others are presumed destroyed.
- Used in Egypt

reference number : E-30

199

denomination	: 6 pence
series	: 3
paper	: plain with vertical metal thread
size	: 11.4 x 5.7 cm
dominant colours	: purple/green
date printed	: September 1948
printed by	: Thomas De La Rue (John Waddington)
number printed	: 4,940,000
prefixes	: none

remarks

- Only 4,779 vouchers of those which actually circulated are unaccounted for. All others are presumed destroyed.
- Used in Egypt

reference number : E-31

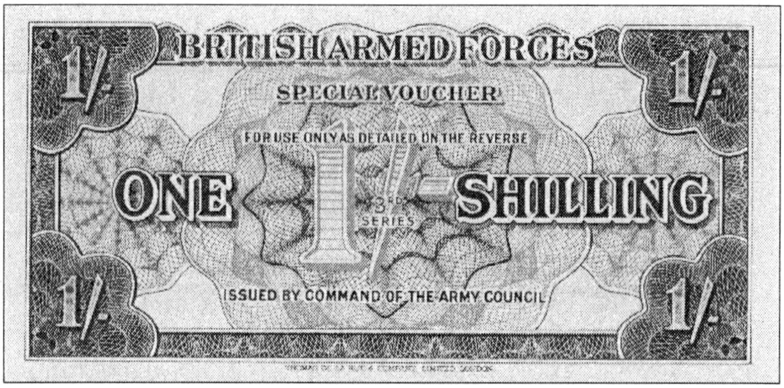

denomination	: 1 shilling
series	: 3
paper	: plain with vertical metal thread
size	: 11.4 x 5.7 cm
dominant colours	: blue/brown/red
date printed	: September 1948
printed by	: Thomas De La Rue (John Waddington)
number printed	: 4,070,000
prefixes	: none

remarks
- Only 3,293 vouchers of those which actually circulated are unaccounted for.
- 100,000 of these vouchers were cancelled by two 6mm perforations and sold by the MoD in 1980 to a London dealer. A small number of notes in this lot inadvertently escaped the hole cancellation. The remaining vouchers were destroyed by the MoD in 1981.
- Used in Egypt

reference number : E-32

denomination	: 2 shillings and 6 pence
series	: 3
paper	: plain with vertical metal thread
size	: 12.6 x 6.3 cm
dominant colours	: green/red
date printed	: September 1948
printed by	: Thomas De La Rue (John Waddington)
number printed	: 3,310,000
prefixes	: J/1 to J/4 inclusive

remarks
- A number of these notes were defective. The paper would split at the metal thread section so the thread could be removed.
- Only 989 vouchers of those which actually circulated are unaccounted for. All others are presumed destroyed.
- Used in Egypt

reference number : E-33

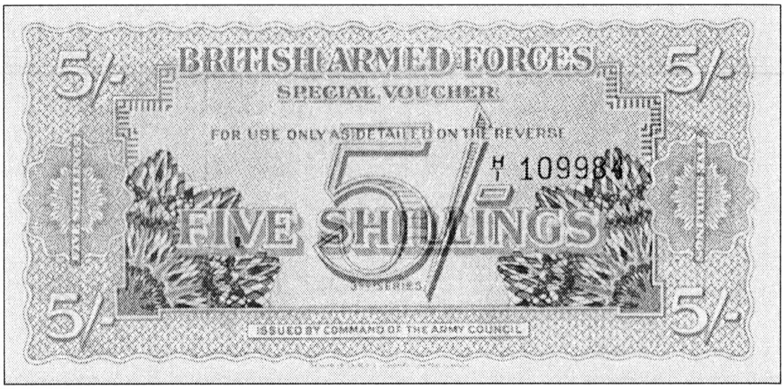

denomination	: 5 shillings
series	: 3
paper	: plain with vertical metal thread
size	: 12.6 x 6.3 cm
dominant colours	: red/green
date printed	: September 1948
printed by	: Thomas De La Rue (John Waddington)
number printed	: 3,040,000
prefixes	: H/1 to H/4 inclusive

remarks

- Only 530 vouchers of those which actually circulated are unaccounted for. All others are presumed destroyed.
- Used in Egypt

reference number : E-34

denomination	: 10 shillings
series	: 3
paper	: plain with vertical metal thread
size	: 14 x 6.9 cm
dominant colours	: red/green
date printed	: September 1948
printed by	: Thomas De La Rue (John Waddington)
number printed	: 2,845,000
prefixes	: G/1 to G/3 inclusive

remarks
- Only 283 vouchers of those which actually circulated are unaccounted for.
- Vouchers numbered G/1 350,000 to 400,000 and G/2 200,001 to 250,000 were cancelled by two 6mm perforations and were sold by the MoD in 1980 to a London dealer. A small number of notes in this lot inadvertently escaped the hole cancellation. The remaining vouchers were destroyed by the MoD in 1981.
- Used in Egypt

reference number : E-35

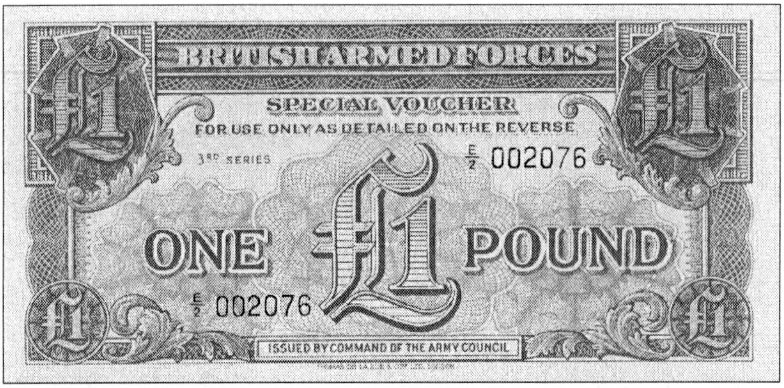

denomination : 1 pound
series : 3
paper : plain with vertical metal thread
size : 14 x 6.9 cm
dominant colours : brown/purple
date printed : September 1948
printed by : Thomas De La Rue (John Waddington)
number printed : 2,490,000
prefixes : E/1 to E/3 inclusive

remarks
- Only 389 vouchers of those which actually circulated are unaccounted for.
- 499,600 vouchers of this type were sold by the MoD by public auction in February 1991.
- Used in Egypt

reference number : E-36

denomination	: 3 pence
series	: 4
paper	: plain with vertical metal thread
size	: 11.4 x 5.7 cm
dominant colours	: slate grey/green
date printed	: 1962
printed by	: Bradbury Wilkinson
number printed	: 9,000,000
prefixes	: none

remarks

- These vouchers were never released for circulation. They were shipped straight to Malta and are believed to have been destroyed locally except for 800,000 vouchers returned to the MoD from Malta and Aden in 1967.

reference number : E-37

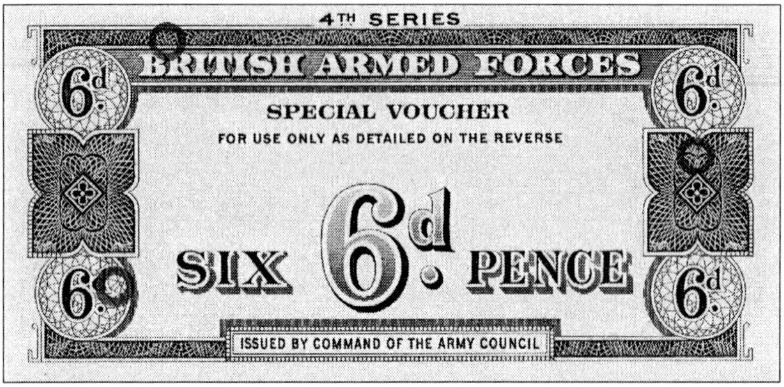

denomination	: 6 pence
series	: 4
paper	: plain with vertical metal thread
size	: 11.4 x 5.7 cm
dominant colours	: blue/violet
date printed	: 1962
printed by	: Bradbury Wilkinson
number printed	: 9,000,000
prefixes	: none

remarks

- These vouchers were never released for circulation. They were shipped straight to Malta and are believed to have been destroyed locally except for 800,000 vouchers returned to the MoD from Malta and Aden in 1967.

reference number : E-38

denomination	: 1 shilling
series	: 4
paper	: plain with vertical metal thread
size	: 11.4 x 5.7 cm
dominant colours	: brown/olive
date printed	: 1962
printed by	: Bradbury Wilkinson
number printed	: 9,000,000
prefixes	: none

remarks

- These vouchers were never released for circulation. They were shipped straight to Malta and are believed to have been destroyed locally except for 900,000 vouchers returned to the MoD from Malta and Aden in 1967.
- 100,000 of these vouchers were cancelled by two 6mm perforations and sold by the MoD in 1980 to a London dealer. A small number of notes in this lot inadvertently escaped the hole cancellation. The remaining 800,000 were destroyed by the MoD in 1981.

reference number : E-39

denomination	: 2 shillings and 6 pence
series	: 4
paper	: plain with vertical metal thread
size	: 12.6 x 6.3 cm
dominant colours	: red-orange/violet
date printed	: 1962
printed by	: Bradbury Wilkinson
number printed	: 4,500,000
prefixes	: M/1 to M/5 inclusive

remarks

- These vouchers were never released for circulation. They were shipped straight to Malta and are believed to have been destroyed locally except for 2,000,000 vouchers returned to the MoD from Malta and Aden in 1967.

reference number : E-40

denomination	: 5 shillings
series	: 4
paper	: plain with vertical metal thread
size	: 12.6 x 6.3 cm
dominant colours	: green/brown
date printed	: 1962
printed by	: Bradbury Wilkinson
number printed	: 4,500,000
prefixes	: N/1 to N/5 inclusive

remarks

- These vouchers were never released for circulation. They were shipped straight to Malta and are believed to have been destroyed locally except for 1,600,000 vouchers returned to the MoD from Malta and Aden in 1967.

reference number : E-41

denomination	: 10 shillings
series	: 4
paper	: plain with vertical metal thread
size	: 14 x 6.9 cm
dominant colours	: purple/blue
date printed	: 1962
printed by	: Bradbury Wilkinson
number printed	: 4,500,000
prefixes	: L/1 to L/5 inclusive

remarks

- These vouchers were never released for circulation. They were shipped straight to Malta and are believed to have been destroyed locally except for 400,000 vouchers returned to the MoD from Malta and Aden in 1967.
- Vouchers numbered L/1 450,000 to 500,000 and L/1 650,001 to 700,000 were cancelled by a two-hole perforation and were sold by the MoD in 1980 to a London dealer. A small number of notes in this lot inadvertently escaped the hole cancellation.The remaining 300,000 vouchers were destroyed by the MoD in 1981.

reference number : E-42

denomination	: 1 pound
series	: 4
paper	: plain with vertical metal thread
size	: 14 x 6.9 cm
dominant colours	: purple-brown/green
date printed	: 1962
printed by	: Bradbury Wilkinson
number printed	: 3,000,000
prefixes	: K/1 to K/3 inclusive

remarks

- These vouchers were never release for circulation. 2,350,000 vouchers of this type were sold by the MoD by public auction in February 1991. Part of these were returned to the MoD from Malta and Aden in 1967

reference number : E-43

denomination	: 3 pence
series	: 5
paper	: not applicable
size	: 11.4 x 5.7 cm
dominant colours	: red-brown/purple
date printed	: not printed
printer	: Bradbury Wilkinson
number printed	: none
prefixes	: none

remarks
- Only proofs and essays are known
- Designed December 1961

reference number : E-44

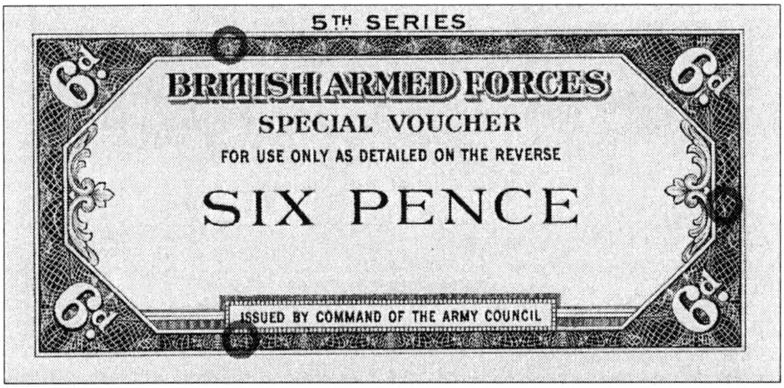

denomination	: 6 pence
series	: 5
paper	: not applicable
size	: 11.4 x 5.7 cm
dominant colours	: green/turquoise
date printed	: not printed
printer	: Bradbury Wilkinson
number printed	: none
prefixes	: none

remarks
- Only proofs and essays are known
- Designed December 1961

reference number : E-45

denomination	: 1 shilling
series	: 5
paper	: not applicable
size	: 11.4 x 5.7 cm
dominant colours	: lilac/green
date printed	: not printed
printer	: Bradbury Wilkinson
number printed	: none
prefixes	: none

remarks
- Only proofs and essays are known
- Designed December 1961

reference number : E-46

215

denomination	: 2 shillings and 6 pence
series	: 5
paper	: not applicable
size	: 12.6 x 6.3 cm
dominant colours	: purple/turquoise
date printed	: not printed
printer	: Bradbury Wilkinson
number printed	: none
prefixes	: S

remarks
- Only proofs and essays are known
- Designed December 1961

reference number : E-47

denomination	: 5 shillings
series	: 5
paper	: not applicable
size	: 12.6 x 6.3 cm
dominant colours	: blue/red
date printed	: not printed
printer	: Bradbury Wilkinson
number printed	: none
prefixes	: R

remarks
- Only proofs and essays are known
- Designed December 1961

reference number : E-48

denomination : 10 shillings
series : 5
paper : not applicable
size : 14 x 6.9 cm
dominant colours : orange/green
date printed : not printed
printer : Bradbury Wilkinson
number printed : none
prefixes : Q

remarks
- Only proofs and essays are known
- Designed December 1961

reference number : E-49

denomination	: 1 pound
series	: 5
paper	: not applicable
size	: 14 x 6.9 cm
dominant colours	: olive/red-brown
date printed	: not printed
printer	: Bradbury Wilkinson
number printed	: none
prefixes	: P

remarks
- Only proofs and essays are known
- Designed December 1961

reference number : E-50

denomination	: 5 new pence
series	: 6
paper	: watermarked (horizontal)
size	: 11.4 x 5.7 cm
dominant colours	: brown/green
date printed	: 1971
printed by	: Thomas De La Rue
number printed	: ?
prefixes	: none

remarks
- < 50,000 vouchers of this type were sold by the MoD by public auction in February 1991.
- This voucher was used in Berlin from 1971 to 1979

reference number : E-51

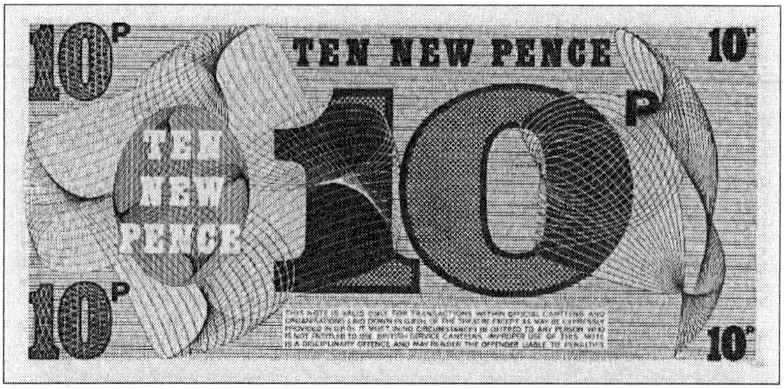

denomination	: 10 new pence
series	: 6
paper	: watermarked (horizontal)
size	: 12.7 x 6.5 cm
dominant colours	: purple/olive
date printed	: 1971
printed by	: Thomas De La Rue
number printed	: 1,000,000
prefixes	: DD/10

remarks

- < 50,000 vouchers of this type were sold by the MoD by public auction in February 1991.
- This voucher was used in Berlin from 1971 to 1979

reference number : E-52

denomination	: 50 new pence
series	: 6
paper	: watermarked (horizontal)
size	: 14 x 7 cm
dominant colours	: green/olive
date printed	: 1971
printed by	: Thomas De La Rue
number printed	: 1,000,000
prefixes	: BB/10

remarks
- < 50,000 vouchers of this type were sold by the MoD by public auction in February 1991.
- This voucher was used in Berlin from 1971 to 1979

reference number : E-53

denomination	: 5 new pence
series	: 6
paper	: watermarked (horizontal)
size	: 11.4 x 5.7 cm
dominant colours	: brown/green
date printed	: 1971
printed by	: Bradbury Wilkinson
number printed	: < 6,000,000
prefixes	: none

remarks
- These vouchers were never put in circulation.
- All available vouchers were sold by public auction in February 1991.

reference number : E-54

denomination	: 10 new pence
series	: 6
paper	: watermarked (horizontal)
size	: 12.7 x 6.5 cm
dominant colours	: purple/olive
date printed	: 1971
printed by	: Bradbury Wilkinson
number printed	: 6,000,000
prefixes	: A/1 to A/6

remarks
- These vouchers were never put in circulation.
- All available vouchers were sold by public auction in February 1991.

reference number : E-55

denomination	: 50 new pence
series	: 6
paper	: watermarked (horizontal)
size	: 14 x 7 cm
dominant colours	: green/olive
date printed	: 1971
printed by	: Bradbury Wilkinson
number printed	: < 1,500,000
prefixes	: B/1 to B/2 inclusive

remarks
- These vouchers were never put in circulation.
- All available vouchers were sold by public auction in February 1991.

CHRONOLOGICAL TABLE OF EVENTS

DATE	EVENT
05.03.1946	First proposal by the War Office to introduce special Canteen money, later to become the BAFSV
01.06.1946	Printing of the First Series Vouchers finished
01.08.1946	Introduction of First Series BAFSV in Germany, Austria, France, Holland, Denmark and Italy
06.05.1947	Introduction of First Series BAFSV in Japan for use with the British Commonwealth Occupation Force
05.09.1947	Printing of the Second Series Vouchers finished
11.12.1947	Shipments of Second Series BAFSVs to Germany, Austria and Trieste Free Territory
06.01.1948	Conversion day of First Series BAFSVs into Second Series BAFSVs in Germany, Austria and Trieste Free Territory
31.03.1948	All First Series BAFSVs are considered collected and sent to Britain to be pulped. First Series is demonetised
01.10.1948	Printing of Third Series vouchers finished

DATE	EVENT
30.05.1949	Third Series BAFSVs are shipped from the printer to the Bank of England
15.09.1949	War Office tries to take the BAFSVs in Japan out of circulation. Fails because of strong opposition by the Australians
26.05.1952	A Fourth Series is planned and destined for storing in Malta
10.08.1956	A number of shipments of Third Series vouchers are made to the Middle East for use during the Suez crisis (Operation Musketeer)
16.04.1957	All Third Series vouchers are returned to the MoD in London. Only a very small number are unaccounted for
1958	A new £5 and 5/- Second Series are introduced for use in West Berlin. All other denominations of the Second Series are re-issued on watermarked paper except the £1 note
01.11.1959	All BAFSVs are taken out of circulation except in the West Berlin arena
07.12.1961	Proofs of Fourth Series notes are ready
14.12.1961	Proofs of Fifth Series notes are ready
1962	Fourth Series notes printed and shipped to Malta
1967	A number of Fourth Series vouchers are returned from Malta and Aden to the MoD

DATE	EVENT
1971	Decimalisation forces the Ministry of Defence to replace the shillings- and pence vouchers still in circulation in Berlin by decimal notes of the Sixth Series
31.12.1979	All BAFSVs taken out of circulation
22.10.1980	Ministry of Defence offers an undisclosed number of surplus shilling- and pence notes of five denominations for sale to British note dealers. Only one of these responds and buys 100,000 notes of each denomination on offer. The remaining notes on offer at the time are destroyed by the MoD
14.02.1991	All remaining BAFSVs are sold by Phillips of London to a British consortium of bank note dealers for £129,000 in one lot of over 17 million notes

SELECT BIBLIOGRAPHY

Bank of England, *OV25/9, OV34/11-12, OV34/14-15, OV34/17-20, C12/109*, Bank of England Archives, 1944 to 1948, London, UK.

Connor, R.D., *The Weights and Measures of England,* HMSO Books, London, UK, 1987

Donnison C.B.E., F.S.V., *Civil Affairs and Military Government, North West Europe, 1944-1946,* HMSO, London, UK, 1961.

Goodbye BAFSVs, The Quadrant, volume IV, number 20, 22 October 1959, London, UK.

Heyman, Charles (ed.), *The British Army, A Pocket Guide,* Pen & Sword Books Ltd., Barnsley, UK, Fourth Edition 1993.

Howard, Michael, *The Central Organisation of Defence*, Royal United Service Institution, London, UK, 1970

Johnson, Franklin A., *Defence by Ministry,* Duckworth,

Laere, A.M.M.van, *Fractional Bank of England Notes*, Banknote News no. 41, Token Publishing Ltd., Honiton, UK.

Mays, James O'Donald, *The Splendid Shilling,* New Forest Leaves, Burley, UK, 1982.

Phillips, *Scripophily and Paper Money*, Auction Catalogue, Sale no. 28520, London, UK, 1991.

Pick, Albert, *Standard Catalogue of World Paper Money*, Vol.II, 6th Ed., Krause Publications, Iola, WI, USA

Rohwer, J. and Hummelchen, G., *Chronology of the War at Sea, 1939-1945: The Naval History of World War Two*, Greenhill Books, London, 1992

Schwan, C.F., Boling, J.E. and, *World War II Military Currency*, BNR Press, Port Clinton, Ohio, USA, 1980

Soldier, The British Army Magazine, volumes 1946, 1947 and 1948, The Soldier Magazine, Aldershot, UK.

Sutton OBE, Brigadier D.J.(ed.), *The Story of the RASC and RCT - 1945-1982*, Leo Cooper/Secker and Warburg, London, UK, 1983.

War Office Files, WO 32/16780, WO 32/16765, WO 32/16776, WO 32/16766, WO 32/16767, WO 32/16793, WO 32/17652, WO 32/16778, PRO, London, UK

War Office, The, *The Soldier's Welfare, Notes for Officers*, 3rd Edition 1944, The War Office, London, UK, 1944

War Office, The, *The War Office - A Newcomer's Guide*, The War Office, London, UK

APPENDICES

ACKNOWLEDGEMENTS

- Appendix A, B, C, D, E © Crown copyright - Reproduced by permission of the Controller of Her Brittanic Majesty's Stationery Office - file WO 32/16765, PRO, London.

- Appendix F © Crown copyright - Reproduced by permission of the Controller of Her Brittanic Majesty's Stationery Office - file WO 32/16778, PRO, London.

APPENDIX A

ROYAL WARRANT

16/General A/361 **A.O. 109/1946**

George RI. **Special Vouchers**

Whereas We deem it expedient to make special provision regarding the issue of pay and allowances to members of our Military Forces;

Our Will and Pleasure is as follows :-

1. This Our Warrant shall apply to such areas abroad as from such dates and for such periods as may be laid down in instructions issued by Our Army Council.

2. No pay or allowances from Army funds receivable by members of Our Military Forces or by their wives or dependants shall be issued in any area to which this Our Warrant applies save in such cases and subject to such conditions as may be prescribed.

3. Members of Our Military Forces or their wives and dependants may if they so desire be issued in any area to which this Our Warrant applies with vouchers denominated in values expressed in terms of the currency of the United Kingdom up to the amount of the pay and allowances from time to time receivable by them from Army funds or up to such other amount as may from time to time be prescribed. Such vouchers shall be subject to such conditions regarding the place and time of their issue, the conditions upon which they may be held, assigned or exchanged for goods or services or the currency of the United Kingdom or of any other territory and otherwise with respect thereto as may be prescribed.

4. The amount represented by the aggregate values denominated on the vouchers issued to any member of Our Military Forces under paragraph 3 hereof or to the wife or dependant of any such member may, except in cases where such voucher have been paid for on their issue, be deducted from any pay or allowances from Army funds which would but for this Our Warrant be receivable by that member or his wife or dependant.

5. The provisions of this Our Warrant shall have effect not-withstanding anything contained in Our Warrant for the Pay, Appointment, Promotion and Non-Effective Pay of Our Army, dated 29th February, 1940, or in any other warrant or regulations or instructions relating to the pay or allowances of members of Our Military Forces.

6. In this Our Warrant the expression "members of Our Military Forces" means members of Our Military Forces for whose pay provision is made by Our Warrant dated 29th February, 1940, aforementioned, or any warrant amending or modifying the same for whose allowances provision is made in the Regulations for the Allowances of the Army, 1944, or any amendment or modification thereof, and includes members of the Nursing or other Auxiliary Services of Our Military Forces; and the expression "prescribed" means prescribed from time to time by instructions issued by Our Army Council or by orders issued by the officer in chief command or other officer in command as may be prescribed by Our Army Council in any area to which this Our Warrant applies.

Given at Our Court at St. James's, this 14th day of July, 1946, in the 10th year of Our Reign.

By His Majesty's Command,

12 | 7 | 46 a505--3 J.J.Lawson.

A-2

BRITISH ARMED FORCES SPECIAL VOUCHERS

OFFICIAL COPY

Crown Copyright Reserved

SPECIAL ARMY ORDER

Nos. 121 and 122

THE WAR OFFICE,
10th August, 1946

29/GENERAL/945 **A.O. 121/1946**

Wearing of Uniform by Officers and Ex-Officers Released from Military Duty who have retained Rank or have been granted Honorary Rank

1. H.M. the King has been graciously pleased to grant permission to the following classes of officers and ex-officers to wear uniform on special occasions when attending cermonials and entertainments of a military nature and on other occasions when the wearing of uniform appears appropriate, as may be defined by the Army Council.*

(a) Officers and ex-officers released from military duty and retained on the unemployed list.
(b) Officers who have resigned or relinguished their commissions and have retained their rank or have been granted honorary rank under the conditions laid down in Army Order 128 of 1945.
(c) Officers of the Home Guard who have been granted honorary rank on the disbandment of the Home Guard under the conditions of Army Order 32 of 1945.
(d) Officers of the Ulster Home Guard who have been granted honorary rank on the disbandment of the Ulster Home Guard under the conditions of Army Order 33 of 1945.
(e) Commissioned officers of the Women's Forces who have been released from duty and retained on the unemployment list, or retired, resigned or relinguished their commissions and have been granted honorary rank under the conditions of Army Order 129 of 1945.

2. When honorary rank granted to officers of the Army and to commissioned officers of the Women's Forces is suspended under Army Order 128, para. 5, and Army Order 129, para. 4, of 1945, respectively, or is withdrawn, the permission to wear uniform by virtue of the grant of such honorary rank will also automatically be suspended or withdrawn, as the case may be.

3. Commissioned officers of the Women's Forces (Officers' Commissions) Order, 1941, for employment with the Royal Army Medical Corps, The Army Dental Corps, the Queen Alexandra's Imperial Military

* *See A.C.I.* 780 *of* 1946.

H.M.Stationary Office, London. Price 1d. net.

B-2

A.O. 121/1946-*contd.*

Nursing Service or Reserve thereof, the Territorial Army Nursing Service or Reserve thereof, or the Auxiliary Territorial Service who retired on retired pay and members of Queen Alexandra's Imperial Military Nursing Service not appointed to a commission, who have retired on retired pay or may in futere so retire, will be permitted to wear uniform after retirement under the same conditions as apply to officers retired from the Army.

4. The uniform to be worn by officers of the Army will be restricted to Service Dress or Battle Dress and will normally be that of the regiment or corps in which the wearer last served. The badges of rank will be those of the honorary rank granted. When an officer has served during the late war in more than one regiment or corps he may, at his option, wear the uniform of any such regiment or corps with the badges of the rank held when serving in that regiment or corps, provided that the rank is not higher than the honorary rank granted.

5. The uniform to be worn by commissioned officers of the Women's Forces will be taht of the Service to which the officer belonged. The badges of rank will be those of the honorary rank granted or of the rank retained on retirement.

6. Army Orders 167, 265 and 420 of 1919 and 206 of 1940 are hereby *cancelled.*

16/GENERAL A/361 **A.O. 122/1946**

Special Vouchers.

With reference to the Royal Warrant dated 17th July, 1946, published as Army Order 109 of 1946, regarding the issue of Special Vouchers to members of the Military Forces, their wives or dependants it is notified that;-

(1) With effect from 1st August, 1946, the arrangements specified therein shall apply until further notice in Denmark, France, Belgium, Germany, Holland, and Luxembourg.

(2) The detailed arrangements shall be as ordered from time to time by the General Officer Commanding-in-Chief, British Army of the Rhine, in the case of Denmark, Belgium, Germany, Holland and Luxembourg; and by the Commander, British Army Staff France, in the case of France.

By Command of the Army Council

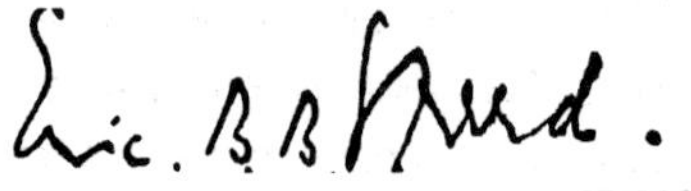

(26148) Wt. - 8/46 W.O.P. Gp. 339 57-9999

APPENDIX C

DRAFT - GENERAL ROUTINE ORDER NUMBER 2489

CURRENCY

1. The amounts of certain Allied currencies and marks received by Paymasters from canteens, Post Offices, etc. and in exchange for men leaving B.A.O.R. have for a long time exceeded the amounts issued as pay. It is therefore clear that black market transactions in goods and currency are taking place on a large scale at the expense of the British taxpayer. The efforts hitherto made to check these transactions have been unsuccessful. More drastic measures are therefore necessary.

2. All ranks and all civilian personnel who are paid from official sources or by officially sponsored organisations are notified that, in the near future, but not earlier than two months from the date of this G.R.O., the British Army of the Rhine, the Naval and Air Forces of Occupation in Germany and the Control Commission for Germany (British Element), while continuing to have their pay credited to them in the U.K., will be able to draw against their pay special vouchers denominated in sterling.

3. These vouchers alone, from the date the scheme is introduced, will be accepted by Army Post Offices, Canteens, Messes, Clubs, Gift Shops, Officers' Shops, Control Commission Shops, Hostels, etc. To enable personnel to make purchases from other than official sources arrangements will be made for the exchange of the vouchers into local currency, but not vice versa.

4. Since local currency will cease to be accepted by official and officially sponsored organisations all ranks are warned that their local currency cash holdings (including Reichsmarks and Allied Military Marks) should be reduced to the absolute minimum before the voucher scheme is introduced. Arrangements will be announced later whereby unexpended balances of pay drawn in local currency may be exchanged, within very small and strictly defined limits, for vouchers. But after this initial exchange, local currencies will not be exchanged in any circumstances.

C-2 5. The voucher ONLY will be exchanges for sterling when personnel proceed to the U.K. from B.A.O.R. on release, posting or on leave. It is illegal for officers and other ranks to take continental currencies into the U.K.

6. This G.R.O. which is a preliminary notice to all concerned will be repeated in all Unit Orders. Detailed instructions will be issued later.

DRAFT PARLIAMENTARY QUESTION AND ANSWER

D-1

QUESTION: To ask the Secretary of State for War whether he has any statement to make regarding the currency in which troops serving in B.A.O.R. draw their pay.

ANSWER: Yes, Sir. Hitherto it has been the practice to pay troops in B.A.O.R. in the currency of the country in which they are serving. Owing to the scarcity on the Continent of goods generally, and particularly of cigarettes, it has been possible for troops to make large profits in local currency by selling canteen goods to civilians at inflated prices. Consequently the amount of local currency received back by Paymasters from canteens and Army Post Offices and exchanged by them for sterling or other currency has been more than that issued as pay. Despite the limits imposed on the amount of exchanges for individuals, which have been some check on these practices, Paymasters have accumulated very considerable balances of German Marks, which will be a direct loss to the Exchequer.

In order to protect the taxpayer, I am arranging for the introduction of special vouchers denominated in sterling which alone will be accepted for purchases in canteens, Army Post Offices, Officers' shops and other official organisations. Troops serving on the continent, while continuing to have their pay credited to them in this country, will be able to draw against their pay these special vouchers which they can use for purchases in the official organisations.

To enable troops to make purchases from other than official sources arrangements will be made for the exchange of these vouchers for local currency, but not vice versa. The vouchers will also be exchangeable into sterling when troops leave the theatre, but local currency will not be so exchangeable. The scheme will apply to all three Services and to the military and civilian staffs of the Control Commission for Germany (British Element).

D-2 The task of printing and distributing the vouchers is considerable and at least two months will elapse before the arrangements can be implemented. I have, however, thought it proper to inform the House of my plan and at the same time to give the troops this provisional notice of the change.

APPENDIX E

GENERAL ROUTINE ORDER NUMBER 2539

PAY - BRITISH ARMED FORCES SPECIAL VOUCHERS

1. With reference to G.R.O. 2489, British Armed Forces Special Vouchers (BAFSV) will be taken into use throughout B.A.O.R. on 1 August 1946. BAFSV are money and in present circumstances are more valuable than some local tender currencies. All safeguards and security measures, and all orders and regulations relating to the loss of Public Funds, which apply to sterling and legal currencies therefore apply also to BAFSV.

2. As from 00.01 hours 1 August 1946 BAFSV only will be used for the following purposes: -

(a) advances against pay to: -

(i) officers and soldiers;
(ii) civilian personnel paid from official sources of by officially sponsored organisations, except locally engaged civilians.

(b) payment for: -

(i) purchases in all official and officially approved establishment such as Army Post Offices, Officers' Shops, Canteens, Gift Shops, Institutes, Hostels, Clubs, etc., and entertainments in Service controlled cinemas and theatres;

(ii) mess bills.

(iii) National Savings Certificates.

(c) BAFSV may be issued only to Officers and soldiers, and civilians and employees (except locally engaged civilians) paid from official sources or by officially sponsored organisations, and to such other persons and organisations as may be specifically authorised by HQ. B.A.O.R.

3. Limitation of Use

E-2

(a) BAFSV are NOT legal tender in the country in which personnel are stationed and must NOT be used for purchases from other than official sources. (see para. 6 below).

(b) It is forbidden to allow BAFSV to enter the private possession of any individual who is not entitled to draw them from official sources. (The Control Commission for Germany (BE) has undertaken to make it illegal for unauthorised persons to be in possession of BAFSV).

(c) Local Commanders will take all practicable steps to ensure compliance with (b) above. Among the steps which it is suggested, should be taken is the exhibition of notices in all establishments officially authorised for use by Service personnel warning all ranks that: -

(i) in the case of all establishments in the categories defined in para. 2 (b) (i) that BAFSV only will be accepted as payment;

(ii) in the case of all establishments which are conducted as businesses for private gain by local civilians, and the use of which is restricted to British and Allied personnel, that it is forbidden to tender BAFSV for goods or services.

4. Denominations

(a) BAFSV are being made available in sterling denominations of £1, 10/-, 5/-, 2/6d., 1/-, 6d. and 3d.

(b) Plastic tokens in denominations of 1d. and 1/2 d. are being made available for use as small change in Institutes, Canteens, etc.

5. Exchange of Unexpended Holdings of Continental currencies.

(a) All military personnel will be permitted, under Unit arrangements, between 29 July 1946 and 1 August 1946 (inclusive), to exchange into BAFSV any unexpended Continental currency not exceeding the amount of the last advance of pay drawn in July 1946 as shown in A.F.W. 3241 (Officer's Advance Book) or A.B. 64 (Soldier's Pay Book) LESS SUMS EXPENDED ON POSTAL ORDERS OR NATIONAL SAVINGS CERTIFICATES, except that: - E-3

(i) personnel posted to B.A.O.R. during the month of July who have not drawn an advance of pay in this theatre during that month, and

(ii) personnel who have returned to B.A.O.R. from leave during the month of July and have not drawn an advance of pay in this theatre since returning from leave, may exchange Continental currency to an amount not exceeding the equivalent of £10 sterling.

(b) Only currency appropriate to the country in which personnel are serving (e.g. Marks in Germany) will be accepted for exchange.

(c) Wherever practicable, Os.C. will complete this exchange for all ranks of the Unit at the same time on a selected day within the period specified above.

(d) Exchange facilities under similar arrangements, subject to the same limitation and control, will be provided during the same period by the employing authority for civilian personnel paid from official sources or by officially sponsored organisations (excluding locally engaged civilians), with the exception that exchanges for civilian personnel who fall within the categories referred to at 5 (a) (i) and (ii) above will not exceed the equivalent of £5 sterling.

(e) Individuals who normally draw advances on special forms of authority will be dealt with by Army Cashiers under the same conditions.

(f) The exchange of personal holdings of Continental currency into BAFSV will NOT be permitted (except as in para. 8 below) after an initial exchange has been made as in (a) to (e) above.

(g) All personnel are again warned that their local currency cash holdings (including Reichsmarks and Allied Military Marks) should be reduced to the absolute minimum before the end of July.

6. Supplies of Continental currency for purchases from other than
E-4 official sources on or after 1 August 1946.

(a) personnel will be permitted at all times, normally under Unit arrangements, to exchange BAFSV into the currency of the country in which they are stationed, for purchases from other than official sources, but it will not be permitted in any circumstances to re-exchange Continental currency into sterling, or into BAFSV except as in para. 8 below.

(b) Imprest Holders will maintain an appropriate sum in local Continental currency for the purpose indicated above, and for the payment of bills for authorised local purchases and services.

7. Exchange of BAFSV for sterling
When personnel proceed to U.K. from B.A.O.R. for any purpose BAFSV alone will be exchanged for sterling

8. Exchange for personnel on Local Leave or temporary duty in liberated countries.

(a) The provision of Continental currency (in exchange for BAFSV) for personnel proceeding on authorised Local Leave or temporary duty in liberated countries will continue as heretofore.

(b) The re-exchange into BAFSV of unexpended balances of Continental currency as provided in (a) will be permitted.

(c) Both exchange and re-exchange under (a) and (b) above will be effected solely by British Army Cashiers.

9. Clubs, Institutions, Canteens, Theatres, Cinemas, etc. controlled by official of voluntary organisations.

(a) As stated in 2 (b) (i) above BAFSV ONLY will be accepted in payment for goods, supplies or services on and after 1 August 1946.

(b) To provide the necessary reserve for change a limited amount of Continental currency held by such organisations may be exchanged for BAFSV, and/or tokens, by Army Cashiers during the period 29th to 31th July 1946.

(c) Surplus Continental currency will be paid into the authorised bank accounts of such organisations in 1 August 1946. Balances on bank accounts or, where a bank account is not maintained, cash balances, may be disposed of in accordance with para. 11.

10. P.R.I., Mess, Regimental and other officially authorised funds.

(a) Continental currency will not be accepted by Presidents Regimental Institutes, Mess, Regimental or other Fund holders after 31 July 1946.

(b) Cash balances in Continental currency will be dealt with and disposed of on the lines indicated in para. 9 (b) and (c) above.

11. Deposit Accounts.

(a) With effect from 1 August 1946, P.R.I., Mess, Regimental and other officially authorised Fund holders, N.A.A.F.I. and officially sponsored voluntary organisations will be authorised to open deposit accounts with District Paymasters.

(b) Currency balances as at 31 July 1946 may be retained in whole or in part for purchases from other than official sources.

(c) Any currency held as at 31 July 1946 which it is not desired to retain, may be transferred through the medium of Army Cashiers for credit to an authorised Deposit Account. Separate instructions will be issued regarding the method of effecting these transfers and the limits to the amounts which may be so transferred.

(d) Subsequently, surplus BAFSV may be similarly transferred to a Deposit Account.

(e) Sums accepted for credit to a Deposit Account may be drawn on in local currency, or in BAFSV, or transferred for credit to a Sterling Account in U.K.

E-6

12. Polish Forces serving under British Command in B.A.O.R.

The foregoing instructions will, in general, apply to Polish Forces serving under British Command. Special accounting instructions will be issued to commanders concerned.

13. ALLIED FORCES SERVING UNDER BRITISH COMMAND IN B.A.O.R.
ALLIED MILITARY MISSIONS ACCREDITED TO HQ., B.A.O.R.
ALLIED LIAISON OFFICERS AND INTERPRETERS SERVING WITH BRITISH ARMY UNITS.

The method of providing BAFSV for such personnel, who are authorised to use British Service Clubs, Canteens, Cinemas, etc., is under consideration.

14. Detailed Instructions

(a) A pamphlet containing detailed instructions will be issued at a later date to all Units and Formations. Its publication will be announced in G.R.Os.

(b)Separate instructions are being applied to the Naval and Air Forces of Occupation in Germany and the Control Commission for Germany (BE) by the authorities concerned.

15. Paras. 1 - 8 of the G.R.O. will be repeated in Unit Orders.

APPENDIX F

FORCE ROUTINE ORDER 33/47
BRITISH COMMONWEALTH OCCUPATION FORCES

INTRODUCTION OF SPECIAL CASH VOUCHERS IN BCOF

1. All BCOF service personnel, non BCOF service personnel and BCOF accredited civilians are warned that with effect from 6 May 1947, the civilian type Japanese Yen currency at present in use by the British Commonwealth Occupation Force will cease to be legal tender in all BCOF establishments.

2. On and from 6 May 1947, special cash vouchers denominated in sterling known as British Armed Forces Special Vouchers (BAFSV) and Australian penny and halfpenny coins usable at sterling rating will become the only legal tender within BCOF for the issue of pay and allowances and for payment of: -

(a) Purchases in all BCOF establishments including Post Offices, Canteens, Gift Shops, Officers Shops, Institutes, Hostel Clubs, cafeterias, messes etc.

(b) Mess bills.

(c) Services, stores, and supplies, provided on prepayment or repayment.

3. BAFSV will be issued in the following denominations: -

£1, 10/-, 5/-, 2/6, 1/-, -/6 and -/3 Sterling

4. BAFSV are legal tender in BCOF officially approved establishments only. BAFSVs are NOT legal tender outside Japan or for transactions with Japanese civilians and will not be tendered as payment for any service of for the payment of any article from non-BCOF establishments.
5. Personnel referred to in para 1 above may exchange BAFSV for Japanese currency with supply officers, paymasters, Field Cashiers and Accountant Officers at the rate of 200 yen to the £1 sterling. Yen currency will not in any circumstances be reconverted to BAFSV.

F–2

6. The exchange of Japanese yen currency in the possession of members will be limited to the unexpended portion of amount of the last pay drawn within the thirty days preceding 6 May 1947.

7. Personnel are advised to limit their drawings of yen currency to not more than their immediate requirements.

8. Detailed instructions regarding the actual conversion to BAFSV will be issued shortly.

9. This notification will be published in all formations and Unit Routine Orders and read to all troops on parade at least twice before 5 May 1947.

APPENDIX G

DEFENCE AND WAR OFFICE ORGANISATION

G-1

When Harold Macmillan took over from Anthony Eden as Prime Minister in January 1957 he inherited a popular disillusionment with the Armed Forces as a result of the Suez adventure. This adventure had cost the British taxpayer £250 million. Macmillan had advocated drastic defence cuts and the end of conscription while still Chancellor of the Exchequer, and now set about putting his ideas into practice.

As part of these reforms Macmillan replaced Antony Head as Minister of Defence with Duncan Sandys, who had served at the War Office and at Supply. Macmillan gave Sandys unusually specific instructions about his views on the organisation of the Ministry and Sandys produced various White Papers outlining the planned changes. Very little actually changed, however, and the departmental arrangements were consolidated into what they had been in 1957.

This changed when Lord Mountbatten took on the post of Chief of the Defence Staff. Besides his unprecedented professional qualifications he was a far more forceful personality than his predecessor. He was not the type of man to be at Sandys back and call and, in his role as Chief of the Defence Staff, he was able to affect revolutionary innovations within the defence organisation. In 1959, the Ministry of Defence began the 'major user principle' which basically meant that in the Far East, Cyprus, Malta and Gibraltar the Army handled the stores, fuel and provisions for all Services, while in Aden this became the responsibility of the RAF. To that effect a number of Commands were established in those arenas. The Near East Command was established in Cyprus in 1960, the Middle East Command at Aden in 1961 and the Far East Command in Singapore in 1962.

In 1962 Peter Thorneycroft took over from Duncan Sandys as Minister of Defence and he faced the task of continuing the momentum of the structural reforms. In July 1963 he tabled a wide-ranging plan to reform the Armed Forces and in that, and the following, year these plans were carried out and the three independent service ministries for the respective armed forces were merged into the Ministry of Defence in its present form.

THE WAR OFFICE AND THE ARMY COUNCIL

G–2

Up to the 1963/1964 reorganisation, and thus covering the best part of the period described in this book, the War Office was a Civil Department of the Crown responsible for the administration of the British Army. Its function was to provide the country with as efficient an Army as possible. This involved recruiting, paying, organising, training, educating, housing, feeding, and clothing the Army in peace and war, and ensuring that it was provided with the ammunition, weapons, transport and equipment necessary for it to operate as an efficient fighting force, whenever and wherever required.

The central control of these matters rested with the War Office, subject to the Cabinet's authority on major issues, and to Parliament's general financial control. Naturally, most decisions taken by the War Office had to be executed in detail by others, chiefly by the military Commands into which the country was divided, or by Commands and Garrisons abroad. But the War Office still had to deal with many small details on a continuing basis.

Figure 101 shows the organisation of the War Office in the form of a family tree in 1945. The following paragraphs focus on the main War Office departments which were involved in the events surrounding the various issues of the BAFSVs.

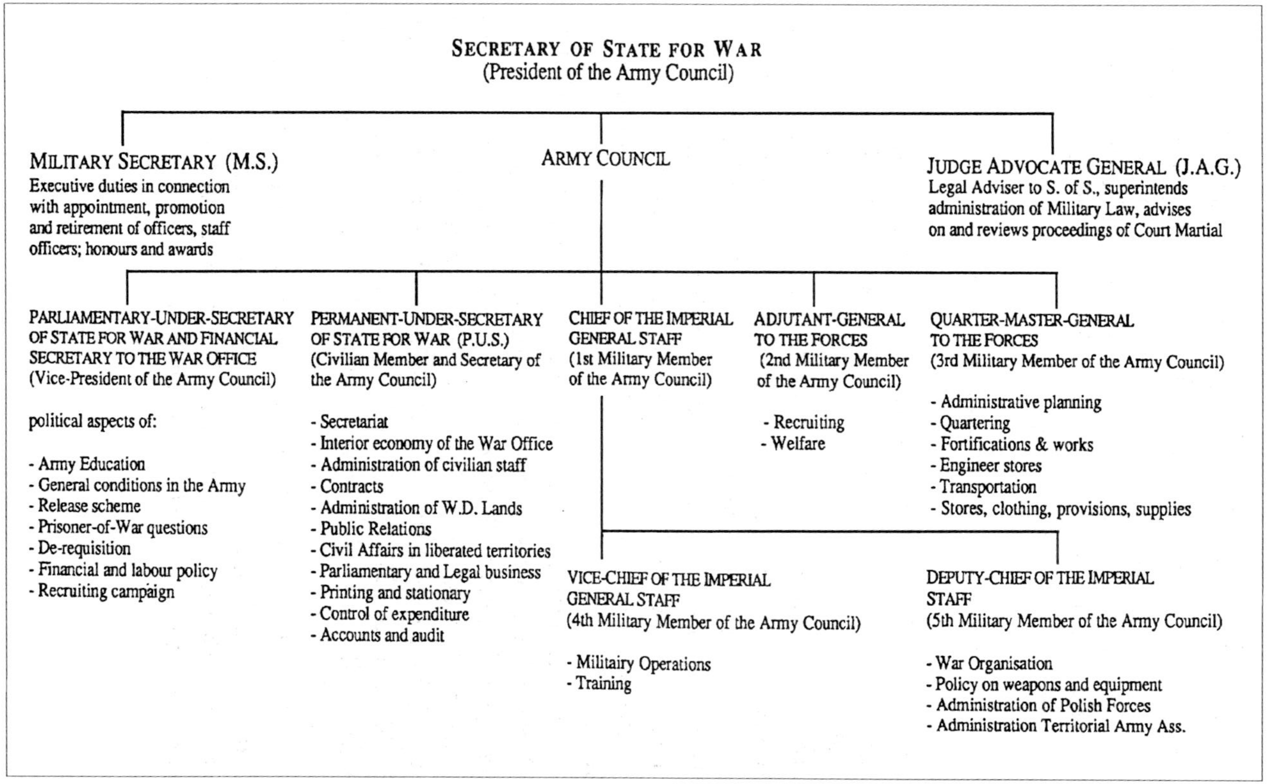

Figure 101. Organisation of the War Office in 1946

THE SECRETARY OF STATE AND THE ARMY COUNCIL

The head of the War Office was the Secretary of State for War (S. of S.) who was directly responsible to the King and to Parliament for the administration of the Army. He was also President of the Army Council, a body composed of military and civilian members, each of whom was responsible to the S. of S. for a particular department of War Office business.

Apart from the military members of the Army Council there
G-4 were two civilian members - the Parliamentary Under-Secretary of State for War and Financial Secretary to the War Office (U.S. of S.), and the Permanent Under-Secretary of State for War (P.U.S.). The U.S. of S. was a junior minister and provided a link between the War Office and Parliament.

The P.U.S. was a permanent Civil Servant. He was the Secretary of the Army Council and was responsible for the general control of War Office procedure. He was also the accounting officer of the Army, responsible for payments and for ensuring that funds were spent to the best advantage. In 1946, the Permanent Under-Secretary of State for War was Sir Eric B.B. Speed, K.C.B., K.B.E., M.C., J.P.

THE P.U.S.'S DEPARTMENT

The work of the P.U.S.'s department connected with the work of every other department of the War Office. One of the largest branches of the P.U.S.'s department was the Registry, which received and distributed all correspondence addressed to the War Office, and held and circulated official papers. Other P.U.S. branches dealt with secretarial work for the Army Council and important War Office committees; official regulations and instructions, printing and stationary requirements; placing of Army Contracts with private firms and relations with the public through the Press. The P.U.S. finance branches were concerned with the expenditure and administration of Army funds.

Today, following the reorganisations of 1963/1964, the lives of almost 1 million servicemen and civilians are directly controlled by the Secretary of State for Defence who chairs the Defence Council. This Defence Council basically makes the political decisions, ensures the efficient running of the three armed services and makes certain that all actions taken are in accordance with the guidelines as laid down by Government. The routine management of the Army is left to a separate body, the Army Board. The Defence Council and the Army Board are manned by the following members:

The Defence Council :
- Minister of State (Armed Forces)
- Minister of State (Defence Procurement)
- Permanent Under-Secretary of State
- Chief Scientific Adviser
- Chief of Procurement Executive
- Chief of Personnel and Logistics
- Chief of Defence Staff
- Vice-Chief of Defence Staff
- Chief of the Naval Staff
- Chief of the Air Staff
- Chief of the General Staff

The Army Board :
- Minister of State (Armed Forces)
- Minister of State (Defence Procurement)
- Quartermaster General
- Master General of the Ordnance
- Second Permanent-Under Secretary
- Chief of the General Staff
- Adjutant General
- Vice-Chief of General Staff
- Controller R&D
- Deputy Under Secretary for the Army.

As far as the subject of this book is concerned these changes mean that, from the moment of the reorganisation of the MoD, the BAFSVs were no longer issued by command of the Army Council, which had ceased to exist, but by command of the Defence Council. Since all vouchers except the Sixth Series were issued or planned before the reorganisation they all carry the inscription 'Issued By Command of the Army Council'. Those that were issued after the reorganisation, i.e. the Sixth Series vouchers (1971), carry the inscription 'Issued By Command of the Defence Council' but this change appears to have had little influence on the issue and running of the voucher scheme.

G-6

APPENDIX H

THE BRITISH £ S D SYSTEM H-1

Up to 15 February 1971 the monetary system in Britain was based on a system of pounds, shillings and pence which had its roots as far back as the sixth century AD.

THE SHILLING

The basic unit of the 'pounds-shillings-and-pence-system' was the shilling which had been used as a unit of account as early as the 6th Century AD. It did not exist as an actual coin until 1504, when the forerunner of the shilling, known as a
testoon, was issued under Henry VII. The testoon derived its name from the Italian *testone* meaning 'coin with a head on it'.

It was not until 1549 that the first true English shilling was issued under King Edward VI who was deeply sensitive about the sorry state of the coinage at the time. His father, Henry VIII, had resorted to debasing the coinage in order to solve his monetary problems. After having spent the money raised by the dissolution of the monasteries he melted down all coins with a precious metal content and re-issued coins of an inferior alloy. Edward VI tried to redress this, but was at the mercy of his 'Protectors', the Lords Somerset and Northumberland, and his resulting 'English shilling' first appeared consisting of 25% silver and 75% base metal.

The last English shilling, except for a souvenir issue in 1970, was issued in 1966, containing no silver at all.

THE PENNY

The testoon was divided into 12 pence, as was the shilling unit. The actual (silver) penny coin was originally called 'denarius' which accounts for the abbreviation 'd.' for penny. This was used until the introduction of the new system in 1971, when the abbreviation 'p' was chosen for 'new penny' to avoid confusion.

THE POUND

H–2

The monetary pound as a coin only came into existence in October 1489 when Henry VII issued his gold piece called a '*soveraign*', worth twenty shillings. But in Norman times the pound already existed as a unit of account. This unit was originally derived from the pound as a measure of weight (Lbs). At the time 240 pence had a weight equal to 20 shillings which in turn was equal to one pound weight (Lbs).

THE NOTATION OF THE OLD £ S D SYSTEM

In popular usage, the notation of the shilling value in the old system was generally shown by adding a slash sign after the number of shillings. An amount of 5 shillings and 4 old pence was therefore commonly shown as 5/4d. Sometimes, however, it was also shown as 5s 4d or even as 5/4. If no pence were present the slash sign was followed by a dash with 5 shillings being written as 5/-. An amount consisting of pence only could also take several forms. For example, 3 pence was sometimes shown as 3d but at other times as -/3 or -/3d, especially in older texts.

The slash sign was also used for separating pounds from shillings but only if pence were also involved. So £3/6/5 might be used but not £3/6 which might be mistaken for £3 and 6 pence. Instead of the slash sign, dashes or full stops were sometimes used so £3/6/5 could be shown as £3-6-5 or, alternatively, £3.6.5.

In a formal context, however, there were certain conventions governing how the currency was represented. In this context the slash was normally avoided and the letter 's' for 'shilling' and 'd' for 'pence' were preferred, for example 5s 6d not 5/6. The figure 0 would be used rather than a dash when there were no shillings or pence, £6 5s 0d, not £6 5s -d. If there were no pounds involved, the £ unit was omitted; it was never written as £0 6s 2d, for example.

In practice, any combination of any of these forms can, however, be found.

THE NEW DECIMAL SYSTEM

Apart from the many realignments in the value, the £ s d system remained in place virtually unchanged from the sixth century onwards. In the 19th century a first attempt was made at decimalisation, however. This was done in 1849 by introducing the Florin which was worth two shillings, being exactly one tenth of a pound. But this experiment never caught on. On 15 February 1971, however, in the reign of Queen Elizabeth II, a decimalised system was finally introduced amidst much opposition. In this new decimal system the pound was the basic unit, subdivided into 100 new pence. The £-sign remained the same but in order to avoid confusion the abbreviation 'd' as it was used for the old penny was dropped and the abbreviation 'p' was chosen for the new penny coin. This was not without reason. Since the value of the new penny was about 0.42 of that of the old penny it was important to state which was which. Five new pence in the new system now was the exact decimal equivalent of one old shilling. The first new five-penny coin had already been issued in 1968 as the successor to the shilling and as a forerunner to decimalisation. H-3

Table 55. £ s d monetary system versus decimal monetary system

old £ s d system (until 1971)			new decimal system (from 1971)		
one penny	=	4 farthings			
one shilling	=	12 'old' pence			
one pound	=	20 shillings			
one pound	=	240 'old' pence	one pound	=	100 new pence

H-4

APPENDIX I

SAMPLE LISTING OF BANKNOTES CONTAINING SECRET MARKS

COUNTRY	PICK 6TH ED..	DENOMINATION	YEAR
Bermuda	13b	5 shillings	1957
Falklands	12-15	£1 through £20	1990
Republic of Ireland	63-69	10/- through £100	1977
Malta	20b	£1	1940
Netherlands	75a	10 guilders	1945
	75b	10 guilders (different marks)	1945
	76	20 guilders	1945
	80	1000 guilders	1945
	83	10 guilders	1949
Northern Ireland	NC9	£1	1949
	NC13	£5	1949
	NC14	£10	1949
	NE13a	£5	1954
	NE14	£1	1970
	NE15	£5	1972

I–2

BRITISH OCCUPATION FORCES IN EUROPE

J-1

GERMANY -THE BRITISH ARMY OF THE RHINE (BAOR)

As had been agreed at the 1944 Potsdam Conference, Germany was split into four occupation zones to be controlled by Britain, the USA, the USSR and France respectively. The British Zone covered the area of Germany from the borders of The Netherlands and Belgium in the west and the North Sea in the north, stretching to the east as far as Hamburg and Bremen. From Bremen, the boundary between the Russian and British occupation zones followed the river Leine southwards down to Hessen. From there the boundary ran west to Cologne, dividing the British zone from the American and French zones which lay to the south. This British zone was to be controlled by an occupation force known as the British Army of the Rhine. From the beginning in May 1945 the core of this Army was formed by the 21 Army Group. This Group consisted of three Corps: 1 (British) Corps, 8 (British) Corps and 30 (British) Corps consisting of more than a dozen divisions as well as a number of separate brigades.

Under the Potsdam agreement the four Allies were to have a shared responsibility in occupying the capital of Berlin which was situated within the Russian Zone. To that end Berlin was divided into a western half and an eastern half. The western half, with its population of over 2 million people, was controlled by the Western Powers and the eastern half was controlled by the USSR. From their respective areas of occupation in the rest of Germany, the Western Powers had the right of access by land and rail to West Berlin.

The task of the occupation forces was a complex one. Not only did they have to disarm and demobilise what was left of the German fighting machine, they also had to cope with a nation on the brink of starvation, with its basic infrastructure shattered and with most of its cities in ruins.

The first and most pressing task was that of housing, feeding and clothing the population of Germany as well as resettling and transporting hundreds of thousands of previously displaced persons to their own areas in other countries. The logistics involved in these
J-2 tasks were breathtaking. A number of operations were started such as Operation Barleycorn, which entailed the demobilisation and the return home of German soldiers to help gather in the harvest and prepare the fields for next year's crop.

Over the years many changes occurred within the structure of BAOR and, as life returned more or less to normal, troops were sent home and the strength of the occupation force was reduced. By 1946 the 30 Corps and the 8 Corps were already disbanded and in 1948 even the 1 Corps disappeared, to be reinstated in 1951, however.

In May 1948 the Russians, flouting international agreements made in Yalta and Potsdam, closed off all road and rail links to Berlin from the Allied occupation zones, without any warning. The result was that a massive air operation was mounted to supply West Berlin with any commodity that a city of over 2 million people might need. The success of this operation caused the Russians to realise that not only could a status quo be maintained but that even reserve supplies could be built up. This led them to lift the blockade and on 11 May 1949 land and rail communications to Berlin were restored to normal.

In October 1992 the HQ of 1 (British Corps) at Bielefeld, Germany was replaced by the HQ of the Allied Command Europe's Rapid Reaction Corps (ARRC) also in Bielefeld. The date for disbanding the HQ of the BAOR in Rheindalen is 31 March 1994. It is replaced by a new HQ called the HQ British Forces Germany (BFG) working alongside the ARRC. From 1 April 1994 both HQ's are situated in Rheindalen. The core of this new BFG is formed by 1 (UK) Armoured Division with a total of about 23,000 troops, and is supported by RAF Germany.

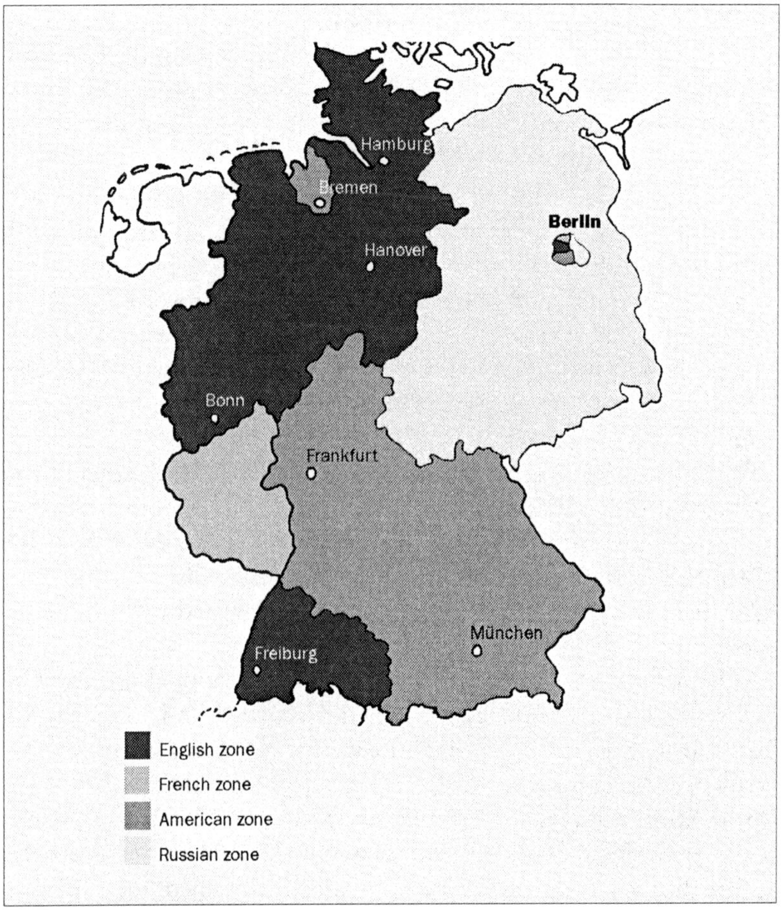

Figure 101. Allied Occupation Zones in Germany

J-3

OTHER EUROPEAN AREAS OF BRITISH OCCUPATION

There were two other areas of occupation in Europe in which Britain was involved which, although technically not part of BAOR, faced many of the same problems. These areas were Austria and the Free Territory of Trieste in Northern Italy.

AUSTRIA - BRITISH TROOPS AUSTRIA (BTA)

The occupation of Austria began when 5 (British) Corps, spearheading the 8th Army, arrived in Austria having fought their way from North Africa through the entire length of Italy. The 5 (British) Corps set up base in Klagenfurt, Austria and from then on faced very much the same task as the BOAR - an endless stream of displaced persons had be housed, fed and clothed.

J-4

As in Germany, the country had been divided into four areas of occupation to be controlled by Britain, the USA, USSR and France respectively. In Vienna the Allied Control Commission Austria was set up as well as an Army Area Headquarters to co-ordinate the various forces. The British zone, comprising the south-west of Austria and Vienna, was controlled by HQ British Troops Austria (BTA) stationed at Klagenfurt.

As with Berlin, Vienna was also divided into four sectors of occupation and, familiar as it may sound, Vienna was an island in the Russian occupation zone! By 1949 the role of the BTA had changed from that of an occupation force to a defensive force. The Russians started to advance through the British zone, aiming towards the Italian border and in 1953 Graz was evacuated and Villach was prepared for evacuation leaving the BTA present only in Vienna and Klagenfurt. Fortunately the Russian threat never became reality and in 1955 the Russian Commission agreed to evacuate their forces from Austria under the strict condition that the country should remain neutral, which would involve the withdrawal of any foreign troops. And so the British occupation forces left Austria on 17 September 1955, handing over their duties to a small Austrian army.

FREE TERRITORY OF TRIESTE - BRITISH ELEMENT TRIESTE FORCE (BETFOR)

The city of Trieste is situated in the north-east of Italy, in a province called Venezia Giulia. Following the collapse of Germany, Yugoslavia was quick to claim the territory as theirs and Yugoslav guerrilla forces occupied the city. But this soon changed when the 8th Army arrived and the Yugoslavians were forced from the city. But they still upheld their claim to the territory of Trieste and keeping them back proved to be a full-time occupation .

The occupation force of Trieste was formed after the HQ 13 Corps, which had fought in North Africa and across Italy into Austria was disbanded in 1946. This led to the formation of HQ British Element Trieste Force or BETFOR. Together with the US Forces in the area BETFOR was to support the Allied Military Government in restoring normality to the area.

In 1953 the Italians became suspicious of British motives for staying so long in Trieste and this led to rioting and unrest by the end of that year. It was then decided to evacuate BETFOR and within 21 days everything had been moved either to the UK, to the BAOR or to the British troops still in Austria. But with the UN decision that a twelve-month delay should be observed prior to withdrawal, a year of tension set in between Italy and Britain before Trieste was finally handed back to Italy. The Italian Army finally took over on 25 October 1954.

BRITISH ARMED FORCES SPECIAL VOUCHERS

Arlette Sirot
photographies et stylisme
Iris Sullivan

Tout est bon
dans le poisson

textes
Colette Gouvion
shopping
John Bentham

Minerva

sommaire

Cuisinière des mers

Voici des effluves iodés, de fraîches senteurs d'eaux calmes et fraîches. Voici que s'irisent des miroitements d'écailles. Voici que s'offre à vous la succulente manne des poissons de mer, de lac, de rivière, dans sa diversité inouïe. Voici qu'enfin, grâce aux recettes mises au point, testées et réunies dans ce livre par Arlette Sirot, images malicieuses à l'appui, vous allez savoir comment en tirer avec brio tous les partis possibles, délicieux, inventifs, malins et souvent économiques.

Arlette Sirot est un cas à part dans le microcosme culinaire. On y trouve de grands chefs dont les toques aux scintillantes étoiles impressionnent tant qu'ils inspirent, d'abord, des complexes. On y rencontre de petits chefs riches de plus de faconde que de talent qui font sourire avant d'agacer. Elle n'appartient à aucune de ces deux galaxies. C'est tout simplement une femme généreuse, fine cuisinière grâce à ses dons, son travail, sa curiosité, sa gourmandise exigeante et son appétit joyeux, qui aime régaler les autres et, loin de garder jalousement pour elle son art de cuisiner, le partage avec tous en toute simplicité.

Au début, en Savoie où les circonstances de sa vie l'avaient amenée, ce fut une maîtresse de maison accueillante, qui aimait cuisiner pour ses amis. Lesquels amis réalisèrent qu'ils ne pouvaient décemment prendre pension à sa table, et lui suggérèrent d'ouvrir un restaurant. Ce qu'elle fit. D'autres suivirent. Jusqu'à Belle-Île-en Mer, où elle s'installa sur un coup de cœur. Tint table ouverte pour les copains. Et le même scénario se reproduisit : « Arlette, ouvre donc un restaurant. » Son Contre quai devint l'une des meilleures tables de la belle île, celle où l'on avait l'impression d'être en famille, la certitude de faire un repas délicieux et la promesse de découvertes gastronomiques tant elle mettait de passion, puisant aussi bien dans les répertoires du terroir que dans les cuisines d'ailleurs, à chercher, tester et servir des plats surprises. Ainsi, par exemple, il n'y eut jamais à sa carte le sempiternel plateau de fruits de mer. Mais son tourteau farci eut bientôt un fan club. Sans parler de ses desserts...

La vie a coulé. Arlette est revenue vivre dans la maison familiale, près de Fontainebleau, en ne conservant que des fonctions de consultante pour ses anciens confrères, et de SOS cuisine pour ses familiers : « Allô Arlette, j'ai dix personnes à dîner, aurais-tu une idée ? Allô Arlette, comment fais-tu ta terrine de lieu aux pommes de terre et à l'aneth ? » Elle conseillait, elle expliquait. Et de nouveau la vox populi s'est exprimée : « Mais qu'attends-tu pour faire des livres ? Ce serait une œuvre d'utilité publique. » C'est ainsi qu'elle a ajouté le stylo à la cuiller en bois.

D'où viennent les thèmes des ouvrages qui se sont succédé ? D'une envie, d'un intérêt pour un type de produits, de propos échangés. Un jour avec une amie Arlette se balade à une manifestation « porte ouverte » au potager de Saint-Jean-de-Beauregard. C'est l'automne. Il fait froid et humide. Pour se réchauffer, il faudrait une bonne soupe. Les deux gourmandes de se mettre à en rêver. Il en naîtra un premier livre, *Recevoir autour d'une soupe*. Des maîtresses de maison lui confient leur souci : « comment recevoir sans avoir, au dernier moment, à s'écheveler seule dans la cuisine tandis que les convives sont à table ? » Réponse : *Recevoir paresseusement*, avec tous les mets qui peuvent se cuisiner à l'avance. Et ainsi de suite.

Ces déclinaisons, cependant, ne se font pas en un coup de cuiller à pot. La cuisinière y pense. Plonge dans sa foisonnante documentation. Se remémore les plats qu'elle a pu goûter au cours de ses voyages, en Italie, en Chine, en Corée ou ailleurs, les saveurs qu'elle a découvertes, les épices et les herbes qui l'ont séduite. Et puis, surtout, elle va au marché. C'est là qu'il y a le plus de plaisir à la suivre, quand les courts copeaux d'argent de sa chevelure s'ébouriffent et que ses yeux brillent comme ceux d'un gamin dans une pâtisserie. Elle hume, contemple, va, vient, attend le coup de cœur pour tel légume magnifique, tel poisson surtout : ce saint-pierre frais sorti de l'océan, ces rougets qui semblent encore frétiller – dont elle se met immédiatement à imaginer comment elle va les accommoder. Dans sa grande cuisine, d'autant plus sympathique qu'elle n'a vraiment rien d'un laboratoire, sans « piano » de chef, sans matériel sophistiqué, elle passe ensuite à l'acte. Essaie. Teste. Invite l'un ou l'autre à venir goûter. Et c'est seulement quand elle est satisfaite qu'elle rédige sa recette, en se mettant totalement dans la peau de celui ou de celle qui voudra la réaliser et n'a pas forcément la virtuosité que sa gourmandise mériterait. Ce n'est pas un chef. C'est une amie qui vous prend la main et vous guide vers la réussite sans angoisse ni migraine.

Son nouveau livre vient à un moment où justement, en France, les poissons sont de plus en plus diversifiés, de plus en plus prisés, mais où souvent l'on ne sait pas encore comment les accommoder. Il est né à la fois d'une vraie passion pour les produits de la mer, de l'envie de la faire partager et d'une espièglerie. Dans le cochon, tout est bon, dit-on. Des oreilles à la queue, des abats aux filets, tout se cuisine, tout se consomme. Le poisson, c'est exactement la même chose : les filets mais aussi les joues, les foies, les têtes, les œufs, les laitances, etc. « Tout est bon dans le poisson » : vous l'allez découvrir. Vous ne le regretterez sûrement pas.

Colette Gouvion

SAMEDI
1
AVRIL
St Hugues
SOL. 5 h 31 à 18 h 19

Faites-en tout un plat

À table. Autour d'un plat de poisson qui sera le cœur du repas. Comment ? Sous toutes les formes possibles, en pot-au-feu, en choucroute, en tourte, en ragoût, en farci… Les poissons rendent ici visite aux recettes traditionnelles qui retrouvent avec eux une nouvelle jeunesse, et même ils s'amusent à prendre l'apparence de gâteaux.

Pot-au-feu de la mer

Comme son cousin classique, il est inratable, mais plus vite cuit, se sert en soupière, réchauffe les corps et les âmes, et s'accompagne de sauces qui, de ce modeste, font un festin.

Pour 6 personnes
Préparation : 45 min
Cuisson : 1 h

- 500 g de filets de lotte
- 4 filets de sole
- 6 langoustines
- 12 grosses crevettes
- 6 noix de Saint-Jacques

Légumes
- 6 carottes
- 2 poireaux
- 2 fenouils
- 250 g de petits oignons blancs
- 6 petits navets ronds

Pour le bouillon
- 1 carotte
- 1 gros oignon
- 1 gousse d'ail
- 1 blanc de poireau
- 20 g de beurre
- 250 g de parures de poisson (têtes et arêtes)
- 1 bouquet garni
- 50 cl d'eau
- 50 cl de vin blanc sec
- sel et poivre

Pour la sauce
- 30 cl de crème liquide
- 2 jaunes d'œufs
- 1/2 citron
- 50 g de beurre

Pour servir, prévoyez 6 rondelles de baguette enduites au pinceau d'huile d'olive, dorées sous le gril et décorées avec un filet d'anchois assaisonné de quelques gouttes de citron.

- **Réalisez le bouillon (éventuellement dès la veille) :** pelez la carotte, l'oignon, l'ail ; nettoyez le blanc de poireau. Émincez tous les légumes. Dans une cocotte (ou un faitout), faites chauffer 20 g de beurre, et mettez-y tous les légumes émincés à fondre sur feu moyen, puis ajoutez les 250 g de parures de poisson. Faites rissoler à feu vif avant d'ajouter le bouquet garni. Salez et poivrez. Versez l'eau et le vin blanc sec. Laissez mijoter 1 heure, filtrez le bouillon et reversez-le dans le faitout en prélevant 50 cl pour la sauce.
- **Préparez tous les légumes de la garniture :** nettoyez-les, épluchez-les et rincez-les. Ôtez les plus grosses côtes externes des fenouils. Tronçonnez tous ces légumes. Portez le bouillon à ébullition et faites-y pocher les légumes pendant une dizaine de minutes. Plongez-y la lotte, laissez frémir pendant 8 à 10 minutes. Ajoutez alors les filets de sole, 3 minutes après les langoustines et les grosses crevettes, 1 minute plus tard les noix de Saint-Jacques. Au bout de 2 minutes, éteignez le feu.
- **Confectionnez la sauce :** faites réduire de moitié le demi-litre de bouillon prélevé. Puis versez-y la crème. Faites bouillir, ajoutez en fouettant les jaunes d'œufs préalablement délayés dans le jus du demi-citron. Incorporez tout en fouettant 50 g de beurre coupé en petits morceaux. Versez la sauce dans la cocotte hors du feu. Vérifiez l'assaisonnement. Mettez le pot-au-feu dans une soupière, et servez-le aussitôt avec les croûtons à l'anchois.

On peut accompagner ce pot-au-feu d'une chantilly à l'estragon réalisée en montant en chantilly 40 cl de crème liquide très froide à laquelle on ajoute 5 ou 6 branches d'estragon ciselé finement, ou d'une sauce vierge (que l'on peut préparer la veille) et dont voici la recette :

• 3 tomates mondées, épépinés et coupées en dés • 2 gousses d'ail non épluchées • 2 cuillerées à soupe de cerfeuil • 2 c. à soupe de persil plat • 1 c. à soupe d'estragon • 1 dizaine de grains de coriandre concassés • 20 cl d'huile d'olive • sel et poivre

- Supprimez le pédoncule des tomates et pelez-les après les avoir ébouillantées.
- Rassemblez tous ces ingrédients dans une casserole : tomates, ail, herbes hachées, grains de coriandre, huile, sel et poivre. Mettez au bain-marie pendant 30 minutes afin de cuire la sauce. Vous pouvez la servir tiède ou froide.

Pour 4 personnes
Préparation : 30 min
Cuisson : 45 min

Choucroute de la mer

- 4 darnes de saumon
- 4 petits filets de haddock
- 12 noix de Saint-Jacques
- 2 boudins de saumon à acheter tout faits
- 100 g de lardons de saumon fumé
- 25 cl de lait
- 1 kg de choucroute crue
- 1 oignon
- 1 gousse d'ail
- 1 l de court-bouillon
- 20 cl de vin blanc
- 15 à 20 baies de genièvre
- 2 feuilles de laurier
- 1 c. à soupe de beurre
- 12 fines tranches de lard fumé

Sauce
- 100 g de beurre demi-sel
- 4 c. à soupe de crème épaisse
- 1 jus de citron
- 1 échalote

Chou et poisson font, on le sait, de bons compagnons. Mais avec quelques compléments qui enrichissent leur duo, la choucroute devient vraiment royale.

- Rincez la choucroute crue à l'eau tiède, puis pressez-la bien entre vos mains pour l'égoutter.
- Faites revenir l'oignon et l'ail épluchés et émincés dans le beurre, puis versez 20 cl de court-bouillon et 20 cl de vin blanc, et ajoutez les baies de genièvre, les feuilles de laurier et les lardons de saumon.
- Laissez cuire pendant 45 minutes sur feu moyen, à couvert.
- Pendant ce temps, pochez les darnes de saumon dans le court-bouillon restant.
- Dans le lait chaud, mettez les filets de haddock à tremper.
- Entourez les noix de Saint-Jacques avec les fines tranches de lard fumé. Dans la poêle, faites dorer à feu moyen dans un peu de beurre les noix et leur corail, 5 minutes sur chaque face.
- Mettez les boudins de saumon à cuire directement dans la choucroute pendant 10 à 15 minutes.
- **Simultanément, réalisez la sauce :** faites fondre 100 g de beurre demi-sel, ajoutez 4 cuillerées à soupe de crème épaisse, le jus d'un citron, 1 échalote hachée. Laissez cuire 10 minutes, à feu moyen.
- Dressez la choucroute sur un plat ainsi que tous les poissons, avec la sauce à part. Servez très chaud.

Chou farci au poisson

Chic et pas cher. La rondeur bon enfant du chou donne le ton. Sa farce insolite lui ajoute un brin d'audace. Une bonne manière d'enrichir les menus de l'hiver.

Pour 4 à 6 personnes
Préparation : 30 min
Cuisson : 1 h 30

- **800 g de filets de poissons blancs (cabillaud, merlan...)**
- **1 beau chou vert frisé**
- **100 g de mie de pain de campagne un peu rassis (ou du pain de mie rassis sans la croûte)**
- **10 cl de lait**
- **1 œuf**
- **2 échalotes (grises si possible)**
- **2 branches de persil plat**
- **1 branche de thym**
- **2 grandes bardes de lard gras larges et très minces**
- **2 oignons**
- **2 carottes**
- **2 gousses d'ail**
- **1 c. à soupe de saindoux (ou de graisse d'oie)**
- **1 bouteille de vin blanc sec**
- **1 bouquet garni**
- **2 clous de girofle**
- **Sel et poivre du moulin**

- Épluchez le chou en éliminant les feuilles extérieures dures et la base du trognon. Lavez-le bien.
- Faites blanchir le chou entier pendant 20 minutes dans de l'eau bouillante salée. Puis plongez-le dans de l'eau très froide pour interrompre la cuisson.
- Retournez-le sur un torchon, dans une passoire et laissez-le égoutter.
- Préparez la farce : mettez le pain à tremper dans le lait. Hachez les filets de poissons, après avoir eu soin d'éliminer les arêtes. Posez les poissons dans un saladier. Malaxez-les avec le pain humecté de lait et émietté, l'œuf entier, les échalotes émincées, le persil haché, le thym effeuillé. Salez et poivrez.
- Ouvrez délicatement les feuilles extérieures du chou en prenant soin de ne pas les casser, et ceci jusqu'au cœur. Ôtez le cœur et remplacez-le par une boule de farce de la même grosseur. Recouvrez-la d'une feuille. Garnissez chaque feuille d'une cuillerée de farce jusqu'à ce que le chou soit reconstitué, en serrant bien les feuilles les unes contre les autres.
- Sur les bardes de lard posées en croix sur le plan de travail, placez le chou. Rabattez les bardes pour bien l'envelopper, puis ficelez l'ensemble.
- Laissez fondre le saindoux dans une grande cocotte sur feu moyen. Faites-y revenir l'un des oignons pelé et émincé, les carottes émincées et les gousses d'ail pelées et écrasées. Ne laissez pas colorer.
- Déposez le chou dans la cocotte. Tournez-le sur toutes ses faces pour l'enrober de gras.
- Mouillez avec le vin blanc et complétez d'eau à hauteur.
- Salez, ajoutez le deuxième oignon épluché et piqué avec les clous de girofle ainsi que le bouquet garni.
- Dès le premier bouillon, couvrez et laissez cuire 1 heure à 1 heure 20 sur feu très doux. Égouttez le chou, posez-le dans un plat creux et découpez-le en quartiers. Arrosez-le de quelques cuillerées de bouillon. Servez chaud.

On peut également présenter ce chou farci avec un coulis de tomates chaud (voir recette page 36).

Pour 4 personnes
Préparation : 45 min
Cuisson : 2 heures
(1 h 30 la veille,
30 minutes le jour
du repas)

- 1 kg d'alose
- 8 cl de vinaigre de vin
- 5 ou 6 jeunes poireaux
- 12 petits oignons nouveaux
- Farine
- 5 cl d'huile d'arachide
- 3 gousses d'ail
- 1,5 l de vin rouge
- 4 morceaux de sucre
- 1 bouquet garni (thym, laurier, persil)
- 8 cl d'armagnac
- Sel et poivre

Civet d'alose

L'alose qui habite les rivières du Sud-Ouest de la France est fort prisée de leurs riverains. Si vous en trouvez, précipitez-vous. Et lancez-vous dans ce civet onctueux.

- La veille, sectionnez l'alose 1,5 cm au-dessus de la queue, jusqu'à l'arête, sans la vider. Suspendez-la au-dessus d'un bol pour recueillir le sang. Ajoutez le vinaigre pour éviter la coagulation. Placez également le foie de l'alose dans le vinaigre.
- Lavez l'alose sous un filet d'eau froide. Séchez-la et détaillez-la en tranches de 2 cm environ. Farinez les tranches sur les deux faces. Faites chauffer dans la poêle 3 cl d'huile et faites-y dorer légèrement les tranches d'alose sur les deux faces. Réservez.
- Épluchez et lavez les poireaux, coupez-les en tronçons d'1 cm environ. Épluchez et ciselez les gousses d'ail ainsi que les oignons nouveaux. Dans une sauteuse, faites chauffer le reste d'huile et faites colorer les tronçons de poireaux sur feu vif, en les retournant à l'aide d'une spatule pour les dorer de toutes parts. Ajoutez ensuite l'ail et les oignons, puis les tranches d'alose. Réservez.
- Dans une grande casserole, amenez à ébullition le vin avec les 4 morceaux de sucre, puis faites-le flamber pendant 30 secondes. Versez-le dans la sauteuse contenant les tranches d'alose et les légumes. Ajoutez le bouquet garni. Salez et poivrez. Couvrez et laissez mijoter pendant 1 h 30 à très petit feu.
- Le lendemain, ajoutez à la préparation le sang et le foie de l'alose, ainsi que l'armagnac. Faites à nouveau cuire pendant 30 minutes, à très petit feu, en évitant de faire bouillir.

Pour 6 personnes
Préparation : 25 min
Cuisson : 25 min

- 3 filets de féra (ou d'un poisson à chair blanche)
- 200 g de champignons de Paris
- 1 belle courgette
- 1 c. à soupe d'huile d'olive
- 1 échalote
- 1 belle gousse d'ail
- 2 c. à soupe de persil
- 15 cl de crème fraîche
- 25 g de beurre
- 1 c. à soupe de chapelure
- 1 lamelle de tome de Savoie (facultatif)

Pour la purée
- 6 pommes de terre BF15
- 25 cl de crème fraîche
- 30 g de beurre salé
- Sel et poivre

Parmentier de féra

Roborative et savoureuse, une variation sur le thème de la brandade et du hachis parmentier avec emprunt à la cuisine traditionnelle savoyarde. Et pourquoi pas ?

- Faites cuire les pommes de terre pour la purée. Pendant ce temps, lavez et hachez les champignons de Paris et la courgette en petits dés.
- Faites revenir à feu vif dans de l'huile d'olive la brunoise de champignons. Dès coloration, ajoutez la courgette, l'échalote, l'ail et le persil hachés. Lorsque les légumes sont rissolés, ajoutez les filets de poisson. Remuez le tout et laissez cuire à couvert pendant 5 minutes environ, toujours sur feu vif. Lorsque le poisson commence à se défaire, incorporez la crème pour faire la liaison. Laissez cuire encore 2 ou 3 minutes.
- Préparation de la purée de pommes de terre. Lorsque les pommes de terre sont cuites, passez-les au presse-purée. Ajoutez la crème, le beurre. Salez et poivrez. Mélangez bien.
- Préchauffez le four à 180 °C (th. 6). Emplissez à mi-hauteur le fond d'un moule de 25 cm de diamètre avec la préparation au poisson. Couvrez de purée et lissez à l'aide d'une spatule. Poudrez de chapelure, posez une noisette de beurre et une lamelle de tome. Enfournez durant 5 minutes, puis faites dorer pendant 3 à 4 minutes sous le gril.

Pour 4 personnes
Préparation : 20 min
Cuisson : 20 min

- 2 filets de lottes de 800 g
- 2 c. à soupe de farine
- 2 grappes de raisins blancs environ (500 g) pour 20 cl de jus (à défaut choisissez du jus de raisin sans sucre ajouté)
- 3 c. à soupe d'huile
- 1 c. à soupe de beurre
- 2 échalotes
- 2 c. à soupe de vinaigre de vin
- 5 c. à soupe de crème fraîche épaisse
- Sel et poivre

En accompagnement
- 250 g de pâtes
- 100 g d'œufs de saumon
- 10 feuilles d'épinards

Fricassée de lotte au jus de raisin

Un authentique mets pour gourmet, à la portée même d'une cuisinière débutante qui goûtera peut-être grâce à lui, qui sait, son premier triomphe.

- Coupez la lotte en fines tranches de 40 g environ. Saler, poivrez et farinez-les.
- Passez les raisins égrenés à la moulinette.
- Hachez les échalotes.
- Faites chauffer dans une poêle le beurre et l'huile, puis faites dorer les morceaux de lotte des deux côtés sur feu vif. Réservez.
- Dans la même poêle, faites revenir les échalotes hachées. Ajoutez le vinaigre, et laissez réduire sur feu vif pendant 5 minutes puis ajoutez le jus des raisins. Salez et poivrez. Laissez réduire de moitié avant d'ajouter la crème fraîche. Amenez à ébullition. Remettez les morceaux de lotte dans la poêle. Laissez cuire 15 minutes.
- Mettez à cuire les pâtes. Ciselez les feuilles d'épinards. Dès que vous avez égoutté les pâtes, ajoutez-y les feuilles d'épinards. Parsemez d'œufs de saumon.
- Servez la fricassée de lotte dans son jus avec le plat de pâtes en accompagnement.

Andouillette de bar

Pour les inconditionnels du *Dicentrarchus labrax* – le nom savant du bar – les adeptes des papillotes et les gourmets en quête de grandes découvertes.

Pour 4 personnes
Préparation : 45 min
Cuisson : 6-7 min

- **800 g à 1 kg de filet de bar sans arêtes**

Pour la farce
- **1 carotte**
- **1 poireau**
- **125 g de champignons de Paris**
- **1 oignon doux**
- **2 œufs**
- **150 g de crème épaisse**
- **Sel et poivre**

Pour la sauce
- **3 échalotes**
- **25 cl de fumet de poisson (déshydraté)**
- **1/2 citron**
- **1 grosse cuillerée de moutarde à l'ancienne**
- **1 c. à soupe de ciboulette hachée**
- **10 cl de crème liquide**

- Découpez dans du papier d'aluminium des rectangles d'environ 21 cm x 15 cm. Beurrez-les avec un pinceau sur les trois quarts de la surface.
- Épluchez tous les légumes et coupez-les en très fine julienne. Faites-les revenir dans une noisette de beurre, pendant quelques minutes, sans leur faire prendre couleur. Réservez.
- À l'aide d'un couteau très fin et très aiguisé – couteau à jambon ou « filet de sole » –, découpez de très fines escalopes sur toute la largeur du filet de bar. Disposez-les sur la partie beurrée du papier d'aluminium ; mettez-en une ou deux, en fonction de la taille des escalopes, qui doivent recouvrir toute la partie beurrée. Réservez 250 à 300 g de filet pour la préparation de la farce.
- **Préparation de la farce.** Dans un mixeur, mettez le filet de bar réservé pour la farce. Salez, poivrez. Mélangez, puis ajoutez les œufs. Mixez de nouveau. Versez la crème petit à petit et, enfin, les légumes. Mélangez bien pour avoir un hachis de bonne tenue. Déposez cette farce au milieu des escalopes en formant un boudin, soit à l'aide d'une cuillère à soupe, soit avec une poche à douille sans douille. Relevez un premier côté de papier aluminium dans le sens de la largeur pour « coller » l'escalope sur le boudin de chair. Reposez la feuille et, avec l'autre extrémité de la feuille, roulez votre andouillette. Vrillez les deux extrémités du papier d'aluminium pour bien fermer.
- **Réalisation de la sauce.** Épluchez et ciselez les 3 échalotes. Faites-les revenir dans un peu de beurre sur feu moyen. Ajoutez les 25 cl de fumet de poisson et la crème. Salez et poivrez. Incorporez un filet de citron, la moutarde et la ciboulette hachée. Parallèlement, dans une grande casserole, mettez à bouillir une grande quantité d'eau. Plongez-y les andouillettes dans leur papier d'aluminium pendant 6 à 7 minutes. Sortez les andouillettes de l'eau, enlevez le papier d'aluminium. Dressez-les sur les assiettes et nappez-les de sauce.
- On peut confectionner ces andouillettes, avec du bar, du saumon, de la truite de mer, ou tout autre poisson ayant une certaine tenue : choisissez des filets pas trop gros mais suffisamment afin de pouvoir y tailler des escalopes.

Pour 4 personnes
Préparation : 15 min
Cuisson : 20 min

- 4 beaux rougets
- 1 oignon
- 3 gousses d'ail
- Huile d'olive
- 1 c. à soupe de graines de fenouil
- 1 tomate bien mûre
- 50 g de beurre

Rougets en bécasses

Surnommés parfois les bécasses de la mer car, comme pour les oiseaux, on peut les cuisiner sans les vider...

Attention, haute gastronomie. Mais pas difficile pour autant. Et clin d'œil au délicat volatile à nobles références et consommation sous haute surveillance.

- Demandez à votre poissonnier d'écailler les poissons et de lever les filets, et de vous réserver les foies, les arêtes centrales, la queue et la tête. Mettez les foies dans une coupelle avec quelques gouttes d'huile.
- **Préparation du fumet.** Rincez soigneusement les parures à l'eau fraîche. Épluchez et émincez 1 oignon ; écrasez les gousses d'ail sans les éplucher. Dans une casserole sur feu doux, faites revenir dans 2 cuillerées à soupe d'huile d'olive, l'oignon émincé, les gousses d'ail, toutes les parures de poisson, pendant 4 minutes. Ajoutez ensuite les graines de fenouil et la tomate coupée en morceaux. Écrasez avec un pilon sur le feu doux et, lorsque tout est réduit en purée, mouillez avec 50 cl d'eau. Couvrez et laissez cuire 10 à 13 minutes.
- Pendant ce temps, retirez les arêtes s'il y en reste sur les filets. Égouttez les foies et écrasez-les à la fourchette. Filtrez le fumet dans une passoire fine. Prélevez-en quelques cuillerées pour la cuisson des filets. Faites réduire le reste de moitié sur feu vif. Salez et poivrez. Faites chauffer, dans une poêle, le fumet réservé. Déposez les filets de poisson côté peau vers le fond du récipient. Après 2 minutes de cuisson à feu doux, éteignez et laissez-les dans la poêle. Incorporez au fumet, en fouettant sur feu doux, 50 g de beurre mou. Hors du feu, ajoutez en fouettant les foies écrasés. Émulsionnez parfaitement. Nappez de sauce le fond des assiettes chaudes, déposez dessus les filets de rouget, côté peau visible et servez aussitôt.

en

Cassoulet de cabillaud

Ô natifs de Castelnaudary, ô fiers habitants de Toulouse la rouge, ne criez pas au crime de lèse-tradition avant d'avoir goûté. Ensuite ? vous en redemanderez.

Pour 4 personnes
Préparation : 30 min
Cuisson des haricots secs : 2 h 30
Cuisson des haricots frais : 30 min à 1 h
Cuisson et finition du cassoulet : 20 min

- 600 g de cabillaud
- 500 g de haricots secs mélangés (ou des haricots frais à écosser)
- 4 gousses d'ail
- 1 carotte
- 2 oignons
- 4 clous de girofle
- 1 bouquet garni
- 3 c. à soupe d'huile d'olive
- 3 tomates bien mûres
- 150 g de lardons de poitrine fumée
- Thym frais effeuillé
- 10 cl de jus de volaille
- 10 cl de jus de crustacé
- 50 g de beurre
- Chapelure
- 1 c. à soupe de persil haché
- Sel et poivre

- Si vous utilisez des haricots secs, mettez-les à tremper la veille dans une grande terrine d'eau froide
- Le lendemain, égouttez-les et mettez-les dans une grande casserole avec 2 litres d'eau froide. Amenez à ébullition.
- Épluchez les gousses d'ail et un oignon, que vous piquez de clous de girofle. Épluchez, lavez et coupez la carotte en morceaux. Ajoutez-les aux haricots ainsi que le bouquet garni. Couvrez et laissez cuire à petits bouillons pendant 2 heures à 2 heures 30 (la durée est fonction de la variété et de la grosseur des haricots. Goûtez pour vous assurer qu'ils sont bien cuits). Si vous utilisez des haricots frais, il n'est pas nécessaire de les faire tremper ; la cuisson durera de 30 minutes à 1 heure selon leur grosseur. Une fois la cuisson terminée, réservez les haricots hors du feu dans leur eau de cuisson.
- Dans une poêle, mettez à dorer les tranches de cabillaud dans 1 cuillerée à soupe d'huile. Réservez.
- Pelez, épépinez les tomates et coupez-les en gros dés.
- Épluchez et émincez l'oignon restant.
- Versez l'huile d'olive restante dans une poêle, et faites revenir l'oignon émincé, les lardons, les dés de tomates avec le thym pendant 2 minutes à feu moyen.
- Égouttez les haricots. Conservez un peu d'eau de cuisson. Remettez les haricots dans la casserole avec le contenu de la poêle. Mélangez avec une cuillère. Assaisonnez de sel et de poivre. Mouillez avec 3 c. à soupe d'eau de cuisson, le jus de volaille et le jus de crustacés.
- Dans un plat allant au four, étalez une couche de haricots, déposez dessus les tranches de cabillaud, et couvrez avec le reste des haricots. Parsemez de noix de beurre. Saupoudrez de chapelure, et faites dorer au gril du four, pendant 12 à 15 minutes.
- Parsemez de persil haché et servez très chaud.

Pour 4 personnes
Préparation : 20 min
Cuisson : 15 min

- **800 g de queue de lotte**
- **2 échalotes**
- **30 g de beurre**
- **10 cl de vin blanc (ou vermouth)**
- **15 cl de crème liquide**
- **20 cl de fumet de poissons (déshydraté)**
- **1 jaune d'œuf**
- **1 c. à soupe d'huile**
- **2 c. à soupe de persil plat ciselé**
- **2 c. à soupe de poivre vert en saumure**
- **3 pincées de poivre**
- **1 pincée de cannelle**
- **1 pincée de piment**
- **2 pincées de curry**
- **Sel**

Blanquette de lotte aux épices

Une chair nacrée sans arêtes. Une sauce onctueuse à s'en lécher les doigts. Des épices savamment dosées. Le régal irrésistible à la portée des débutants.

- Demandez à votre poissonnier de vous préparer la queue de lotte en une douzaine de médaillons de 50 à 60 g.
- Dans une casserole, faites revenir sur feu moyen les échalotes hachées dans 10 g de beurre jusqu'à ce qu'elles soient translucides. Mouillez avec le vin blanc (ou le vermouth). Laissez un peu réduire. Puis ajoutez le fumet et 5 cl de crème. Laissez épaissir sur feu doux pour obtenir une sauce onctueuse. Puis assaisonnez de poivre, cannelle, piment et curry en poudre. Mélangez.
- Délayez le jaune d'œuf avec 10 cl de crème liquide dans une terrine, et incorporez progressivement la sauce très chaude. Gardez la sauce au chaud au bain-marie.
- Chauffez le reste de beurre et l'huile dans une grande poêle. Faites saisir les médaillons à feu moyen pendant 1 minute de chaque côté, et poursuivez la cuisson pendant 2 minutes. Salez en fin de cuisson.
- Mettez les médaillons de lotte dans un plat chaud et nappez-les de sauce.
- Parsemez de persil ciselé et de poivre vert.
- Accompagnez ce plat de riz créole.

Pour 4 personnes
Préparation : 45 min
Marinade : 2 h
Cuisson : 15 min

- 1 filet de cabillaud d'environ 600 g
- 300 g de pommes de terre
- Huile d'olive
- 1 gousse d'ail
- 15 cl de crème liquide
- 50 cl de lait
- Thym et laurier
- 8 poivrons rouges, ou jaunes, ou verts (vous pouvez panacher les couleurs)
- Sel et poivre

Poivrons farcis à la brandade de cabillaud

Coup de cœur au marché pour des poivrons tentateurs, si colorés, brillants, dodus ? Ne restez pas sur votre faim, et cuisinez-les en poivrons farceurs.

- Faites cuire les pommes de terre épluchées dans de l'eau salée. Écrasez-les ensuite au presse-purée. Versez dans la purée avec 1 cuillerée à soupe d'huile d'olive, une gousse d'ail pressée et de la crème liquide chaude.
- **Préparation de la brandade.** Mettez à mariner pendant 2 heures le filet de poisson avec du gros sel et du poivre. Puis rincez-le. Dans un plat allant au feu, recouvrez le poisson d'une quantité égale d'eau et de lait, ajoutez le thym et le laurier. Amenez à ébullition et retirez du feu. Effeuillez le filet de cabillaud et incorporez-le à la purée, dans les proportions suivantes : un tiers de pommes de terre, deux tiers de cabillaud. Laissez refroidir.
- **Préparation des poivrons.** Préchauffez le four à 180 °C (th. 6). Piquez chaque poivron au bout d'une fourchette et passez-les sur la flamme du gaz en les tournant de tous côtés jusqu'à ce que la peau devienne noire. Rafraîchissez-les sous l'eau froide, pelez-les, retirez le pédoncule et épépinez-les, sans crever la chair. Mettez les poivrons dans un plat allant au four. Arrosez-les avec un peu d'huile d'olive, salez-les des deux côtés, puis enfournez pendant une quinzaine de minutes. Laissez-les refroidir à température ambiante, avant de les farcir de brandade.
- Servez avec une sauce tomate classique ou un coulis de poivrons jaunes que vous préparez comme suit : pour 4 personnes, prenez 4 poivrons jaunes pelés. Épépinez-les, coupez-les grossièrement en morceaux, mixez-les avec du sel, du poivre et 2 cuillerées à soupe d'huile d'olive.

Soupe de carpe et ses quenelles

Pour recevoir autour d'une soupe de poisson originale, un plat vraiment complet qui puise aux sources chaleureuses de la cuisine savoyarde.

Pour 4 personnes
Préparation : 45 min
Cuisson : 1 h

Pour la soupe
- 2 échalotes
- 100 g de champignons de Paris
- 80 g de beurre
- 20 cl de vin blanc sec
- 1 botte de cerfeuil
- 1 botte de persil
- 10 cl de crème fraîche
- Sel et poivre

Pour les quenelles
- 1 carpe de 800 g
- 50 g de purée d'olive
- 10 cl de crème fraîche
- 1 l de bouillon de volaille réalisé avec du bouillon déshydraté
- Sel et poivre

Pour la brunoise de légumes
- 1 carotte
- 50 g de courgette
- 20 g de beurre

- Demandez à votre poissonnier de lever les filets du poisson en enlevant la peau, et de vous donner la tête et les arêtes.
- **Préparation de la soupe.** Hachez finement les échalotes et les champignons de Paris. Faites-les revenir avec les arêtes dans 30 g de beurre. Mouillez avec le vin blanc et complétez avec autant d'eau. Ajoutez les queues de persil et de cerfeuil. Salez et poivrez. Laissez cuire à petit feu pendant 30 minutes, puis passez au chinois. Faites réduire ce bouillon pendant 30 minutes à petit feu. Ensuite, incorporez 50 g de beurre et la crème fraîche, ainsi que les pluches de cerfeuil hachées finement.
- **Préparation des quenelles.** Passez la chair du poisson au mixeur. Salez, poivrez, et placez-la durant 30 minutes au congélateur. Au bout de ce temps, incorporez doucement la crème fraîche à la cuillère en bois. Partagez cet appareil en deux parts, incorporez à l'une la purée d'olives, laissez l'autre nature. Faites chauffer le bouillon de volaille sur feu vif. À ébullition, réduisez le feu. À l'aide de deux cuillères à café, formez des petites quenelles que vous ferez glisser rapidement dans le liquide frémissant. Au bout de 4 à 5 minutes, retournez-les délicatement, laissez à nouveau 5 minutes puis égouttez-les. Poursuivez l'opération jusqu'à épuisement des deux.
- **Réalisation de la brunoise de légumes.** Détaillez les légumes lavés et épluchés, en très petits dés. Étuvez-les doucement au beurre une dizaine de minutes. Réservez au chaud.
- Passez la soupe chaude au mixeur pour la faire « mousser », et versez-la dans les assiettes à soupe bien chaudes. Placez dedans les quenelles des deux sortes et la brunoise de légumes. Et servez aussitôt.

Pour 4/6 personnes
Préparation : 30 min
Cuisson de la pâte : 15 min
Cuisson de la tourte
une fois garnie : 35 min

- **1 rouleau de pâte brisée**
- **225 g de filet de haddock**
- **110 g de filet de kippers (harengs fumés)**
- **250 g de lardons de saumon fumé (ou chutes de saumon)**
- **5,5 cl de lait**
- **1 feuille de laurier**
- **1 pincée de macis en poudre**
- **2 gros œufs entiers et 2 jaunes**
- **Poivre noir fraîchement moulu**
- **20 cl de crème fraîche liquide**
- **1 râpée de noix de muscade**
- **1 c. à café de câpres au vinaigre**
- **2 cornichons finement hachés**

Tourte aux trois poissons fumés

Pas de poisson frais ? Peu de temps ? Proche de la quiche lorraine, mais plus dépaysante, à vous la tourte aux riches saveurs nordiques. Effet garanti.

- Préchauffez le four à 200 °C (th. 6-7).
- Garnissez un moule à tarte avec la pâte brisée. Faites cuire la pâte sans garniture (après l'avoir légèrement piquée avec une fourchette) jusqu'à ce qu'elle soit bien dorée (15 minutes environ).
- Mettez les filets de haddock et de kippers dans une casserole avec le lait, le laurier et le macis. Portez à ébullition, couvrez et laissez pocher 2 minutes. Sortez les filets de poissons de la casserole. Enlevez la feuille de laurier et réservez le lait.
- Mettez les œufs entiers ainsi que les jaunes dans une terrine, poivrez mais ne salez pas – les poissons fumés sont en général assez salés –, ajoutez le lait de cuisson refroidi, ainsi que la crème fraîche. Mélangez.
- Coupez les filets de haddock et de kippers en morceaux de 1 cm environ. Déposez-les ainsi que les lardons de saumon sur la pâte à tarte précuite. Ajoutez les câpres égouttées et hachées et les cornichons hachés. Versez dessus, petit à petit, l'appareil de façon à couvrir les poissons et les condiments.
- Enfournez pendant 35 minutes environ, toujours à 200 °C, jusqu'à ce que la tourte soit bien dorée et la crème bien prise.

Pour 8/10 personnes
Préparation : 30 min
Cuisson : 1h30

- 500 g de filets de poisson (lieu, colin, cabillaud...)
- 1 kg de tomates
- 4 gros poivrons rouges
- 6 gousses d'ail (ou 6 échalotes)
- Court-bouillon
- 2 branches de thym
- 2 feuilles de laurier
- 1 bouquet de basilic (ou de fines herbes)
- 6 œufs
- 8 c. à soupe d'huile d'olive
- Sel et poivre

Gâteau de poisson

Du salé cuisiné sous le signe de la pâtisserie. Ainsi ce gâteau doré, truffé de légumes ensoleillés, bon aux papilles des grands et des petits.

- Passez les poivrons sous le gril du four en les exposant sur toutes les faces, de sorte que la peau noircie se décolle. Pelez et épépinez-les. Coupez-les en tout petits dés.
- Plongez les tomates dans l'eau bouillante pour les éplucher facilement. Coupez-les en petits morceaux. Mélangez-les avec les gousses d'ail concassées. Salez et poivrez.
- Faites chauffer l'huile d'olive dans une sauteuse et versez-y les dés de poivron ainsi que le mélange de tomates et d'ail. Faites réduire pendant 40 minutes sur feu doux.
- Pendant ce temps, faites pocher les filets de poisson dans un court-bouillon parfumé de thym et de laurier, pendant 10 minutes sur feu moyen.
- Hachez ces filets cuits et mélangez-les aux légumes. Ajoutez les feuilles de basilic émincées.
- Préchauffez le four à 180 °C (th. 6).
- Battez les œufs en omelette. Incorporez-les, hors du feu, à la préparation précédente.
- Beurrez un grand moule à manqué, ou à charlotte, ou même un moule à cake.
- Enfournez durant 45 minutes en ayant posé le moule dans un plat rempli d'eau bouillante.
- Démoulez le gâteau lorsqu'il est froid et servez-le avec une mayonnaise.

Pour 8/10 personnes
Préparation : 30 min
Cuisson : 45 min

- 700 g de filets de poisson (daurade, merlan, etc.)
- 200 g de thon en boîte
- 1 sachet de court-bouillon
- 1 pincée de paprika
- 2 tranches de pain de mie
- Quelques cuillerées de lait
- 4 œufs
- 3 c. à soupe d'huile
- Sel et poivre

Pour la sauce verte

- 1 poignée de persil, d'épinards et d'oseille mélangés
- 2 jaunes d'œufs
- 1 c. à soupe de moutarde au citron
- 15 cl d'huile
- 1 citron
- Sel et poivre

Savarin de poisson

Dans le même esprit que précédemment, ce savarin malin fait équipe avec la sauce verte en toute bonhomie, et peut partir gaiement en pique-nique.

- Mettez les filets de poisson pendant une vingtaine de minutes dans un court-bouillon frémissant bien aromatisé. égouttez-les puis pilez-les avec le thon. Assaisonnez de sel, poivre et paprika.
- Préchauffez le four à 180 °C (th. 6).
- Incorporez le pain de mie que vous avez fait tremper dans du lait et réduit en panade.
- Travaillez bien pour faire un hachis. Incorporez les œufs battus et 2 à 3 cuillerées à soupe d'huile.
- Versez la pâte dans un moule à savarin beurré. Et enfournez pendant 45 minutes, en posant le moule dans un plat rempli d'eau bouillante.
- Démoulez-le à chaud et laissez-le refroidir.
- **Préparez la sauce verte :** lavez, équeutez les herbes et plongez-les durant 3 minutes dans de l'eau bouillante salée. Égouttez-les et passez-les au mixeur. Réalisez une mayonnaise avec les jaunes d'œufs, la moutarde, l'huile et le jus de citron. Salez et poivrez. Incorporez la purée verte. Vérifiez l'assaisonnement.
- Servez avec le gâteau refroidi.

Pour 4 personnes
Préparation : 15 min
Cuisson : 35 min

- **250 g de lardons de saumon fumé**
- **500 g de tomates cerises**
- **2 c. à soupe d'huile d'olive**
- **4 œufs**
- **40 cl de crème liquide**
- **100 g de parmesan râpé**
- **2 pincées de noix de muscade**
- **2 c. à soupe de ciboulette**
- **Sel et poivre**

Clafoutis aux tomates cerises et aux lardons de saumon fumé

À servir doré sur tranche, sans rien révéler de la vraie nature de cette version malicieuse d'un grand classique des desserts « maison ». Les enfants vont adorer.

- Préchauffez le four à 150 °C (th. 5).
- Lavez les tomates cerises, essuyez-les, ôtez le pédoncule. Posez-les dans un plat allant au four et pouvant les contenir en une seule couche. Arrosez les tomates d'huile d'olive. Déposez dessus les lardons de saumon fumé. Enfournez pendant une vingtaine de minutes.
- Cassez et fouettez les œufs en omelette. Incorporez la crème, le parmesan, la muscade, la ciboulette ciselée, le sel et le poivre. Répartissez la préparation dans 4 petits plats, ajoutez les tomates et les lardons cuits, qui doivent sortir de moitié de la préparation à base d'œufs. Enfournez pendant une quinzaine de minutes, toujours à 150 °C.
- Les clafoutis doivent juste prendre et dorer légèrement. Décorez-les avec quelques brins de ciboulette.
- Servez chaud.

Pour 4/6 personnes,
soit 12 fish cakes
Préparation : 45 min
Cuisson : 10 min
Repos : 2 h

- 425 g de filet de saumon (ou du saumon en boîte au naturel)
- 275 g de pommes de terre à purée
- 2 c. à soupe de mayonnaise
- 2 c. à soupe bien remplies de câpres au vinaigre
- 6 cornichons au vinaigre égouttés et hachés
- 2 gros œufs durs hachés
- 1/4 c. à café de macis en poudre
- 1/4 c. à café de poivre de Cayenne en poudre
- Sel et poivre du moulin
- 1 c. à dessert de pâte d'anchois (ou 4 anchois)
- 2 c. à soupe de jus de citron
- 2 c. à soupe bien pleines de persil
- 1 court-bouillon

Fish Cakes

Les Britanniques ont leur « fish pie », une tourte aux pommes de terre et cabillaud. Voici son cousin à la mode de Bretagne, un pané original et bien relevé.

- Si vous utilisez du poisson frais, pochez le filet de saumon pendant quelques minutes dans un court-bouillon de poisson. Pelez les pommes de terre, coupez-les en gros dés, et faites-les cuire dans de l'eau salée pendant 25 à 30 minutes. Égouttez-les et réduisez-les en purée. Avec un batteur électrique ou un fouet, incorporez à cette purée les 2 cuillerées de mayonnaise. Dans un grand saladier, mélangez le saumon effeuillé, les câpres égouttées et hachées, les cornichons hachés, les œufs durs, toutes les épices et la pâte d'anchois. Couvrez le saladier et mettez-le au réfrigérateur pendant 2 heures.
- Pendant ce temps, préparez la sauce au persil. Dans une casserole, mettez le lait avec les queues de persil, le laurier, l'oignon, le macis et les grains de poivre. Faites chauffer sur feu doux jusqu'à ébullition, puis versez dans un saladier, et laissez infuser jusqu'à complet refroidissement. Au moment de confectionner la sauce, passez le lait. Dans une casserole sur feu doux, faites fondre le beurre, puis incorporez la farine et, petit à petit, le lait en travaillant avec un

Pour paner les fish cakes
- 50 g de farine
- 1 œuf
- 75 g de chapelure blanche (je conseille la chapelure blanche, la chapelure dorée risquant de trop foncer à la cuisson)

Pour la cuisson
- 3 c. à soupe d'huile
- 50 g de beurre

Pour la sauce au persil
- 42 cl de lait
- 1 bouquet de queues de persil
- 1 feuille de laurier
- 1 petit oignon
- 1 pincée de macis en poudre
- 10 grains de poivre noir
- 40 g de beurre
- 25 g de farine
- 4 c. à soupe très pleines de feuilles de persil finement haché
- 1 c. à soupe de crème liquide
- 1 c. à café de jus de citron
- Sel et poivre noir du moulin

fouet jusqu'à ce que le mélange soit bien lisse. Amenez à ébullition. Laissez cette sauce sur le feu doux pendant environ 5 minutes en remuant de temps en temps jusqu'à épaississement. Hors du feu, ajoutez les feuilles de persil haché, la crème et le jus de citron. Salez et poivrez.

Au bout du repos de deux heures, sortez le saladier du réfrigérateur, farinez légèrement vos mains et formez des rouleaux de poisson de 5 à 6 cm de diamètre. Découpez ensuite ces rouleaux en rondelles de 2 cm d'épaisseur environ. Répartissez dans 3 assiettes de la farine, 1 œuf battu et la chapelure. Roulez chaque fish cake dans la farine, puis dans l'œuf battu et, en dernier, dans la chapelure. Faites ces opérations des deux côtés. Dans une grande poêle, mettez les fish cakes à cuire dans le mélange d'huile et de beurre sur feu moyen, pendant 4 à 5 minutes de chaque côté. Lorsqu'ils sont bien dorés, posez-les sur du papier absorbant. Répétez l'opération jusqu'à finition de l'appareil, en rajoutant éventuellement dans la poêle de l'huile et du beurre. Servez chaud sans attendre avec la sauce au persil.

Pour 4 personnes
Préparation : 30 min
Cuisson : 45 min

- 300 g de chair de poisson cuite (peu importe la variété, utilisez un reste !)
- 100 g de filet de poisson cru
- 100 g de filet de maquereau fumé
- 400 à 500 g de pain de campagne rassis
- 1 l de lait
- Thym et laurier
- 3 œufs
- Herbes mélangées (aneth, persil, cerfeuil, ciboulette…)
- Un peu de calvados
- Sel et poivre

Pain perdu de poisson de Nicolas

Une recette de Nicolas Vagnon

Les chefs talentueux ne travaillent pas que les produits de luxe. Preuve : cette recette d'un fou de poisson, belle démonstration de l'art d'utiliser les restes.

- Faites chauffer le lait avec le thym et le laurier. Hors du feu ajoutez le pain rassis.
- Réalisez un hachis avec tous les poissons.
- Préchauffez le four à 210 °C.
- Lorsque le pain est bien imprégné, malaxez-le bien sans l'égoutter. Incorporez le hachis de poisson ainsi que les œufs. Assaisonnez de sel et poivre. Ajoutez les herbes hachées. Parfumez avec un trait de calvados. Mélangez de nouveau avec les mains de façon à obtenir une pâte homogène.
- Beurrez un moule à cake ou un plat à clafoutis. Enfournez à 210 °C pendant 15 minutes, puis à 180 °C pendant 30 minutes.
- Vous pouvez servir ce pain perdu à l'apéritif après l'avoir découpé en petits carrés.

La fête du poisson

Des rillettes, des terrines, des pâtés, des boudins, des saucissons... Lorsqu'à la ferme se célèbre la fête du cochon, on prépare tous ces compléments des morceaux nobles qui deviendront provende des pique-niques, petites faims, repas sur le pouce et apéritifs inventifs. Le poisson s'y prête tout autant. En plus surprenant.

LES RILLETTES INRATABLES, PRÊTES EN UN CLIN D'ŒIL, ÉTONNANTES PAR LA DIVERSITÉ DE LEURS SAVEURS SOUVENT COMPOSÉES : LE MÊME USAGE QUE LEURS COUSINES ISSUES DU COCHON, AVEC LA LÉGÈRETÉ EN PRIME.

Pour 6 personnes
Temps de préparation : 15 min
Cuisson : 5 min
Conservation : 48 h

- 1 kg de maquereaux
- 1 maquereau fumé
- 1 c. à soupe de coriandre hachée
- 1 c. à soupe d'aneth haché
- 15 cl de crème fraîche
- 2 c. à soupe de moutarde de Meaux
- 1 c. à café de moutarde de Dijon
- 1 citron
- Sel et poivre

Rillettes de maquereaux

Ou comment surprendre avec le plus sympathique des poissons de mer, parfois injustement traité en parent pauvre, alors qu'il a tout pour plaire, y compris son prix.

- Demandez à votre poissonnier de lever les filets des maquereaux.
- Préchauffez le four à 210 °C (th. 7). Ôtez les arêtes des filets des maquereaux, avant de les poser sur une plaque antiadhésive humide. Mettez-les à cuire au four pendant 5 bonnes minutes et laissez-les refroidir. Enlevez la peau des poissons qui se détache maintenant facilement.
- Lavez les herbes, séchez-les et hachez-les. Dans la crème fraîche chauffée sur feu doux, mettez les herbes et arrêtez la cuisson. Lorsque la crème a refroidi, ajoutez les 2 moutardes et le jus du citron. Rectifiez l'assaisonnement.
- Enlevez les arêtes du maquereau fumé.
- Mixez tous les ingrédients. Rectifiez de nouveau l'assaisonnement, si c'est nécessaire.
- Tassez les rillettes dans une terrine et mettez celle-ci au frais. Dégustez de préférence au bout de 48 heures.

Rillettes
de

Pour 6 personnes
Préparation : 15 min
Conservation : 48 h

- 400 g de saumon
- 200 g de saumon fumé
- 100 g d'œufs de saumon
- 2 jaunes d'œufs
- 150 g de beurre mou
- Sel et poivre
- 75 cl de court-bouillon

Rillettes de saumon

Ce qui change tout : le mélange saumon frais, saumon fumé et œufs de saumon. C'est ainsi que se marient sur les tartines de pain grillé l'élégance et la simplicité.

- Faites cuire le saumon dans le court-bouillon pendant dix minutes, puis écrasez-le à la fourchette.
- Ajoutez le saumon fumé coupé en dés minuscules (on trouve des dés de saumon tout prêts dans les grandes surfaces), les 2 jaunes d'œufs et les 150 g de beurre mou.
- Assaisonnez, puis incorporez les œufs de saumon.
- Moulez dans une terrine et mettez au frais.

Pour 6 personnes
Préparation : 10 min
Marinade : 1 h
Pas de cuisson
Conservation : 48 h

- 12 sardines levées en filets
- 1 citron
- 2 c. à soupe d'huile d'olive
- 2 oignons
- 20 g d'amandes effilées
- 1 bouquet de persil
- 4 c. à soupe de crème fraîche
- 1 pointe de Tabasco®
- Sel et poivre

Rillettes de sardines fraîches

Pourvu que ces sardines soient impeccablement fraîches, une manière de se régaler de poisson cru que même les Japonais vont nous envier.

- Faites mariner les filets de sardines dans un plat pendant 1 heure avec le jus du citron, l'huile d'olive, 1 oignon émincé et une pincée d'amandes effilées.
- Au bout d'1 heure, égouttez les sardines. Mixez-les avec l'autre oignon et le persil (feuilles et tiges). Ajoutez la crème fraîche et le Tabasco®. Mixez de nouveau, salez et poivrez.
- Mettez dans une terrine que vous gardez au frais.

Pour 6 personnes
Préparation : 15 min
Marinade : 12 h
Cuisson : 5 min
Réfrigération : 12 h

- 300 g de filet de carpe sans arêtes
- 250 g de sandre
- 2 oignons
- 2 citrons
- 25 cl de vin blanc sec
- 1 c. à café d'aneth
- 1 c. à café de cerfeuil
- 1 c. à café de persil plat
- Sel et poivre

Rillettes de poissons de rivière

Pour combler de contentement le pêcheur revenu triomphant de son expédition halieutique ou pour consoler celui qui a plus rêvé au bord de l'eau que pêché.

- Préparez la marinade : dans un plat creux, mettez les oignons finement émincés, le jus des 2 citrons, le vin blanc, les herbes hachées, les poissons coupés en dés de 1 cm de côté. Mélangez et laissez mariner durant 12 heures au réfrigérateur.
- Au bout de ce temps, égouttez les dés de poissons, déposez-les dans le panier d'un cuit vapeur, et faites-les cuire pendant 5 minutes.
- Puis écrasez-les à la fourchette. Salez et poivrez.
- Mettez les rillettes dans une terrine au réfrigérateur pendant 12 heures avant de déguster.

Pour 4 personnes
Préparation : 15 min
Marinade : 4 h
Pas de cuisson

- 250 g de filets de harengs
- Lait
- 4 échalotes ciselées
- 1 oignon émincé
- 1 petit pain au lait
- 1 c. à café de sucre
- 1 bouquet de persil
- 1 c. à café de moutarde
- 2 c. à soupe de crème fraîche
- 350 g de beurre mou

Rillettes de harengs fumés

Rien à dépiauter, rien à cuire. En deux temps trois mouvements, les saveurs de l'Europe du Nord vont jeter l'ancre sur la table. Elles ne manquent pas d'amateurs. Dans le même esprit : le pâté de harengs fumés (recette page 20). Pain noir, bonne bière ou petit verre de genièvre lui vont bien au teint.

- Mettez à tremper les filets de harengs, pendant 4 heures, dans du lait (le lait doit recouvrir les filets).
- Faites tremper le pain au lait dans du lait tiède et réduisez-le en panade.
- Égouttez les filets de harengs. Coupez-les et mettez-les dans le mixeur avec les échalotes et l'oignon.
- Broyez-les en farce fine, puis ajoutez la panade de pain au lait, le sucre, le persil haché, la moutarde, la crème fraîche et le beurre mou.
- Amalgamez bien ces rillettes et mettez-les dans une terrine que vous placez au frais.

Pour 6 personnes
Préparation : 15 min
Pas de cuisson

- **400 g de haddock**
- **1 tranche de pain de mie**
- **2 c. à soupe de crème fraîche épaisse**
- **1 c. à soupe d'huile d'olive**
- **1 citron vert**

Tarama de haddock

Botte magique pour maîtresse de maison pressée. Instantanément prêt, ou presque. Avec le parfum du citron vert pour dépayser le délicat filet fumé.

- Mixez le haddock très fin, puis, en continuant à mixer, ajoutez le pain de mie, la crème, l'huile et le jus du citron vert.
- Mélangez bien et versez dans des petits ramequins individuels. Gardez-les au réfrigérateur jusqu'au moment de les servir.

Pour 4 personnes
Préparation : 10 min
Cuisson : 10 min
Réfrigération : 1 nuit

- 750 g de harengs fumés entiers
- 225 g de beurre mou en morceaux
- 3 c. à café de purée d'anchois
- 1 pincée de macis broyé
- 1 petite pincée de poivre de Cayenne

Pâté de harengs fumés

À servir à des gens du Nord pour les réjouir, ou à des gens du Sud pour les étonner, avec du pain noir, une bonne bière ou une petite lichette de genièvre.

- Préchauffez le four à 210 °C (th. 7).
- Beurrez un plat allant au four, mettez-y les harengs et enfournez durant 8 à 10 minutes jusqu'à ce que la chair se détache facilement des arêtes.
- Retirez les arêtes et la peau des poissons.
- Mixez les chairs avec le beurre, la purée d'anchois, le macis et le poivre.
- Mettez la préparation dans une terrine et gardez-la au réfrigérateur pendant une nuit.

TERRINES ET PÂTÉS NOUVELLE ÉTAPE DANS LA DÉCOUVERTE DE SUCCULENTES CHARCUTERIES DE POISSON. SANS CONTRESENS À LA CLEF. L'ÉTYMOLOGIE DU MOT « CHARCUTERIE » EST « CHAIR COUPÉE ». C'EST BIEN DE CELA QU'IL S'AGIT.

Terrine de raie au concombre

Elle demande un peu de temps mais se prépare 24 heures à l'avance. Ce qui permet de goûter une satisfaction paisible quand on la sert dans toute sa subtilité.

- Épluchez et lavez la carotte, le poireau, le céleri, l'échalote. Émincez-les très fins. Pelez le citron à vif et coupez-le en tranches. Mettez le tout dans une casserole, mouillez avec le vin blanc et l'eau. Salez au gros sel. Ajoutez 10 à 15 grains de poivre, le bouquet garni et portez à ébullition 15 minutes pour obtenir un court-bouillon.
- Lavez la raie et plongez-la dans le court-bouillon chaud. Faites-la cuire, sans bouillir, pendant 15 à 20 minutes.
- Épluchez le concombre et, avec un économe, faites des lamelles de 2 à 3 millimètres les plus longues possibles jusqu'au cœur du concombre. Disposez ces lamelles dans une assiette creuse et saupoudrez-les de sel fin. Laissez-les dégorger au frais pendant une trentaine de minutes.
- Mettez les feuilles de gélatine à tremper dans de l'eau froide.
- Retirez la raie du court-bouillon, égouttez-la bien. Enlevez la peau fine qui la recouvre puis levez les filets en suivant le cartilage du poisson. Disposez une première couche de filet de raie dans la terrine recouverte d'un film alimentaire (cela facilitera le démoulage).
- Passez au chinois le court-bouillon de cuisson et prélevez-en un demi-litre. Rectifiez l'assaisonnement et incorporez-y, pendant qu'il est encore chaud, les feuilles de gélatine essorées.
- Égouttez soigneusement les lamelles de concombre. Disposez-en la moitié sur la première couche de raie. Remettez une couche de filet de poisson. Étalez de nouveau une couche de concombre et terminez avec la raie. Versez dans la terrine le demi-litre de court-bouillon gélatiné en tapotant la terrine afin qu'il s'infiltre bien entre les différents ingrédients. Le court-bouillon doit recouvrir tous les éléments jusqu'au-dessus de la dernière couche de raie. Réfrigérer jusqu'au lendemain.

Pour 4 personnes
Préparation la veille : 1h30
Cuisson : 35 min

- 500 g d'aile de raie
- 1 carotte moyenne
- 1 blanc de poireau
- 1 petite branche de céleri
- 1 échalote
- 1 citron
- 25 cl de vin blanc
- 25 cl d'eau
- 1 ou 2 concombre(s)
- 2 feuilles de gélatine
- 1 bouquet garni (thym, laurier, queues de persil)
- Gros sel
- Sel fin et poivre en grains

Pour une dizaine de personnes
Préparation : 45 min
Cuisson : 1 h
Dessalage : 48 h

- 400 g de morue sèche salée
- 15 pommes de terre rattes
- 500 g de belles feuilles de blettes
- 400 g de crème liquide
- 1 c. à soupe d'ail haché
- 80 g de beurre
- 1 pincée de quatre-épices
- 20 olives noires dénoyautées
- Sel et poivre

Terrine de morue aux pommes de terre

La morue est du cabillaud salé. Il doit donc être longuement dessalé pour donner des mets solides et délicieux, comme cette terrine évoquant à la fois brandade et aïoli. Vous pouvez du reste servir cette terrine avec un aïoli allégé avec de la crème fouettée.

- Dessalez la morue pendant 48 heures. Changez l'eau plusieurs fois.
- Au moment de la préparation, épluchez les pommes de terre rattes et coupez-les en fines tranches. Rincez-les et séchez-les dans un torchon.
- Prélevez les feuilles des blettes en les gardant en grands morceaux. Faites-les blanchir 1 minute dans de l'eau bouillante salée, transvasez-les dans une passoire et rafraîchissez-les en les passant sous l'eau froide. Réservez.
- Dans une casserole, faites chauffer doucement la crème avec la morue dessalée, coupée en gros tronçons avec les arêtes et la peau. Salez légèrement, poivrez, ajoutez l'ail haché. Laissez frémir environ 10 minutes.
- Préchauffez le four à 150 °C (th. 5).
- Sortez la morue de la crème : ôtez la peau – sans la trouer – et les arêtes, effeuillez le poisson. Réservez la peau et la crème.
- Déposez les tranches de pommes de terre dans un grand plat creux. Faites fondre le beurre à feu doux et écumez la mousse puis versez doucement le beurre clarifié sur les rondelles de pommes de terre, en laissant le dépôt dans le fond de la casserole. Salez, poivrez, ajoutez une pincée de quatre-épices et remuez.
- Beurrez une terrine longue. Habillez le fond et les parois avec le vert des blettes, côté mat à l'intérieur. Formez une couche de pommes de terre et une couche de morue. Disposez un rang d'olives noires sur toute la longueur de la terrine. Arrosez de 3 cuillerées à soupe de crème de cuisson. Recommencez la même opération deux fois et, pour finir, couvrez avec la peau de la morue. Refermez le tout avec du vert des blettes et versez un petit verre de crème de cuisson.
- Recouvrez d'une feuille de papier de cuisson. Enfournez 1 heure. Laissez refroidir. Tassez la terrine avec un poids et mettez-la au réfrigérateur.

Persillé de poisson façon jambon persillé

Plusieurs opérations à enchaîner la veille demandent un peu de temps mais aucune virtuosité. Le résultat est un plat parfait pour repas froid très raffiné.

Pour 10 personnes
Préparation : 30 à 45 min
Cuisson du poisson : 10 à 12 min
Repos : 24 h

- 1,1 kg de filet de cabillaud
- 1,1 kg de saumon cru
- 10 branches de persil plat
- 3 brins d'estragon
- 3 brins de cerfeuil
- 3 brins de ciboulette
- 3 brins de coriandre fraîche
- 4 gousses d'ail
- Sel et poivre
- 60 cl de nage de légumes
- 6 feuilles de gélatine

Pour la nage

- 1 bulbe de fenouil
- 5 blancs de poireaux
- 10 échalotes
- 10 gousses d'ail
- 3 brins d'estragon
- 4 brins de cerfeuil
- 4 brins d'aneth
- Beurre et huile
- 50 cl de vin blanc sec
- 5 grains de coriandre
- 5 grains de poivre

- **Préparation de la nage.** Épluchez, lavez et émincez tous les légumes et les herbes. Faites-les suer à feu doux dans un mélange de beurre et d'huile. Versez le vin. Faites réduire à feu vif, puis ajoutez de l'eau pour couvrir les légumes. Portez à ébullition. Assaisonnez avec les grains de coriandre et de poivre concassés. Laissez cuire durant 30 minutes à feu doux. Passez au chinois. Cette nage se conserve au réfrigérateur pendant 3 à 4 jours. On peut également réaliser cette nage à partir de produits déshydratés que l'on trouve dans les grandes surfaces.
- Mettez la terrine au réfrigérateur. Préchauffez le four à 150 °C. Hachez finement toutes les herbes. Ciselez les gousses d'ail, faites-les blanchir et réservez. Retirez les arêtes des filets de poisson à l'aide d'une pince à épiler. Salez-les et poivrez-les sur les deux faces. Recouvrez votre plaque de four de papier d'aluminium, huilez-le et déposez-y les filets. Enfournez pendant 10 à 12 minutes. Effeuillez ensuite les poissons sans les mélanger. Portez à ébullition les 60 cl de nage de légumes et incorporez-y les feuilles de gélatine (préalablement trempées dans de l'eau froide et essorées). Mélangez et laissez refroidir jusqu'à ce que la préparation ait une consistance huileuse. Incorporez toutes les herbes hachées et l'ail. Dans la terrine très froide, versez une couche de gelée. Remettez la terrine au réfrigérateur durant quelques minutes puis répartissez dessus une couche de saumon effeuillé, puis une couche de gelée aux herbes, puis une couche de cabillaud, puis de nouveau des herbes, puis du saumon… et, ainsi de suite, jusqu'à épuisement des ingrédients. Laissez reposer pendant 24 heures au réfrigérateur.
- On peut pour faciliter le démoulage, avant de mettre les ingrédients, tapisser la terrine de papier film. Au moment du service, coupez des tranches plutôt épaisses, si possible avec un couteau électrique ou un couteau fin et très bien aiguisé, style couteau à jambon. Servez soit avec une sauce rémoulade soit avec une vinaigrette aux herbes.

Marbré de foie de lotte

Un hors-d'œuvre élégant, où se superposent et se fondent l'évocation des algues, le croquant du céleri-rave, le moelleux du foie dans le velouté d'une gelée.

- Une variante de la terrine de foie de lotte (recette page 31). Selon le principe de cette recette, garnissez le fond d'une terrine d'une feuille reconstituée de paillettes de porphyra, arrosez avec un peu de gelée froide, recouvrez d'une tranche de foie de 1,5 cm d'épaisseur puis de tranches de céleri-rave légèrement cuit à la vapeur et enfin d'une couche de gelée. Posez une autre tranche de foie de lotte puis de nouveau une algue précuite, de la gelée, une autre tranche de foie, et ainsi de suite. Terminez en versant une couche de gelée, pressez légèrement et placez ainsi au réfrigérateur pendant une nuit.

* Marbré de foie de lotte

Pour 6 personnes
Préparation : 20 min
Cuisson : 20 min

- 800 g de lieu jaune
- 4 petits poireaux
- 1 bouquet d'aneth
- 90 g de gelée en poudre
- 10 pistils de safran
- 150 g de crème fraîche
- 1/2 citron
- Sel et poivre

Terrine de lieu aux poireaux et à l'aneth

Banal, ce brave lieu ? Son mariage avec les poireaux et l'aneth, sa touche safranée et sa parure de crème fouettée vont vous faire changer d'avis.

- Demandez à votre poissonnier de lever les filets de lieu. Salez et poivrez-les. Lavez les poireaux ainsi que le bouquet d'aneth. Émincez-les et faites-les cuire pendant une dizaine de minutes dans un cuit-vapeur, sans les mélanger. De la même façon, cuisez les filets de lieu pendant une dizaine de minutes. Dans un bol, mélangez délicatement la gelée avec le safran et 10 cl d'eau tiède. Dans une terrine rectangulaire, déposez une couche d'aneth, puis une couche de lieu puis une couche de poireaux, recommencez l'opération jusqu'à épuisement des ingrédients. Versez le bol de gelée sur la terrine ainsi préparée. Couvrez-la d'un film alimentaire et mettez-la au réfrigérateur pendant 12 heures.
- Le lendemain : battez la crème fraîche avec le jus de citron. Démoulez la terrine, coupez-la en tranches. Servez-la avec la crème fouettée citronnée.

Hure de saumon au citron

Hure : nom donné à la tête de certains animaux comme le sanglier, le brochet ou le saumon et au pâté de tête de sanglier. Ici c'est un pâté épatant pour tablée en appétit.

Pour 8 à 10 personnes
Préparation : 35 min
Marinade : 2 h
Cuisson du poisson : 5 min
Montage de la terrine : 15 min

- **500 g de saumon en filet**
- **6 œufs entiers**
- **40 g de gelée en poudre**
- **4 citrons**
- **60 g de piments rouges en conserve**
- **2 échalotes**
- **1/2 bouquet de persil plat**
- **1 bouquet de cerfeuil**
- **8 brins d'estragon**
- **15 g de poivre vert**

Pour la marinade

- **10 cl de vin blanc sec**
- **6 brins d'estragon**
- **10 cl de court-bouillon**
- **Sel et poivre**

- Placez la terrine dans le réfrigérateur.
- Coupez le saumon en lanières de 1,5 cm, mettez-les dans un plat allant au feu. Mélangez les éléments de la marinade et versez-les sur le saumon. Laissez pendant 2 heures au froid.
- Mettez les œufs à cuire durant 8 minutes à l'eau bouillante. Laissez-les refroidir avant de les écaler et de hacher séparément les blancs et les jaunes.
- Préparez la gelée dans un demi-litre d'eau bouillante. Laissez-la refroidir à température ambiante en remuant de temps en temps.
- Pelez les citrons à vif pour en prélever les quartiers que vous taillez en petits dés.
- Posez le plat contenant le saumon sur le feu et faites pocher le saumon pendant 3 minutes dans sa marinade portée à ébullition, puis égouttez le poisson sur un linge.
- Détaillez les piments en petits dés. Épluchez et hachez les échalotes. Effeuillez le persil, le cerfeuil et l'estragon. Hachez-les séparément.
- Pour faciliter le démoulage de la terrine, tapissez-la (fond et parois) avec du film alimentaire.
- Parsemez au fond de la terrine les blancs et jaunes d'œufs hachés, les dés de citron et de piment, le poivre vert en grains, le persil, le cerfeuil et l'estragon hachés. Recouvrez d'un peu de gelée. Mettez la terrine au réfrigérateur durant quelques minutes, puis sortez-la et déposez quelques lanières de saumon, salez et poivrez, parsemez d'échalotes hachées, recouvrez d'une nouvelle couche d'ingrédients, de saumon, de gelée. Recommencez ces opérations jusqu'à ce que le moule soit rempli.
- Réservez au frais pendant 24 heures.
- Servez en tranches de 1 cm d'épaisseur.

Pour 6 personnes
Dénervage du foie : 15 min
Marinade : 1 nuit + 2 h
Cuisson : 45 min
Repos : 48 h

- **500 g de foies de lotte**
- **Lait**
- **Sel**
- **Poivre blanc**
- **Paprika**
- **1 pincée de sucre semoule**
- **Laminaires ou algues kombu (de quoi chemiser la terrine)**
- **25 g de gelée Maggi®**
- **1 c. à soupe de cognac**

Foie gras de la mer

Les lottes aussi ont un foie. Succulent. Surtout si l'imagination s'en mêle. Assurez-vous un peu à l'avance d'en trouver chez votre poissonnier, ou passez-lui commande.

- Laissez dégorger les foies toute une nuit dans du lait refroidi de glaçons (le lait doit recouvrir les foies). Le lendemain matin, pelez et dénervez soigneusement les foies et passez-les à l'eau fraîche. Remettez-les ensuite dans un nouveau bain de lait frais pendant 2 heures puis égouttez-les parfaitement. Salez, poivrez de poivre blanc en poudre, et saupoudrez très légèrement de paprika et d'une pincée de sucre semoule.
- Préchauffez le four à 150 °C (th. 5).
- Délayez à froid la gelée Maggi dans 30 cl d'eau puis portez à ébullition en remuant lentement. Ajoutez la cuillerée de cognac. Réservez.
- Chemisez une terrine avec des algues. Ajoutez un peu de gelée, posez les foies et enveloppez-les soigneusement d'algues.
- Selon la taille de la terrine, mettez à cuire au four moyen pendant 45 minutes, sur une lèchefrite avec un peu d'eau.
- Dès la sortie du four, versez le reste de gelée, pressez légèrement et laissez reposer au frais pendant 48 heures avant de déguster.
- Servez le foie de lotte sur des toasts au pain de seigle par exemple.

Pour 6 à 8 personnes
Préparation : 45 min
Cuisson : 40 min

- **800 g de filet de saumon ou de darnes**
- **300 g de parures de saumon (peau et arêtes)**
- **2 jus de citron**
- **250 g de riz long grain**
- **3 branches d'aneth**
- **200 g de beurre**
- **250 g de champignons de Paris**
- **4 échalotes**
- **5 œufs durs**
- **1 œuf pour la dorure**
- **800 g de pâte feuilletée à étaler**
- **1 verre de vin blanc sec**
- **Sel et poivre**

Koulibiac de saumon

Un classique russe. Facile à réussir si on utilise une pâte feuilletée toute prête. Hors d'œuvre ou plat principal, sa vue suffit à provoquer une faim qu'il comble délicieusement.

- Retirez les arêtes et la peau du saumon, et mettez-les dans un saladier d'eau citronnée (conservez le deuxième jus de citron pour les champignons).
- Dans une casserole, placez les filets de saumon et le vin blanc. Salez et poivrez. Recouvrez d'eau froide et laissez mijoter 15 minutes à petit feu. Laissez refroidir le saumon dans son eau de cuisson, puis égouttez-le et réservez-le dans un torchon.
- Faites cuire les parures de saumon pendant 30 minutes à feu doux dans l'eau de cuisson des filets. Filtrez le fumet obtenu. Versez-en la moitié dans une grande casserole et portez-le à ébullition. Jetez-y le riz et laissez-le cuire durant 20 minutes. Laissez-le refroidir, puis mélangez-le avec l'aneth haché et 50 g de beurre fondu.
- Lavez et hachez les champignons, arrosez-les avec du jus de citron pour éviter qu'ils noircissent. Épluchez et hachez les échalotes. Faites-les revenir au beurre puis ajoutez-y les champignons. Salez et poivrez. Laissez cuire pendant 15 minutes. Coupez le saumon en lanières. Écalez les œufs durs.
- Préchauffez le four à 240 °C (th. 8). Étalez la pâte feuilletée sur 1 cm d'épaisseur (c'est la pâte qui fait office de terrine, d'où l'épaisseur de l'abaisse), en rectangle de 30 x 50 cm environ, et placez-la sur une tôle recouverte d'un papier sulfurisé beurré. Déposez au milieu de la pâte en une bande de 10 cm de large une couche de riz, des champignons, et des lanières de saumon. Alignez ensuite les œufs durs entiers au centre de cette farce, couvrez-les de saumon, de champignons et de riz. Rabattez les deux bords de la pâte par-dessus la farce en lui donnant une forme rectangulaire, soudez-les avec un peu d'œuf battu. Avec un pinceau, badigeonnez de l'œuf battu sur tout le pâté. Décorez éventuellement de feuilles ou de tout autre motif réalisé dans les chutes de pâte.
- Faites cuire durant 20 minutes à 240 °C, puis baissez la température du four à 180 °C (th. 6) et laissez cuire encore 20 minutes.
- Servez le koulibiac en tranches avec le reste du beurre fondu en saucière. Vous pouvez accompagner ce plat d'une purée de céleri ou de carottes.

ANDOUILLES, SAUCISSONS ET BOUDINS UN PAS DE PLUS DANS NOTRE PETIT JEU DU CHARCUTIER, AVEC DES AJOUTS SUCCULENTS AU RÉPERTOIRE DES TAPAS, ANTI-PASTI, ET AUTRES AMUSE-GUEULE OU DES PLATS À PART ENTIÈRE.

Pour une dizaine de personnes
Préparation : 30 min
Cuisson : 15 min
Trempage : 1 nuit
Repos : 2 jours

- 100 g de foie de lotte
- Lait
- 50 g de beurre
- 100 g d'oignons
- 500 g de chair de maigre de porc
- 800 g de lard
- 4 œufs
- 20 cl de crème fraîche
- 25 g de sel fin
- 5 g de poivre blanc
- 10 g de farine de porphyra (farine d'algues)
- 1 c. à soupe d'eau de fleur d'oranger
- 1 bouquet garni marin (queues de persil, thym, laurier, lanières d'algues)
- 1 boyau de porc (chez le charcutier)

Boudin blanc de foie de lotte

Variation sur des saveurs océanes. La farine de porphyra (une algue) se trouve dans les boutiques bio, et le boyau prêt à l'emploi chez le charcutier.

- Mettez les foies de lotte à dégorger toute une nuit dans du lait (le lait doit recouvrir les foies), puis pelez-les et dénervez-les.
- Dans le beurre fondu, faites revenir les oignons ciselés, la chair de maigre de porc et le lard.
- Hachez finement l'ensemble avec les foies de lotte. Passez cette farce au tamis et travaillez-la avec 4 œufs entiers et 20 cl de crème fraîche. Ajoutez la farine de porphyra et l'eau de fleur d'oranger. Assaisonnez avec 25 g de sel fin et 5 g de poivre blanc. Emplissez le boyau de porc avec cette farce et placez les attriaux au réfrigérateur pendant 2 jours.
- Faites-les pocher à l'eau pendant 15 minutes avec un bouquet garni marin. Puis poêlez-les ou cuisez-les au gril.

Saucisson de calmar

Une bonne farce pour surprendre, dépayser et régaler autour du même plat les amateurs du très maritime calmar et ceux du très terrien saucisson chaud de Lyon.

Pour 4/6 personnes
Préparation : 40 min
Cuisson : 15 min

- 500 g de calmars
- 4 c. à soupe d'huile d'olive

Pour la farce
- 500 g de moules
- 200 à 250 g de viande de porc hachée (morceau pris dans la gorge – ou chair à saucisse)
- 1 botte de ciboulette
- 1 gousse d'ail
- sel et poivre

Pour la sauce
- 4 petits oignons hachés
- 3 c. à soupe d'huile d'olive
- 400 g de concassée de tomates (surgelée ou en boîte)
- 15 cl de vin blanc
- Thym frais

- Lavez bien les calmars à l'eau courante, retirez la peau noire, videz-les (le poissonnier peut le faire pour vous). Coupez les tentacules et hachez-les finement.
- **Préparation de la farce.** Faites ouvrir les moules en les plaçant dans une casserole sur feu moyen, sans eau. Sortez-les de leur coquille. Filtrez le jus et réservez-le. Dans un saladier, mettez la viande de porc hachée, les moules, la botte de ciboulette ciselée, l'ail finement haché, les tentacules hachés, du sel et du poivre. Mélangez bien. Tassez la farce à l'intérieur des calmars, puis cousez l'ouverture avec du fil et une aiguille, ou fermez les calamars à l'aide d'une petite pique de bois. Dans une poêle, mettez les calmars à cuire dans 3 ou 4 cuillerées à soupe d'huile d'olive chaude pendant 4 à 5 minutes. Réservez.
- **Confection de la sauce.** Dans une casserole, faites revenir les petits oignons hachés dans 2 ou 3 cuillerées à soupe d'huile d'olive, puis ajoutez les tomates concassées, et mouillez avec 15 cl de vin blanc et le jus des moules. Parsemez de thym frais. Déposez les calmars farcis dans cette sauce, et laissez cuire une dizaine de minutes – un peu plus si les calmars sont très gros.
- Coupez-les en rondelles et servez-les avec la sauce.

Boudin blanc de poisson

Pour 4 personnes
Préparation : 15 min
Cuisson : 30 min

- 100 g de filet de poisson haché (perche, merlan, lieu...)
- 100 g de chair de crabe
- 50 cl de lait
- 30 g de riz
- 75 g de saindoux
- 2 gros oignons hachés
- Sel et poivre
- 1 petite truffe ou une petite boîte de pelures de truffe (facultatif)
- 1 pincée de muscade
- 1 œuf
- 1 boyau de porc (en charcuterie) ou de bœuf

L'arme absolue pour surprendre les enfants (et les grands) et les convaincre qu'il existe, et sans arêtes, bien meilleur que le fade et tristounet « poisson carré ».

- Faites cuire le riz dans le lait.
- Faites fondre le saindoux et mettez-y à cuire les oignons sans leur laisser prendre de couleur. Ajoutez le hachis de poisson et de crabe. Laissez cuire 15 minutes à feu vif.
- Ajoutez le riz, éventuellement les truffes, du sel, du poivre, de la muscade. Liez avec l'œuf battu.
- Introduisez le tout dans le boyau en vous aidant d'un entonnoir.
- Faites pocher le boudin dans de l'eau bouillante salée et aromatisée pendant 15 à 20 minutes.
- Sortez le boudin de l'eau, essuyez-le doucement, mettez-le sur une grille. Couvrez-le avec un linge pour l'empêcher de se racornir. Laissez refroidir.
- Piquez légèrement le boudin avec une aiguille à brider pour éviter qu'il n'éclate et faites-le griller sur feu doux durant 12 à 15 minutes avant de servir.

Saucissons maigres

Pour 12 personnes
Préparation : 20 min
Cuisson : 20 min

- 1 kg d'anguille de rivière
- 750 g de colin
- 600 g de grosses queues de crevettes
- 150 g de mie de pain rassis avec un peu de croûte
- Sel et poivre
- 2 boyaux de bœuf
- 2 litres de court-bouillon

Manifestement, il y a anguille sous roche. Et tout pour faire découvrir à une tablée d'affamés un plat sympathique et roboratif auquel on aurait pu ne jamais penser.

- Hachez séparément les poissons crus débarrassés de leurs arêtes et de leur peau. Réunissez-les, ajoutez le pain. Hachez encore à nouveau. Salez et poivrez et travaillez bien le tout. Coupez les crevettes en dés.
- Prenez deux boyaux de bœuf, remplissez-les de hachis et de crevettes. Ficelez et faites cuire pendant une vingtaine de minutes dans un court-bouillon de poisson.
- Vous pouvez servir ces saucissons avec une salade de pommes de terre relevée d'une sauce moutarde à l'estragon.

Pour 4 personnes
Préparation : 30 min
Cuisson : 5 min
Marinade : 12 h

- 4 filets de féra
- 20 cl de vin blanc de Savoie
- 2 échalotes
- 10 g de sel
- 2 g de poivre
- 500 g de crépine de porc
- 10 cl de crème
- 1 l de bisque

Pour la garniture
- 500 g de cèpes
- 20 g de beurre
- 1 échalote
- 10 g de persil
- 1 pointe d'ail
- sel et poivre

Attriaux de féra aux cèpes

Étymologie montagnarde, et on ne quitte pas les cimes : le fera est un poisson des lacs et rivières alpins qui descend parfois de ses hauteurs.

- Demandez à votre poissonnier de lever les filets de féra sans la peau. Coupez-les grossièrement en morceaux et mettez ceux-ci à mariner avec le vin blanc, les échalotes ciselées, le sel et le poivre pendant 12 heures au froid. Au bout de ce temps, mettez la crépine à tremper dans de l'eau froide. Passez les filets marinés et égouttés au hachoir à grosse grille, et ajoutez la crème petit à petit. Formez 8 petits tas ronds avec ce hachis. Enveloppez-les de crépine. Réservez au froid.
- **Préparation de la garniture.** Faites sauter les cèpes émincés dans le beurre sur feu vif, ajoutez 1 échalote ciselée, le persil haché, la pointe d'ail. Aux trois quarts de la cuisson, assaisonnez de sel et poivre. Réservez au chaud.
- Préchauffez le four à 200 °C (th. 7). Poêlez les attriaux des deux côtés avec une noix de beurre pour les faire dorer. Mettez les cèpes dans un plat allant au four, posez dessus les attriaux. Nappez de bisque.
- Enfournez pendant 5 minutes et servez.

Pour 4 personnes
Préparation : 15 min
Cuisson : 20 min

- 1 carpe de 1 kg
- 32 écrevisses
- 1 blanc d'œuf
- 5 cl de crème fraîche
- 1 bouquet de persil
- 1 crépine
- 4 échalotes
- 25 cl de vin rouge
- 50 cl de jus de veau
- 100 g de beurre
- 500 g de bolets ou cèpes
- 100 g de brunoise de légumes (carottes, navets, haricots verts)
- Sel et poivre
- 1 litre de court-bouillon

Attriaux

de carpe aux écrevisses et aux bolets

En Savoie, on appelle attriaux des saucisses plates réalisées avec les abats du cochon. Ici, c'est la carpe qui a la parole et se pare de subtiles saveurs.

- Levez les filets de carpe et enlevez toutes les arêtes à l'aide d'une pince à épiler. Hachez la chair du poisson. Mélangez-la avec le blanc d'œuf, la crème fraîche et le persil haché. Assaisonnez et réservez.
- Faites cuire les écrevisses pendant 3 minutes dans un court-bouillon. Mettez-en 8 de côté. Décortiquez les autres, et confectionnez un petit fumet avec les carcasses et 15 cl d'eau que vous ferez réduire fortement jusqu'à obtention de 5 cl de liquide. Filtrez celui-ci.
- Étalez la crépine et coupez-la en 8 carrés de 10 cm de côté environ. Déposez une grosse cuillerée de farce de carpe au milieu, enfoncez-y 2 écrevisses décortiquées et refermez la crépine en forme de petits paquets rectangulaires.
- **Préparez la sauce :** mettez à suer 2 échalotes hachées dans un peu de beurre, versez dessus le vin rouge, le jus de veau et la réduction d'écrevisses. Laissez réduire jusqu'à obtention de 15 à 20 cl de liquide. Ensuite, montez cette sauce au beurre en fouettant le beurre bien froid et en l'incorporant par petits morceaux.
- Épluchez les bolets, émincez-les et poêlez-les avec 2 échalotes hachées.
- Dans un peu de beurre, faites sauter rapidement la brunoise de légumes préalablement blanchie et les écrevisses réservées.
- Dans une poêle antiadhésive légèrement beurrée, mettez les attriaux à cuire pendant 5 minutes environ. Retournez-les à mi-cuisson.
- Dressez les attriaux dans un plat, disposez autour les bolets et la brunoise de légumes. Nappez de sauce.
- Servez chaud.

Pour 6 personnes
Préparation : 20 min
Cuisson : 20 min

- 800 g de calmars
- 1 crépine
- 1 pied de porc cuit
- 5 petits piments (piquillos)
- 10 brins de persil plat
- Huile d'olive
- Sel et poivre

Pour la sauce
- 500 g de chorizo
- 20 cl de bouillon de volaille

Crépinettes
de calmars au pied de porc

Le calmar est plein de ressources insuffisamment exploitées. Le voilà dans un mariage insolite qui pique la curiosité et réveille les appétits les plus blasés.

- Préchauffez le four à 200 °C (th. 7).
- Mettez la crépine à tremper dans de l'eau froide.
- Lavez les calmars, épongez-les, coupez-les en lanières, puis faites-les caraméliser à la poêle dans de l'huile d'olive bien chaude (5 à 6 minutes).
- Désossez le pied de porc et découpez toute la chair en petits dés (1 cm). Mélangez-la aux calmars. Ajoutez les piments coupés en lanières et le persil plat lavé, séché et effeuillé. Salez et poivrez.
- Rincez soigneusement la crépine, séchez et détaillez-la en 6 grands carrés.
- Répartissez la farce au centre de chaque carré. Fermez-les bien en forme de petits paquets. Placez ceux-ci dans un plat allant au four et sur le feu (ne rincez pas votre poêle, vous en aurez besoin pour la préparation de la sauce). Faites dorer ces crépinettes des deux côtés sur feu vif dans un peu d'huile d'olive puis terminez la cuisson au four chaud pendant 5 à 6 minutes. Réservez-les au chaud.
- **Préparez la sauce :** épluchez le chorizo, coupez-le en fines rondelles puis en bâtonnets que vous faites revenir 5 minutes dans la poêle de cuisson des calmars, sur feu vif. Déglacez avec le bouillon de volaille et laissez légèrement réduire.
- Servez les crépinettes avec cette sauce.

Le thon
cochon de la mer

Un sédentaire terrien dodu, un aristocrate sauvage, éternel voyageur des océans, mais tous deux, depuis des millénaires, d'inlassables nourriciers des humains. Et le thon offre tant de ressources que cru, poêlé, rôti, mijoté, grillé, on pourrait le servir chaque jour sans jamais lasser.

Pour 4 personnes
Préparation : 25 min
Cuisson : 25 min

- **4 morceaux de ventrèche de thon de 150 g environ chacun**
- **4 tranches de poitrine de cochon de 100 g chacune**
- **2 poivrons rouges**
- **4 tomates**
- **2 grosses échalotes**
- **2 gousses d'ail**
- **10 cl d'huile d'olive**
- **1 bouquet garni**
- **25 cl de vinaigre de xérès**
- **5 g de piment d'Espelette en poudre**
- **Sel et poivre**

Ventrèches
de thon et de cochon, sauce aux poivrons

En version terre et mer. La ventrèche, c'est le lard. Du cochon et du thon. Les deux réunis, sur fond pimenté, s'entendent comme « lardrons » en foire.

- Préparation de la sauce aux poivrons. Videz et taillez les poivrons en gros dés. Ébouillantez les tomates, épluchez-les, épépinez-les et découpez-les en gros morceaux. Épluchez et hachez les échalotes et les gousses d'ail. Dans l'huile d'olive chaude, mettez les échalotes et les morceaux de poivrons. Laissez mijoter 10 minutes sans faire colorer, puis ajoutez les tomates et le bouquet garni. Poursuivez la cuisson 25 minutes à feu doux en remuant. Versez 5 cl de vinaigre de xérès. Rectifiez l'assaisonnement. Enlevez le bouquet garni et mixez cette préparation.
- 20 minutes avant de passer à table : saisissez les tranches de poitrine de cochon des 2 côtés dans une poêle à feu doux, sans matière grasse. Réchauffez la sauce aux poivrons sur feu doux. Saisissez les morceaux de ventrèche de thon dans la poêle ayant servi à la cuisson du cochon. Faites-les dorer 6 à 8 minutes à feu vif (le thon doit être mi-cuit).
- Répartissez la sauce aux poivrons dans de grandes assiettes, et posez dessus les morceaux thon et de cochon côte à côte. Déglacez la poêle de cuisson avec le vinaigre restant, en remuant avec une spatule. Versez cette sauce sur chaque assiette. Saupoudrez d'une pointe de piment d'Espelette.

Pour 4 personnes
Préparation : marinade : 2 à 4 h
Cuisson du poisson : 10 min
Préparation de la sauce : 10 min
Pas de cuisson pour la sauce

- 4 filets de thon d'environ 180 g chacun
- 1/4 bouquet de thym
- 2 c. à café de graines de fenouil
- 1 c. à café de poivre en grains
- 1/2 citron non traité
- 4 c. à soupe d'huile d'olive

Pour la sauce

- 2 bouquets de persil
- 6 filets d'anchois à l'huile
- 4 gousses d'ail
- 3 c. à soupe de câpres
- 2 c. à café de pulpe de tomates
- 10 cl d'huile d'olive
- 1 c. à soupe de jus de citron (ou de vinaigre de vin)
- Sel et poivre

Filet de thon grillé mariné au poivre et au thym

Un steak de thon cuisiné comme un steak au poivre

Ensoleillé par des senteurs méditerranéennes. Or c'est en Méditerranée que les thons se reproduisent. Les Grecs le savaient déjà voilà 2 000 ans et en faisaient grand cas.

- Effeuillez le thym et mélangez-le aux graines de fenouil et aux grains de poivre pilés. Ajoutez le zeste du citron émincé et 2 cuillerées à soupe d'huile. Nappez les filets de thon de ce mélange, recouvrez-les avec du film alimentaire et mettez-les au réfrigérateur de 2 à 4 heures.
- **Préparation de la sauce.** Mélangez le persil effeuillé, les filets d'anchois égouttés et coupés en dés, l'ail entier épluché. Passez ce mélange au mixeur avec les câpres, la pulpe de tomates et l'huile. Assaisonnez de jus de citron ou de vinaigre. Rectifiez l'assaisonnement en sel et poivre.
- Préchauffez le four à 180 °C (th. 6). Salez les filets de thon, posez-les sur une plaque que vous placez à environ 10 cm du gril du four pendant environ 4 minutes de chaque côté.
- Servez avec la sauce accompagnée de pommes gaufrettes ou de chips de pommes de terre.

La simplicité
d'un court-bouillon.
L'onctuosité des poivrons
confits dans les parfums
d'épices. Du vert,
du rouge, du rose nacré :
technicolor pour
temps d'été.

Effeuillé de thon au confit de poivrons rouges

Pour 4 personnes
Préparation : 35 min
Cuisson : 20 min
Repos : 2 h

- 1 morceau de thon de 500 g et 5 cm d'épaisseur, sans peau, ni arêtes
- 4 poivrons rouges charnus
- 1 tête d'ail nouveau
- 2 tomates
- 12 feuilles de laurier
- 1/3 de c. à café de piment d'Espelette en poudre
- 1 c. à café de cumin en poudre
- 1 c. à café d'origan en poudre
- 1 c. à café de sucre semoule
- 2 c. à soupe d'huile d'olive
- Gros sel de mer et poivre

- Couvrez le morceau de thon de gros sel et laissez-le macérer pendant 30 minutes au frais. Versez 1,5 litre d'eau dans une casserole de 20 cm de diamètre. Mettez dedans les feuilles de laurier et 1 cuillerée à soupe de gros sel. Portez à ébullition. Lorsque le thon a macéré 30 minutes, rincez-le et plongez-le dans l'eau bouillante. Dès que l'ébullition reprend, comptez 5 minutes, puis éteignez le feu et laissez tiédir le thon dans son bouillon de cuisson pendant 1 heure à 1 heure 30.
- **Préparation du confit de poivrons.** Lavez les poivrons, pelez-les avec un économe, coupez-les en 4 et débarrassez-les des graines et filaments intérieurs. Coupez chaque quartier de poivrons en lamelles de 1 cm dans la longueur. Détachez les gousses d'ail et pelez-les. Ébouillantez les tomates, pelez-les, coupez-les en quartiers puis en lamelles de 0,5 cm. Versez 2 cuillerées à soupe d'huile d'olive dans une sauteuse antiadhésive posée sur feu moyen. Jetez-y les lamelles de poivron et laissez-les cuire durant 5 minutes en tournant souvent. Ajoutez alors les gousses d'ail et 5 minutes plus tard les tomates, le piment, le cumin, l'origan, le sucre. Salez et poivrez. Laissez cuire 25 minutes environ jusqu'à ce qu'il n'y ait plus de liquide et que les poivrons soient moelleux et légèrement caramélisés.
- Égouttez le thon et détachez-le en feuilles tendres et goutteuses. Servez-le sur un lit de poivrons tièdes nappé du jus de cuisson. Accompagnez ce thon de ciboules, d'oignons frais émincés et de roquette.

Pour 4 personnes
Préparation : 30 min
Marinade : 1 h
Cuisson : 4 min

- 1 tranche épaisse de thon d'environ 600 g (sans la peau, ni les arêtes)
- 2 c. à soupe de graines de sésame
- 2 oignons nouveaux avec leurs tiges vertes
- 1 tige de citronnelle
- 1 c. à soupe de gingembre frais râpé
- 1 citron
- 2 c. à soupe d'huile de sésame
- 200 g de mesclun
- Sel et poivre

Pour la marinade
- 2 c. à soupe d'huile de tournesol
- 2 c. à soupe de vinaigre de cidre
- 1 c. à soupe de gingembre frais
- 1 tige de citronnelle

Thon en croûte de sésame

Métamorphosé par sa panure de sésame, enrichi de fraîcheur citronnée et de gingembre, diététiquement irréprochable et gastronomiquement délectable.

- **Préparation de la marinade.** Dans un bol, mélangez l'huile de tournesol avec le vinaigre de cidre, le gingembre râpé, la tige de citronnelle finement ciselée. Déposez la tranche de thon dans un plat creux et arrosez-la avec la marinade. Couvrez avec un film alimentaire et laissez mariner au moins 1 heure au frais en retournant le thon de temps en temps pour que la chair soit bien imprégnée.
- Émincez finement les oignons et leurs tiges vertes, ainsi qu'une tige de citronnelle. Dans un bol, mélangez la citronnelle, 1 cuillerée à soupe de gingembre râpé, un peu de jus de citron, l'huile de sésame. Salez et poivrez.
- Égouttez le thon, recouvrez-le de graines de sésame en appuyant pour bien les incruster dans la chair. Saisissez le thon sur toutes ses faces dans une poêle anti-adhésive non graissée, sur feu vif : les graines doivent dorer et le thon rester rouge à cœur. Découpez-le en tranches, arrosez-le de sauce à l'huile de sésame (gardez suffisamment de sauce pour la salade), parsemez d'oignons émincés.
- Servez avec le mesclun assaisonné de sauce à l'huile de sésame.

Pour 6 personnes
Préparation : 30 min
Cuisson : 1 h

- 1,5 kg de thon sans peau, ni arêtes
- 1 tête de thon (pas trop grosse) coupée en deux
- 4 oignons
- 1 kg de pommes de terre
- 3 c. à soupe d'huile d'olive
- 4 grosses tomates
- 10 gousses d'ail
- 4 piments d'Espelette
- 50 cl de vin blanc sec
- 1 bouquet garni
- Sel

Marmitako

Spécialistes de la pêche au thon, les pêcheurs des côtes basques conservaient les têtes dont on faisait une soupe, le « marmitako ». Tradition à maintenir.

- Épluchez les oignons. Épluchez les pommes de terre et réservez-les dans de l'eau.
- Dans une poêle, faire revenir dans un peu d'huile d'olive 3 oignons émincés, sans coloration.
- Coupez les tomates en quartiers et ajoutez-les aux oignons ainsi que les gousses d'ail épluchées. Couvrez et laissez cuire à feu doux pendant 15 minutes. Réservez.
- Rincez les deux moitiés de tête de thon et déposez-les dans un faitout, ajoutez 1 oignon émincé, les piments entiers et le bouquet garni.
- Versez le vin blanc, ajoutez de l'eau pour couvrir à hauteur. Salez. Portez à ébullition. Écumez et laissez cuire durant 20 minutes à feu doux.
- Coupez le thon en petits dés.
- Tamisez le bouillon de cuisson de la tête et réservez les légumes de garniture.
- Décortiquez la tête dont vous mettez la chair dans le bouillon.
- Coupez les pommes de terre en gros dés.
- Passez la sauce tomate au mixeur, avec les piments. Versez l'ensemble dans le faitout contenant le bouillon et poursuivez la cuisson durant 30 minutes, à couvert, sur feu moyen.
- Cinq minutes avant de servir, ajoutez les dés de thon. Laissez reprendre l'ébullition. Goûtez, et rectifiez l'assaisonnement si besoin est.
- Servez bouillant.

Pour 8 personnes
Préparation : 40 min
Cuisson : 35 min
Réfrigération : 1 nuit

- 800 g de ventre de thon
- 5 feuilles de gélatine
- 8 belles tomates bien mûres
- 1 oignon
- 3 poivrons rouges
- 350 g d'olives farcies aux anchois
- Vinaigre de xérès
- Huile d'olive
- Sel et poivre

Terrine de ventre de thon

Le ventre, parfaitement comestible, y aviez-vous pensé ? Ici, pour une fraîche terrine, le voici copin-copines avec tomates et poivrons, les vieux alliés du beau fuselé.

- Mettez les feuilles de gélatine à tremper dans de l'eau froide. Émondez les tomates, épépinez-les et coupez-les en petits morceaux. Pelez et émincez l'oignon. Dans une casserole, faites revenir l'oignon à l'huile d'olive puis ajoutez la chair des tomates. Laissez cuire à feu doux pendant 30 minutes. Incorporez les feuilles de gélatine essorées. Salez et poivrez.
- Préchauffez le four à 180 °C (th. 6). Saisissez les poivrons au four, pendant 15 minutes. Sortez-les et pelez-les. Coupez le ventre du thon en tranches de 1 cm d'épaisseur. Faites-les revenir sur feu vif dans une poêle avec de l'huile d'olive, de chaque côté. Laissez-les cuire durant 5 minutes.
- Tapissez une terrine de papier sulfurisé. Étalez-y une couche de fondue de tomates, puis une couche de poivrons, d'olives aux anchois et enfin de thon. Renouvelez l'opération jusqu'à ce que vous ayez rempli la terrine. Mettez-la au réfrigérateur jusqu'au lendemain.
- Préparez une vinaigrette à base de vinaigre de xérès et d'huile d'olive. Démoulez la terrine et coupez-la en tranches régulières à l'aide d'un couteau fin très bien aiguisé. Servez avec un peu de vinaigrette.

Pour 4 personnes
Préparation : 15 min
Cuisson : 20 min

- 4 darnes de thon de 200 g chacune
- 4 filets d'anchois à l'huile d'olive
- 2 citrons
- 2 gousses d'ail
- 3 bulbes de fenouil
- 5 cl de vermouth sec
- 7 c. à soupe d'huile d'olive
- 1 c. à café de graines de fenouil
- Sel et poivre

Thon braisé au fenouil

En direct du four à la table, le bel accord entre une chair imprégnée de goût anisé, le trait tonique du vermouth et la vivacité bien tempérée de l'anchois.

- Préchauffez le four à 180 °C (th. 6).
- Coupez les citrons en rondelles.
- Frottez un grand plat à rôtir avec une gousse d'ail pelée et graissez-le d'1 cuillerée à soupe d'huile d'olive.
- Disposez les rondelles de citron dans le fond. Ajoutez les fenouils épluchés et émincés. Salez et poivrez.
- Déposez les darnes de thon sur ce lit de légumes. Poivrez-les mais ne les salez pas. Arrosez avec le vermouth sec et 3 cuillerées à soupe d'huile d'olive. Recouvrez d'une feuille de papier d'aluminium. Enfournez pendant 10 minutes.
- Écrasez les filets d'anchois à la fourchette avec 1 gousse d'ail pressée et 3 cuillerées à soupe d'huile d'olive. Étalez cette préparation sur les darnes. Parsemez de graines de fenouil.
- Poursuivez la cuisson encore 10 minutes au four sans couvrir et servez.

Pour 4/6 personnes
Préparation : 25 min
Cuisson : 15 min

- 1 ventrèche de 800 g
- 1 c. à soupe d'huile d'olive
- Fleur de sel et mignonnette
- 2 c. à soupe de farine
- 5 oignons nouveaux

Pour la sauce
- 3 c. à soupe de sauce soja
- 6 c. à soupe de vinaigre de vin rouge
- 1 gousse d'ail
- 3 c. à soupe d'huile d'olive
- 1 c. à soupe de câpres
- 1 c. à soupe d'olives vertes
- 1 c. à soupe d'olives noires
- 1 c. à café de poivre vert
- 1 c. à soupe de poivrons confits
- Thym

Ventrèche
de thon aux aromates

Réunissez les aromates. Faites frire les oignons. Et constatez que le lard de poitrine du thon n'est pas moins goûteux que celui du cochon de nos traditions.

- Faites réduire la sauce soja et le vinaigre. Ajoutez la gousse d'ail pelée et coupée en 4 dans la longueur, et l'huile d'olive, puis les câpres, les olives vertes et noires dénoyautées et hachées, le poivre vert, les lamelles de poivron, le thym effeuillé.
- Assaisonnez les deux faces du poisson de mignonnette et de fleur de sel. Faites-le saisir sur feu vif dans l'huile d'olive sur les 2 faces puis découpez le poisson en une douzaine de fines tranches que vous nappez de sauce aux aromates chaude.
- Parallèlement, roulez dans la farine les oignons épluchés et coupés en fines rondelles. Trempez-les dans l'huile pour les faire frire. Posez ces oignons frits sur les tranches de ventrèche.

Pour 4 personnes
Préparation : 15 min
Marinade : 4 h
Pas de cuisson

- 2 rouelles de thon blanc soit 500 à 600 g
- 2 citrons verts non traités
- 1 c. à café de chili
- 8 à 10 petits oignons nouveaux
- 2 c. à soupe d'huile d'olive
- 2 branches de persil plat
- 200 g de perce-pierre ou de criste-marine (boutiques bio)
- Poivre du moulin

Salade
de thon blanc aux algues

Le thon blanc se nomme aussi germon. Il est beaucoup utilisé en conserve. Mais frais, cru, accompagné d'algues, il nous met l'océan à la bouche.

- Parez le thon en retirant la peau et les arêtes, et coupez-le en dés d'environ 2 cm.
- Déposez les dés de thon dans un grand saladier. Arrosez-les avec le jus des 2 citrons verts.
- Mélangez avec délicatesse en soulevant pour que le jus de citron imprègne parfaitement le thon.
- Ajoutez le chili et mélangez de nouveau. Émincez finement les oignons. Incorporez-les au thon.
- Versez l'huile sur le poisson. Réservez au réfrigérateur pendant au moins 4 heures.
- Avant de servir, mélangez encore une fois très délicatement.
- Arrosez les algues séchées avec un filet d'huile d'olive (ces algues séchées se présentent sous forme de paillettes et se composent de dulse, laitue de mer, nori… Elles ont en outre de très jolies couleurs). Assaisonnez avec le poivre du moulin. Saupoudrez de persil haché.
- Servez la salade d'algues avec les dés de thon blanc marinés.

Pour 4 personnes
Préparation : 30 min
Réfrigération : 20 min
Pratiquement pas de cuisson

- **300 g de thon frais**
- **1,5 l de bouillon de légumes instantané (ou fait maison)**
- **2 c. à café de pâte wasabi (épiceries asiatiques)**
- **1 c. à café de sucre**
- **4 c. à soupe de sauce de poissons (épiceries asiatiques)**
- **Poivre**
- **4 c. à soupe de sauce soja foncée**
- **50 g de pousses de soja**
- **1/2 bouquet de coriandre**
- **3 carottes**
- **6 petits oignons blancs**
- **4 cœurs de céleri branche**
- **4 champignons de Paris**

Soupe au thon

C'est en particulier avec le thon que les Japonais préparent leurs sushis. Condiments du Sud-Est asiatique et bouillon, voilà le sushi occidentalisé.

- Mettez le filet de thon au congélateur durant une vingtaine de minutes.
- Dans le bouillon chaud, déposez la pâte wasabi, le sucre et la sauce de poissons. Poivrez. Laissez mijoter 5 minutes et réservez au chaud.
- Sortez le filet de thon du congélateur et découpez 4 tranches d'au moins 2 cm d'épaisseur. Découpez le reste en petits dés. Déposez les tranches les unes à côté des autres sur une assiette, poivrez, arrosez de sauce soja.
- Épluchez les carottes et coupez-les en julienne. Épluchez et émincez les petits oignons. Coupez les cœurs de céleri en julienne. Posez les légumes sur les tranches de thon que vous roulez autour des légumes.
- Déposez un roulé de thon aux petits légumes dans chaque assiette.
- Portez le bouillon à ébullition et versez-le bouillant dans les assiettes sur les rouleaux de thon. Garnissez avec les champignons de Paris coupés en très petits dés, les feuilles de coriandre et parsemez de pousses de soja ainsi que de petits dés de thon.
- Dégustez aussitôt.

Pour 4 personnes
Préparation : 40 min
Cuisson : 50 min

- 800 g de filet de thon pris dans un morceau épais
- 4 tranches fines de jambon de Bayonne
- 6 branches de thym frais
- Huile d'olive

Pour l'accompagnement
- 300 g d'épinards
- 4 petites courgettes
- 4 oignons nouveaux
- 10 cl d'huile d'olive
- 3 gousses d'ail
- 1 c. à soupe de curcuma
- Sel et poivre

Pour la sauce
- 4 échalotes
- 5 cl d'huile d'arachide
- 2 gousses d'ail
- 1 bouquet garni
- 70 g de poitrine fumée en dés
- 50 cl de vin rouge
- 25 cl de fumet de poisson
- Sel et poivre

Rôti de thon rouge au jambon de Bayonne

Réunies en une seule merveille, deux des plus fameuses spécialités du pays Basque, le thon et le jambon. À l'évidence ils étaient faits l'un pour l'autre.

- Entourez le filet de thon avec les tranches de jambon de Bayonne. Ficelez-le comme un rôti et réservez-le au réfrigérateur. Lavez et équeutez les épinards. Lavez et taillez les courgettes et les oignons en gros dés. Dans une grande poêle, faites revenir à feu vif dans 10 cl d'huile d'olive chaude les oignons, les gousses d'ail épluchées et les courgettes. Laissez colorer pendant quelques minutes, puis ajoutez les épinards et le curcuma. Salez et poivrez ; Laissez cuire durant 25 minutes à feu doux, tout en remuant. Préchauffez le four à 180 °C (th. 6). Déposez le filet de thon dans un grand plat avec le thym. Arrosez d'huile d'olive et enfournez pendant 25 minutes.
- **Préparez la sauce au vin rouge :** épluchez et hachez les échalotes. Dans une casserole, faites revenir les échalotes dans l'huile d'arachide. Remuez avec une spatule et laissez colorer. Ajoutez les gousses d'ail entières avec la peau, le bouquet garni, la poitrine fumée et le vin rouge. Laissez réduire de moitié. Versez le fumet de poisson tout en remuant. Et faites de nouveau réduire de moitié. Rectifiez l'assaisonnement.
- Sortez le rôti de thon du four. Enlevez la ficelle et disposez le poisson dans un grand plat entouré des légumes croquants. Servez avec la sauce au vin.

Pour 4 personnes
Préparation : 30 min
Cuisson : 50 min

- 300 à 400 g de thon cuit au naturel (ou en boîte)
- 2 ou 3 aubergines
- Huile d'olive

Pour la ratatouille
- 2 courgettes
- 4 tomates
- 1 poivron rouge
- 1 poivron rouge
- 4 feuilles de basilic
- 2 c. à soupe d'huile d'olive
- Sel et poivre

Il vous faudra des moules à soufflé de 12 cm de diamètre

Charlotte
de thon aux aubergines

Si vous savez préparer une ratatouille et ouvrir une boîte de thon, ces jolies charlottes en ramequins ne seront pour vous qu'un jeu d'enfant gourmand.

- **Préparation de la ratatouille.** Coupez tous les légumes en petits dés et faites-les revenir dans une poêle avec 2 cuillerées à soupe d'huile d'olive pour obtenir une compote de légumes dans le style d'une ratatouille. Laissez cuire à feu doux environ 20 minutes. Ajoutez éventuellement un peu d'eau si cela attache. Salez et poivrez.
- Préchauffez le four à 160 °C (th. 5). Lavez les aubergines et coupez-les en tranches fines, sans les éplucher. Poêlez ces tranches dans un peu d'huile d'olive bien chaude afin qu'elles soient bien rissolées. Épongez-les entre deux feuilles de papier absorbant Chemisez les petits moules très légèrement beurrés avec ces tranches d'aubergines en les disposant joliment : rosace au fond, en remontant sur les côtés, en les faisant se chevaucher et en les laissant dépasser Déposez dans les moules le thon émietté mélangé à la compote de légumes. Rectifiez l'assaisonnement. Mettez les charlottes au four, au bain-marie, pendant 30 minutes. Elles doivent être bien fermes et dorées sur le dessus.
- Démoulez et servez avec une sauce tomate bien chaude.

Tout est bOn

dans le poisson

Têtes, joues, foies, parures… Lorsque leurs hommes rentrent de la pêche, les femmes de marins savent fort bien, de ces menus fretins, faire bouillir la marmite. Les vrais cuisiniers, de leur côté, les utilisent pour renforcer les goûts et innover. Sagesse des unes, inventivité des autres : à vous de jouer.

Pour 6 personnes
Préparation : 30 min
Cuisson : 30 min

- 6 têtes de poisson (saumon ou bar)
- 500 g de spaghettis
- 2 branches de céleri
- 1 carotte
- 4 gousses d'ail écrasées
- 1 gros oignon
- 2 branches de thym
- 1 feuille de laurier
- 3 c. à soupe d'huile d'olive
- 2 branches de basilic
- Sel et poivre du moulin

Sauce tomate

- 1,5 kg de tomates bien mûres
- 2 gousses d'ail
- 1 gros oignon
- 2 c. à soupe d'huile d'olive
- 1 brin de thym
- Sel et poivre
- 1 pincée de sucre
- 1 c. à café de curry

LA TÊTE

Spaghetti à la tête de poisson

Suggérez à votre poissonnier de vous conserver ces têtes que souvent il jette, faute d'amateurs. Et si vous êtes une cliente fidèle, il se pourrait même qu'il vous les offre.

- Lavez et coupez le céleri et la carotte en petits tronçons. Pelez l'ail et l'oignon, coupez-les en deux. Mettez les têtes de poissons dans un faitout. Ajoutez 4 litres d'eau, les légumes, les herbes, du sel. Portez à ébullition, et poursuivez la cuisson 15 à 20 minutes à feu doux. Laissez tiédir.
- **Préparation de la sauce tomate.** Ébouillantez, pelez et concassez les tomates. Pelez l'ail et l'oignon et hachez-les. Dans l'huile d'olive chaude, faites revenir l'ail et l'oignon pendant 5 minutes. Ajoutez les tomates et le thym. Salez, poivrez et ajoutez une pincée de sucre. Laissez cuire durant une quinzaine de minutes puis incorporez le curry, remuez et réservez.
- Égouttez les têtes de poissons. Détachez soigneusement les chairs, c'est-à-dire les joues, l'arrière des ouïes, le cou, et mettez-les à chauffer dans la sauce tomate. Filtrez le bouillon et portez-le à ébullition, plongez-y les spaghettis et faites-les cuire al dente. Égouttez rapidement. Incorporez 3 cuillerées à soupe d'huile d'olive et le basilic haché. Arrosez de sauce au poisson, et servez sans attendre dans des assiettes chaudes.

Pour 4 personnes
Préparation : 30 min
Cuisson : 1 h

- 2 kg de têtes de poissons blancs de grande taille (lieu jaune, morue, bar, etc.)
- 100 g de saumon fumé
- 30 g de gingembre frais épluché et émincé
- 2 piments oiseaux
- 1 peau d'orange séchée, réhydratée et coupée en morceaux
- Quelques brins de ciboulette hachés
- Sel et poivre

Trois plus à ce bouillon d'une simplicité paléolithique : la note de saumon fumé, les touches d'orange et de gingembre, ses quenelles qui en font un plat complet.

Soupe de têtes de poissons

- Mettez les têtes de poissons dans une cocotte avec le gingembre, les piments et la peau d'orange. Recouvrez d'eau. Salez. Faites cuire durant 1 heure à petit feu sans bouillir.
- Filtrez le bouillon.
- Sortez les têtes, épluchez-les et hachez les chairs (jetez le reste). Réservez au chaud les parties comestibles.
- Hachez le saumon et mélangez-le à la chair des têtes. Salez et poivrez.
- Formez de petites boulettes de poisson.
- Remettez le bouillon sur le feu jusqu'à ébullition, baissez alors le feu et déposez-y les boulettes une à une. Retirez-les lorsqu'elles remontent à la surface.
- Servez-les dans des bols et parsemez-les de ciboulette.

LES JOUES

Joues de raie au chou

L'art de conjuguer des ingrédients a priori peu faits pour se rencontrer. Chou croquant, joues pochées, tomates et oignons crus, vinaigrette tiède s'entendent cependant à merveille.

Pour 4 personnes
Préparation : 30 min
Cuisson : 15 min

- 12 grosses joues de raies (800 g environ)
- 8 belles feuilles de chou vert
- 4 petites tomates
- 4 petits oignons nouveaux
- 9 c. à soupe de vinaigrette
- 15 cl de vinaigre d'alcool coloré
- 1 bouquet garni
- Gros sel
- 1 c. à soupe rase de poivre en grains
- 9 graines de coriandre
- 1/2 botte de ciboulette
- 2 brins de cerfeuil

- Éliminez la grosse côte centrale des feuilles de chou, blanchissez-les 1 minute à l'eau bouillante salée. Rafraîchissez-les à l'eau froide et égouttez-les bien à plat sur un linge.
- Ébouillantez les tomates après les avoir entaillées en croix et avoir retiré le pédoncule. Pelez-les, coupez-les en deux pour les vider de leurs graines et coupez la chair en petits dés. Épluchez les oignons et émincez-les très finement.
- Préparez une vinaigrette classique.
- Préparez le court-bouillon : dans une casserole, versez 1 litre et demi d'eau et le vinaigre, ajoutez le bouquet garni, 2 bonnes pincées de gros sel, le poivre en grains, les graines de coriandre. Portez à ébullition et plongez les joues de raie dans ce court-bouillon en ébullition, laissez reprendre un premier bouillon, retirez du feu et laissez tiédir 3 à 4 minutes avant de sortir les joues à l'aide d'une écumoire. Retirez le cartilage au milieu de chaque joue.
- Déposez les feuilles de chou dans une passoire que vous plongez dans une casserole d'eau bouillante pour les réchauffer. Laissez-les s'égoutter.
- Versez 3 cuillerées de vinaigrette dans une petite casserole, ajoutez les dés de tomate, et faites juste tiédir sur feu très doux.
- Mettez les feuilles de chou égouttées dans une sauteuse avec la vinaigrette restante. Faites également tiédir sur feu très doux.
- Dans le fond de chaque assiette chaude, posez 3 joues sur 2 feuilles de chou. Sur chaque joue, placez un petit tas de dés de tomates, 1 pincée d'oignons émincés, 1 pincée de gros sel, 1 pincée de poivre moulu. Parsemez le tout de ciboulette ciselée et de pluches de cerfeuil.

Pour 4 personnes
Préparation : 20 min
Cuisson : 10 min

- 500 g de joues de lotte
- 500 g de petits pois
- 60 g de beurre
- 1 bouquet d'estragon
- 10 cl de vin blanc (ou de fumet de poisson)
- 20 cl de crème fraîche
- 1/2 citron
- Sel et poivre

Joues
de lotte sautées à l'estragon

Les joues, le plus fin du poisson, tous les amateurs le savent. On en trouve désormais dans toutes les bonnes poissonneries et même dans les grandes surfaces.

- Lavez et épongez les joues. Assaisonnez-les de sel et poivre.
- Écossez les petits pois et cuisez-les à l'eau salée en les maintenant fermes.
- Dans une sauteuse, saisissez dans le beurre chaud toutes les joues de lotte. Retournez-les, couvrez et laissez suer doucement avec la moitié du bouquet d'estragon effeuillé.
- Lorsqu'il se forme un petit jus au fond de la sauteuse, détendez-le avec le vin blanc. Portez à ébullition puis ajoutez la crème. Salez et poivrez. Débarrassez les joues de lotte dans une autre sauteuse, couvrez-les avec les petits pois et le reste de l'estragon. Passez dessus la sauce au chinois.
- Terminez la cuisson en ajoutant une noix de beurre et le jus d'un demi-citron.

Pour 4 personnes
Préparation : 30 min
Cuisson : 5 min

Fricassée de joues de cabillaud aux dés de légumes

Poisson pour les protéines, petits légumes croquants pour les vitamines, avec une sauce de haute volée que les convives seront, bien sûr, conviés à saucer.

- 20 belles joues de morue
- 1 carotte
- 1 courgette
- 1 fenouil
- 1 petit céleri-rave
- 3 branches de persil
- 2 échalotes
- 2 gousses d'ail
- 40 g de beurre
- 1/2 c. à café de concentré de tomates
- 10 cl de muscadet ou de vin blanc sec
- 20 cl de bouillon de légumes réalisé avec du bouillon déshydraté
- Sel et poivre

- Ôtez la petite peau qui enveloppe les joues. Réservez à température ambiante.
- Épluchez tous les légumes et coupez-les en petits cubes. Faites-les cuire séparément dans de l'eau bouillante salée, en les rafraîchissant rapidement en fin de cuisson pour les garder fermes et croquants. Égouttez-les et mélangez-les.
- Hachez finement le persil et les échalotes, écrasez l'ail et faites étuver le tout à feu doux avec une noisette de beurre et le concentré de tomates. Mouillez avec le vin blanc, laissez évaporer le liquide, puis ajoutez le bouillon de légumes, laissez réduire d'environ un tiers, et pour finir passez ce jus d'aromates dans une petite casserole en pressant bien les herbes afin de récupérer tous les sucs. Laissez réduire de nouveau de moitié sur feu vif, puis à feu très doux incorporez 20 g de beurre en fouettant pour émulsionner l'ensemble. Rectifiez l'assaisonnement et gardez au chaud.
- Salez et poivrez les joues de morue, et faites-les cuire à feu vif dans une poêle antiadhésive pas plus de 2 minutes de chaque côté, en les retournant à mi-cuisson lorsque la première face est bien dorée.
- Réchauffez les petits légumes en les faisant suer doucement avec le reste de beurre.
- Disposez les joues de cabillaud en cercle sur des assiettes bien chaudes, répartissez la julienne de légumes, nappez de sauce et servez aussitôt.

Pour 4 personnes
Préparation : 10 min
Cuisson : 5 min
Dessalage : 1 nuit

- 600 à 800 g de langues de morue salées
- 1 l de lait
- 1 l d'eau
- 2 c. à soupe de farine
- 10 cl d'huile d'olive

Pour le pistou
- 8 gousses d'ail
- 1 bouquet de basilic, si possible à grandes feuilles
- 6 c. à soupe d'huile d'olive
- 2 c. à soupe de fumet déshydraté de poisson

Pour le coulis de tomates
- 6 tomates bien mûres
- 2 gousses d'ail
- 2 c. à soupe d'huile d'olive
- 1 petit bouquet garni
- 1 c. à café de sucre
- Sel et poivre du moulin

LA LANGUE

Langues de morue sauce pistou

Prenez un produit qui vient du froid : ces langues de morue. Offrez-leur une petite cure de potager provençal : ail, tomates, basilic. Elles vont adorer ce dépaysement. Vous aussi.

- **La veille :** mettez les langues de morue à dessaler en changeant l'eau 1 ou 2 fois.
- **Le lendemain :** Préparez le coulis de tomates : pelez, épépinez et concassez les tomates. Pelez l'ail. Sur feu doux, dans une sauteuse, faites revenir tout d'abord l'ail, puis les tomates concassées et le bouquet garni dans l'huile chaude. Laissez cuire doucement 6 à 8 minutes sans couvrir et en remuant de temps en temps. Assaisonnez d'1 cuillerée à café de sucre. Salez et poivrez.
- Préparez le pistou : épluchez les gousses d'ail. Écrasez-le un peu avec la lame du couteau. Effeuillez le basilic.
- Hachez-les dans le bol du mixeur et hachez jusqu'à obtention d'une pommade. Versez alors l'huile en filet, puis ajoutez le fumet de poisson jusqu'à ce que la sauce soit bien homogénéisée. Ajoutez le coulis de tomates et mélangez bien.
- Égouttez les langues de morue et pochez-les dans le mélange d'eau et de lait pendant 3 à 4 minutes sans jamais les faire bouillir. Égouttez-les. Séchez-les sur du papier absorbant puis passez-les dans la farine. Secouez pour faire tomber l'excédent de farine. Dans une poêle antiadhésive, faites rissoler sur feu vif, dans l'huile chaude, les langues pendant 1 minute environ. Posez-les sur du papier absorbant.
- Jetez l'huile et sans laver la poêle, essuyez-la. Versez dedans la sauce pistou. Laissez chauffer sur feu moyen durant 1 minute avant d'y incorporer les langues en mélangeant avec une cuillère de bois.

Pour 4 personnes
Préparation : 10 min
Cuisson : 6 min
Dessalage : 1 nuit

- 24 langues de morue
- 50 cl de lait
- 50 cl d'eau
- 10 cl d'huile d'olive

Pour la pâte à frire
- 2 blancs d'œufs
- 4 c. à soupe de farine de riz
- 1 pointe de sel de céleri

Pour le coulis de tomates
- 6 tomates bien mûres
- 2 gousses d'ail
- 2 c. à soupe d'huile d'olive
- 1 petit bouquet garni
- 1 c. à café de sucre
- Sel et poivre du moulin

Beignets
de langues de morue

Ne donnez surtout pas ces langues au chat, sauf s'il a été vraiment sage. Faites-en plutôt des beignets bien dorés, à croquer tout chauds un jour froid en se brûlant gaiement les doigts.

- On trouve en général les langues de morue salées, il faut donc, la veille de la préparation, les mettre à tremper dans de l'eau fraîche afin de les dessaler.
- Le lendemain, faites-les pocher dans le mélange d'eau et de lait pendant 3 à 4 minutes. Égouttez-les aussitôt sur du papier absorbant.
- Préparez le coulis de tomates : pelez, épépinez et concassez les tomates. Pelez l'ail. Sur feu doux, dans une sauteuse, faites revenir tout d'abord l'ail, puis les tomates concassées et le bouquet garni dans l'huile chaude. Laissez cuire doucement 6 à 8 minutes sans couvrir et en remuant de temps en temps. Assaisonnez d'1 cuillerée à café de sucre. Salez et poivrez.
- Mélangez au fouet dans une jatte les trois ingrédients de la pâte. Trempez les langues de morue dans cette pâte à frire. Dans une poêle antiadhésive, faire rissoler les beignets dans l'huile d'olive chaude sur feu vif pendant 1 minute de chaque côté. Lorsqu'ils sont bien dorés, égouttez-les sur du papier absorbant.
- Servez-les aussitôt avec le coulis de tomates chaud ou froid.

Pour 4 personnes
Préparation : 30 min
Cuisson : 4 min

Dentelle de skrei de Norvège, sabayon aux huîtres et langues de skrei

Une recette de Christian Têtedoie, restaurant Têtedoie à Lyon

Le skrei est le seigneur norvégien des cabillauds, familier des rêveuses îles Lofoten. On le sèche, on le sale, et consommé extra-frais, c'est une rare merveille. Il est ici en tenue de fête.

- 500 g de skrei de Norvège
- 2 douzaines d'huîtres n° 3
- 16 langues de skrei
- 8 jaunes d'œufs
- 200 g de beurre
- 1 filet d'huile d'olive
- 1 jus de citron
- 1 pincée de gingembre
- 1 pincée d'anis vert
- 1 pincée de poivre blanc
- 1 c. de miel mille fleurs
- 1 bouquet d'herbes (aneth, cerfeuil, ciboulette, persil...)

Fumet de poisson

- 1 arête de poisson blanc
- 1 oignon
- 1 bouquet garni (persil, thym, laurier)
- 25 cl de vin blanc

- Préparez le fumet de poisson en réunissant tous les ingrédients dans 1 litre d'eau. Portez à petite ébullition pendant 20 minutes, puis filtrez.
- Coupez le poisson en longues tranches fines. Mélangez les jaunes d'œufs et le jus des huîtres (sabayon). Incorporez le beurre bien froid en petits morceaux puis les huîtres hachées finement, le miel et les épices. Portez les langues de skrei à ébullition dans le fumet. Laissez refroidir dans le fumet. Après cuisson, si cela est nécessaire, épluchez les langues.
- Nappez le fond des assiettes avec le sabayon. Déposez dessus les fines tranches de skrei. Passez quelques instants sous le gril du four jusqu'à belle coloration. Ajoutez les langues, assaisonnez avec l'huile d'olive et le jus de citron, ajoutez les herbes finement hachées.

Pour 6 personnes
Préparation : 20 min
Cuisson : 30 min

- 900 g de langues de cabillaud
- 6 grosses pommes de terre
- 3 gros oignons
- 10 cl de lait
- 100 g de farine
- 2 œufs
- 125 g de beurre
- Sel et poivre
- Muscade

Langues
de cabillaud poêlées aux oignons

Chaque terre-neuvas conservait les langues de cabillaud dans un tonnelet, ce qui lui permettait de comptabiliser ses prises. Ensuite, il les mangeait. Cuisiner ces langues, c'est revivre une épopée.

- Épluchez les pommes de terre et les oignons. Émincez les oignons grossièrement et taillez les pommes de terre en petits cubes.
- Faites cuire les cubes de pommes de terre une quinzaine de minutes dans de l'eau bouillante salée et égouttez-les.
- Dans trois assiettes différentes : versez le lait, la farine et les œufs battus à la fourchette.
- Lavez les langues et essuyez-les bien dans un torchon propre. Passez-les une à une dans le lait, puis dans les œufs et, en dernier, dans la farine.
- Dans une poêle, sur feu vif, mettez dans 50 g de beurre fondu la moitié des oignons émincés. Laissez cuire pendant 5 minutes en remuant, puis ajoutez les pommes de terre et faites dorer le tout.
- Une dizaine de minutes avant de passer à table, faites fondre dans une autre poêle le reste du beurre, déposez-y les langues de cabillaud panées et laissez colorer sur feu vif, 5 minutes de chaque côté.
- Assaisonnez de sel, poivre et muscade.
- Servez avec les pommes de terre.

Pour 4 personnes
Préparation : 25 min
Cuisson : 45 min
Dessalage : 12 h

- **800 g de langues de morue salées**
- **8 tomates**
- **4 gros oignons**
- **4 à 8 piments verts selon le goût**
- **4 c. à soupe d'huile**

Rougail
de langues de morue

- **La veille :** faites dessaler les langues de morue en changeant l'eau 2 à 3 fois.
- **Le lendemain :** Épluchez les oignons et coupez-les en rondelles. Ébouillantez les tomates, pelez-les et coupez-les en gros dés. Coupez les piments en fines rondelles.
- Dans une cocotte, mettez les 4 c. à soupe d'huile puis disposez les langues de morue après les avoir émiettées. Recouvrez avec les oignons et les tomates concassées. Couvrez et faites suer à feu doux. Quand les oignons et les tomates ont ramolli, poursuivez la cuisson à feu moyen pendant 30 minutes environ : les oignons doivent devenir translucides.
- Découvrez et terminez la cuisson à feu vif jusqu'à évaporation du liquide. Ajoutez alors les rondelles de piments et rectifiez l'assaisonnement : ajoutez du poivre mais soyez prudent avec le sel, les langues de morue étant salées !
- Servez bien chaud avec du riz blanc.

La langue, disait le fabuliste grec Ésope, est la meilleure et la pire des choses. C'est l'une des meilleures avec ce rougail, interprétation d'un plat traditionnel de l'île de la Réunion.

Pour 6 canapés
Préparation : 15 min
Cuisson : 10 min

- 150 à 200 g de foies de raie
- 2 c. à soupe de fines herbes (ciboulette, cerfeuil, estragon, persil...) et de persil hachés
- 1 c. à soupe de câpres au vinaigre
- 20 g de beurre
- 6 tranches de pain de mie
- 1 c. à soupe de chapelure
- 1/2 citron
- Sel

LE FOIE

Toasts de foie de raie

Vite faits, faciles et même, grâce au foie, riches en oméga 3. Comme ces toasts originaux sont aussi délicieux, en fonction de vos convives, voyez grand. Il y a peu de risques qu'il vous en reste.

- Les foies de raie sont à commander chez votre poissonnier, car en général ils sont jetés. Attention, ils doivent être très frais !
- Préchauffez le four à 180 °C (th. 6).
- Hachez les fines herbes et le persil. Hachez les câpres.
- Dans une casserole, mettez 15 g de beurre, laissez-le fondre doucement, puis ajoutez les fines herbes et le persil hachés, ainsi que les câpres et un peu de sel. Couvrez et laissez cuire sur feu très doux durant 2 à 3 minutes.
- Pendant ce temps, dans une autre casserole, déposez les foies bien lavés, couvrez-les d'eau froide avec un peu de sel. Placez la casserole sur le feu et, dès que l'eau commence à bouillir, couvrez, retirez du feu, et laissez ainsi les foies pendant 3 à 4 minutes.
- Parallèlement, faites griller les tranches de pain.
- Égouttez les foies, épongez-les, coupez-les en tranches d'1 cm.
- Sur chaque tranche de pain grillé, étendez une couche de fines herbes puis une couche de foie, une autre couche de fines herbes, et pour finir saupoudrez de chapelure.
- Posez dessus une noisette de beurre.
- Placez les toasts l'un à côté de l'autre sur une plaque que vous mettez dans le four à 180 °C pendant 2 à 3 minutes.
- Au moment de servir, versez sur chaque rôtie quelques gouttes de jus de citron.

Paté de foie
dé

Pour 4 personnes
Préparation : 30 min
Cuisson : 30 min

- 300 g de foie de raie
- 1 l de court-bouillon réalisé avec du court-bouillon déshydraté
- 4 carrés de pâte feuilletée de 15 cm x 15 cm

Pour la sauce
- 20 g de beurre
- 1 c. à café de farine
- 125 g de champignons de Paris
- 1 oignon
- 1 échalote
- 20 cl de fumet de poisson
- 15 cl de vin blanc
- Sel
- Poivre de Cayenne
- 1 c. à soupe de câpres au vinaigre
- 1 c. à soupe de persil haché
- 1 c. à soupe d'estragon haché
- 80 g de beurre d'anchois
- 40 g de parmesan râpé fin

Croustades
de foie de raie gratinées

Elles embaument, elles croustillent, elles appellent la fourchette. Encore une utilisation raffinée du modeste foie de raie, en hors-d'œuvre copieux ou plat principal savoureux.

- Faites dégorger les foies de raie 15 minutes dans de l'eau froide. Dans une casserole, amenez le court-bouillon à ébullition. Puis mettez-y les foies. Réduisez le feu et laissez cuire pendant 20 minutes sans ébullition. Laissez refroidir les foies dans le liquide. Ensuite, essuyez-les et coupez-les en morceaux.
- Préchauffez le four à 180 °C (th. 6). Mettez les carrés de pâte feuilletée sur une plaque recouverte d'un papier sulfurisé beurré. Formez un petit bord tout autour en pliant la pâte, et pour éviter qu'elle ne se boursoufle à la cuisson : soit vous la piquez avec une fourchette, soit vous y déposez des haricots secs. Mettez la plaque dans le four chaud pendant une dizaine de minutes. Puis sortez les croustades du four.
- **Préparation de la sauce.** Dans une casserole, laissez fondre un morceau de beurre d'environ 20 g, faites-y revenir la farine jusqu'à ce qu'elle soit bien dorée, puis ajoutez les champignons émincés, ainsi que l'oignon et l'échalote ciselés. Mouillez avec le fumet de poisson et le vin blanc. Laissez cuire à petit feu durant une vingtaine de minutes. Puis salez, poivrez, et ajoutez les câpres, le persil et l'estragon hachés. Donnez quelques bouillons. Incorporez alors le beurre d'anchois (soit acheté tout fait, soit obtenu en mixant 30 g de beurre avec 50 g d'anchois), ainsi que les morceaux de foie de raie. Chauffez encore quelques instants sur feu moyen, emplissez les croustades de cette préparation, saupoudrez-les de parmesan, déposez dessus quelques copeaux de beurre et passez-les quelques minutes sous le gril pour les faire gratiner.

Pour 4 personnes
Préparation : 15 min
Cuisson : 10 min
Réfrigération : 2 h
Repos : 1 nuit

- 500 à 700 g de foie de lotte
- Poivre noir
- Gros sel gris
- 1 c. à soupe d'oignons blancs
- Fleur de sel

Foie de lotte « au torchon »

Comme pour le foie gras de canard ou d'oie, la cuisson au torchon, bien plus facile à réussir pour la lotte que pour les volatiles, permet de conserver à ce produit noble sa saveur la plus authentique.

- **À préparer la veille.** Enlevez comme pour un foie gras de canard les nerfs, mais superficiellement pour ne pas abîmer la chair, puis assaisonnez les morceaux de foie de poivre du moulin à mouture très grosse, de gros sel gris concassé et d'oignon haché très fin. Façonnez ces morceaux que vous avez bien imprégnés avec les épices dans un papier sulfurisé que vous roulez en serrant bien. Donnez-leur la forme d'un boudin, fermez chaque extrémité en tortillant le papier. Enveloppez ces boudins de papier d'aluminium en rabattant les deux extrémités. Placez-les au réfrigérateur pendant 2 heures, puis faites-les cuire à la vapeur dans leur papillote pendant une dizaine de minutes. Laissez-les refroidir, mettez-les au frais et attendez le lendemain pour les déguster.
- Servez en tranches fines. Parsemez dessus un peu de fleur de sel et accompagnez-les d'un chutney de rhubarbe et pomme, de rondelles de radis roses ou de crudités.

Pour 4 personnes
Préparation : 40 min
Cuisson : 1 h 30

- Les barbes de 24 coquilles Saint-Jacques
- 100 g de gros sel
- 1 gros oignon
- 2 carottes
- 2 noix de beurre
- 4 c. à soupe de vinaigre de xérès
- 4 c. à soupe de porto blanc
- 10 cl de vin blanc sec
- 10 petites pommes de terre nouvelles
- 1/4 de botte de ciboulette

LES TRIPES

Tripes de Saint-Jacques à la façon d'Olivier Roellinger

Inscrites au menu du « trois étoiles » de Cancale. Pour l'imiter chez vous, un jour d'envie de ce beau produit, pourquoi pas un repas tout Saint-Jacques, d'abord les barbes, ensuite les noix ?

- Demandez à votre poissonnier de vous réserver les barbes des coquilles. Frottez-les avec du gros sel, puis rincez-les abondamment pour retirer tout le sable. Alignez-les sur une planche et taillez-les en lanières de 1 cm.
- Coupez l'oignon et les carottes en petits dés.
- Démarrez la cuisson des tripes : faites saisir une première fois les barbes pendant 4 minutes avec une noix de beurre. Égouttez-les et réservez le jus.
- Dans la même casserole, faites revenir l'oignon et les carottes avec l'autre noix de beurre, ajoutez les barbes, déglacez avec le vinaigre et le porto blanc. Laissez réduire de moitié avant d'ajouter le vin blanc et cuire à couvert pendant 1 heure à très petit feu.
- Mettez les pommes de terre à cuire avec la peau. Ensuite, épluchez-les et coupez-les en deux. Réservez au chaud.
- Ciselez très finement la ciboulette.
- Mettez les pommes de terre et la ciboulette dans les tripes.
- Servez immédiatement dans des assiettes creuses, en répartissant le jus.

Pour 6 personnes
Préparation : 20 min
Cuisson : 3 h

- 2,5 kg de coquilles Saint-Jacques
- 2 gros oignons
- 2 grosses carottes
- 100 g de beurre
- Huile d'olive
- 75 cl de cidre brut
- 25 cl de fond de veau (fond déshydraté)
- 1 bouquet garni
- Gros sel et poivre du moulin
- 3 c. à soupe de vinaigre de cidre

Tripes de Saint-Jacques au cidre brut

Si les noix de Saint-Jacques jouissent d'une réputation justifiée, les barbes - les tripes - se cuisinent aussi excellemment. Faute d'amateurs, souvent les poissonniers les jettent. Halte au gâchis !

- Ouvrez les coquilles ou faites-les ouvrir par votre poissonnier : séparez les noix des barbes. Mettez de côté les noix qui serviront pour une autre recette.
- Lavez à plusieurs eaux les barbes, qui sont en général très sableuses, parez-les soigneusement puis égouttez-les.
- Épluchez et lavez les oignons et les carottes, et taillez ces légumes en brunoise : c'est-à-dire en tout petits dés.
- Dans un faitout, mettez le beurre à chauffer sur feu moyen, ajoutez la brunoise de légumes et laisser cuire 4 à 5 minutes en remuant.
- Pendant ce temps, faites sauter les barbes à la poêle dans un peu d'huile d'olive pour qu'elles rejettent leur eau. égouttez-les, incorporez-les aux légumes, et mouillez avec le cidre et le fond de veau. Salez et poivrez. Ajoutez le bouquet garni. Couvrez et cuisez au four préalablement chauffé à 150 °C pendant 3 heures.
- À la sortie du four, rectifiez l'assaisonnement et ajoutez 2 à 3 cuillerées à soupe de vinaigre de cidre.

Pour 4 personnes
Préparation : 10 min
Cuisson : 2 h à 2 h 30

- 4 kg de coquilles Saint-Jacques
- 4 gousses d'ail
- 1/2 bouquet de persil
- Sel, poivre

Tripes de Saint-Jacques à la façon de Nicolas

Recette de Nicolas Vagnon

Pas fous, les cuisiniers inventifs. Ils tirent parti des noix et des barbes. Imitez-les. Et, pour commencer, en faisant les yeux doux à votre poissonnier pour qu'il vous mette ces barbes de côté.

- Pour réaliser cette recette, il faut utiliser des coquilles très fraîches, pratiquement vivantes, dont on n'utilisera que les barbes – les noix seront employées dans une autre recette. Vous pouvez également demander à votre poissonnier de vous réserver les barbes. Comme il prépare très souvent les coquilles pour ses clients et ne garde que les noix, il devrait vous en fournir sans difficulté.
- Coupez la partie noire des barbes, et mettez-les sans les laver dans une casserole pas trop grande. Couvrez d'eau froide. Amenez à frémissement, écumez et laissez infuser pendant 30 minutes en mettant le feu en veilleuse. Passez alors au chinois et laissez décanter ce bouillon.
- Lavez les barbes 3 à 4 fois, et mettez-les à mijoter dans le bouillon en couvrant, d'abord sans sel pendant environ 1 heure et demie à 2 heures, puis ôtez le couvercle et laissez un peu évaporer. Ajoutez de l'ail cru haché très fin et du persil frisé ciselé. Salez et poivrez.
- On peut accompagner ce plat de purée de potimarron.

Pour 6 personnes
Préparation : 15 min
Cuisson : 3 min

- 500 g environ d'œufs de bars en petits sachets
- 2 œufs entiers
- 100 g de farine
- 10 cl d'huile d'olive
- 2 citrons
- Sel et poivre

LES ŒUFS

Croquettes d'œufs de bar

Il n'y a pas que le caviar. La plupart des poissons produisent des œufs qui méritent d'être cuisinés. On trouve la plupart d'entre eux en poches, dans les poissonneries ou les grandes surfaces.

- Prenez les sachets qui contiennent les œufs de poisson, coupez-les en tranches de 2 cm de large environ.
- Battez les 2 œufs entiers, assaisonnez-les de poivre et de sel, et plongez-y les œufs de poisson.
- Égouttez-les et roulez-les dans la farine.
- Mettez à chauffer l'huile d'olive dans une poêle.
- Faites frire les tranches d'œufs de poisson, tournez-les lentement sur toutes les faces jusqu'à ce qu'elles soient bien dorées et croustillantes.
- Après environ 3 minutes, retirez-les et déposez-les sur du papier absorbant.
- Servez aussitôt avec des quartiers de citron.

d'

Pour 4 personnes
Préparation : 5 min
Cuisson : 10 min

- 4 poches d'œufs d'alose
- 3 c. à soupe d'huile d'arachide
- 2 c. à soupe de farine

Pour la vinaigrette

- 5 c. à soupe d'huile d'olive
- 2 c. à soupe de vinaigre de vin
- Sel et poivre
- 2 échalotes
- 1 bouquet de ciboulette

Œufs d'alose à la vinaigrette

Au printemps, dans le Sud-Ouest, l'alose, migrateur proche du hareng, fait comme le saumon : elle remonte les rivières pour se reproduire. Ses œufs sont délicats. On le sait du côté de Bordeaux.

- **Préparation de la sauce vinaigrette.** Mélangez l'huile, le vinaigre, le sel et le poivre, et ajoutez les échalotes finement ciselées.
- Séchez soigneusement les poches d'alose, farinez-les et assaisonnez-les. Dans une poêle, faites dorer, de chaque côté, les poches d'œufs dans l'huile chaude. Réduisez le feu et laissez cuire encore 5 minutes de chaque côté. Déposez-les dans un plat chaud. Ajoutez la ciboulette ciselée dans la vinaigrette. Arrosez les poches d'œufs d'alose avec la vinaigrette.
- Servez aussitôt.

Pour 4 personnes
Préparation : 10 min
Cuisson : 15 min

- 1 poche d'œufs de cabillaud
- 2 tranches de pain de mie
- 1 c. à soupe de persil plat ciselé
- 1 citron
- 2 œufs
- 10 cl de crème fraîche
- 1 pincée de muscade
- Sel et poivre

Ramequins d'œufs de cabillaud

Prête en 25 minutes chrono, préparation et cuisson comprise, mais la saveur et la belle apparence d'un mets de grande cuisine, est-ce qu'une maîtresse de maison débordée peut trouver mieux ?

- Enlevez les œufs de la poche et écrasez-les à la fourchette avec le pain émietté.
- Salez, poivrez et poudrez de muscade.
- Ajoutez le persil, le jus de citron et les jaunes d'œufs battus avec la crème fraîche.
- Montez les blancs en neige, incorporez-les à la préparation précédente.
- Versez cet appareil dans des ramequins préalablement beurrés et mettez-les à cuire pendant 15 minutes à four moyen (140 °C).
- Servez immédiatement.

Pour 4 personnes
Préparation : 45 min
Cuisson : 20 min

- 400 g de filets de skrei levés dans la partie épaisse du dos (avec la peau)
- 4 œufs
- 15 g de beurre
- 20 cl de crème
- 120 g d'œufs de skrei
- 200 g d'airelles
- 1 c. à soupe de fécule
- 20 cl d'huile de pépins de raisin
- 1 bouquet de roquette
- 1 bouquet de ciboulette
- 1 bouquet d'aneth
- 1 bouquet de cerfeuil
- 1 bouquet de mâche
- 1 citron
- Sel et poivre

Effeuillé de skrei de Norvège

Recette de Christian Têtedoie, restaurant Têtedoie à Lyon

Pour faire souffler chez vous l'air tonique des fjords, une recette où le poisson culte des marins norvégiens est savamment revisité, avec airelles et œufs brouillés, par un grand chef de Lyon.

- Mettez les filets de skrei avec leur peau à cuire au four à 180 °C, juste salés dans un plat beurré, pendant 6 minutes.
- Faites fondre le beurre et mettez-y cuire les 4 œufs en brouillade. À la fin, ajoutez la crème et les œufs de skrei. Laissez cuire pendant 2 minutes afin de lier la crème et les œufs à la brouillade, puis laissez refroidir légèrement.
- Écrasez les airelles pour en extraire le jus, mettez celui-ci à chauffer sans bouillir, ajoutez un peu de fécule mélangée à de l'eau froide pour le lier, salez et poivrez. Laissez refroidir. Ajoutez 10 cl d'huile au jus d'airelles, mélangez à la fourchette pour ne pas amalgamer l'huile dans sa totalité.
- Assaisonnez le bouquet d'herbes mélangées avec l'huile restante et le jus de citron, le sel et le poivre.
- Au dernier moment, disposez la brouillade au centre de l'assiette, en vous aidant éventuellement d'un cercle pour une présentation plus soignée. Dans ce cas, tassez bien avant de retirer le cercle. Disposez dessus les herbes en bouquet, et, tout autour, le skrei effeuillé en petites lamelles, puis versez la vinaigrette au jus d'airelles par petites touches.

Pour un bol de tarama (8 personnes)
Préparation : 15 min
Pas de cuisson

- 1 poche d'œufs de cabillaud fumés
- 5 tranches de pain de mie
- 10 cl de lait
- 5 cl de crème fraîche liquide
- Le jus d'un demi-citron
- 25 cl d'huile de pépins de raisin
- Quelques gouttes de Tabasco®

Tarama
d'œufs de cabillaud fumés

Ne dites pas « du » mais « des » taramas. Il en existe de plusieurs sortes dans le commerce, prêts à être tartinés. Mais les taramas maison, si vite prêts sans cuisson, sont autrement bons.

- Retirez les croûtes des tranches de pain de mie. Émiettez-les et arrosez-les avec le lait et la crème. Laissez imbiber le pain 1 minute puis essorez-le entre vos mains.
- Fendez la poche d'œufs de cabillaud et, à l'aide d'une cuillère, grattez délicatement pour récupérer les œufs et les mettre dans le bol d'un mixeur.
- Arrosez-les avec le jus de citron. Mixez quelques secondes et, dès que la préparation est un peu fluide, incorporez la mie de pain essorée. Versez l'huile en filet jusqu'à ce que le tarama soit onctueux. Disposez-le dans un bol.
- Assaisonnez de quelques gouttes de Tabasco®.
- Mettez-le au réfrigérateur jusqu'au moment de servir.

Pour 4 personnes
Préparation : 15 min
Pas de cuisson
Repos : 36 h

- 250 g d'œufs de poissons frais (colin, daurade, hareng, etc.)
- 1 c. à soupe de gros sel de mer gris
- 1 gros citron
- Thym et laurier
- 1 pincée de piment de Cayenne en poudre
- 1 pincée de paprika
- 4 c. à soupe d'huile d'olive

Tarama
frais d'œufs de poissons

L'occasion fera la larronne ou le larron. Si, en faisant votre marché, vous trouvez ces œufs de poissons frais, faites main basse sur le butin. Et trois jours plus tard, chez vous on se régalera.

- Faites mariner les œufs avec une grosse cuillerée à soupe de gros sel gris.
- Écrasez-les ensuite avec une fourchette en ajoutant le jus d'un gros citron ou de 2 petits.
- Ajoutez du thym, du laurier, 1 pincée de piment de Cayenne, 1 pincée de paprika ainsi que les 4 cuillerées d'huile d'olive bien fruitée.
- Laissez-les mariner au frais pendant 24 heures, puis mixez au maximum ou passez au presse-purée grille fine de façon à obtenir une pâte.
- Laissez reposer le tarama durant 12 heures avant de le servir avec des tartines de pain légèrement grillées.

Pour 4 personnes
Préparation : 10 min
Cuisson : 5 à 6 min

- 50 g de poutargue râpée
- 2 gousses d'ail
- 5 c. à soupe d'huile d'olive
- 1 piment sec oiseau
- 400 g de spaghettis fins ou toutes autres pâtes
- Sel et poivre

Pâtes à la poutargue

Le plus connu des œufs de poisson, la poutargue est, selon le dictionnaire Robert, « une sorte de caviar fait avec les œufs du mugle ». Un banal plat de spaghettis ou autres tagliatelles en est transfiguré.

- Pelez l'ail en éliminant le germe et hachez-le très fin.
- Dans une sauteuse sur feu doux, faire revenir l'ail haché et le piment dans l'huile d'olive. Laissez cuire jusqu'à ce que l'ail blondisse légèrement.
- Faites cuire les pâtes al dente à l'eau bouillante salée. égouttez-les et versez-les dans la sauteuse. Assaisonnez avec l'huile parfumée et retirez du feu.
- Poudrez de poutargue. Poivrez. Mélangez et servez aussitôt.

en

Pour 4 personnes
Préparation : 30 min
Cuisson : 10 min

- 4 escalopes de laitance
- 30 g de beurre
- 1 pincée de farine
- 8 feuilles de laitue ciselées
- 4 champignons de Paris émincés
- 1/2 échalote hachée finement
- Quelques gouttes de vin blanc
- 2 c. à soupe de crème
- Sel et poivre
- 2 c. à soupe de sauce hollandaise
- Le jus d'un quart de citron

LES LAITANCES

Laitances de carpe en apéritif

À la saison où les poissons se reproduisent, entre septembre et janvier selon les espèces, les laitances abondent. Dans l'antiquité, et au Moyen Âge encore, on leur attribuait des vertus reconstituantes.

- Colorez au beurre les laitances farinées.
- Dans une petite casserole, faites suer à couvert avec le jus de citron les feuilles de laitue et les champignons puis ajoutez la demi-échalote hachée. Arrosez de quelques gouttes de vin blanc, crémez, et laissez cuire doucement pendant quelques minutes.
- Rassemblez les laitances et les laitues.
- Passez la sauce, et poivrez-la légèrement.
- Incorporez 2 cuillerées à soupe de sauce hollandaise mousseuse.
- Servez dans de petites assiettes chaudes.

Sauce hollandaise

Préparation : 5 min Cuisson : 10 min • **2 jaunes d'œufs** • **3 cuillerées à soupe d'eau** • **150 g de beurre clarifié (ou de beurre cru)** • **1 pincée de sel**

- Mettez les jaunes d'œufs dans l'eau et battez-les avec un fouet – sur feu très doux – jusqu'à ce qu'ils soient bien épais et qu'ils collent au fouet. Incorporez alors soit le beurre clarifié tiède (beurre fondu doucement au bain-marie : il devient clair et libère un dépôt blanchâtre au fond du récipient – dépôt que l'on jettera), soit du beurre cru (à la température de la pièce mais pas trop mou) coupé en parcelles, tout en continuant de fouetter.
- Salez et gardez au chaud à température très douce.

Pour 4 personnes
Préparation : 40 min
Dégorgement : 1 h
Cuisson : 20 min

- **600 g de laitances de hareng**
- **10 cl de vinaigre blanc**
- **100 g de tomates**
- **1 pomme**
- **100 g de champignons de Paris**
- **2 c. à soupe de farine**
- **50 g de beurre**
- **Huile**
- **10 g de câpres**
- **20 cl de verjus**
- **8 c. à café de vinaigre de cidre**
- **2 brins de persil plat**
- **Sel et poivre du moulin**

Laitances de hareng au verjus

On trouve des laitances entre septembre et janvier.

- Mettez les laitances à dégorger pendant 1 heure dans de l'eau froide, additionnée d'un filet de vinaigre blanc.
- Ébouillantez les tomates, pelez-les, videz-les de leurs graines, et détaillez la chair en petits dés. Pelez la pomme et détaillez-la également en petits dés. Lavez les champignons et coupez-les, eux aussi, en petits dés.
- Les laitances ayant dégorgé, regardez l'aspect du filament sanguinolent qui les traverse et, s'il est trop gros, retirez-le, à l'aide d'un petit couteau pointu, en entaillant légèrement le long du filament. Faites aussi 3 incisions en biais pour sectionner le nerf, puis rincez les laitances dans l'eau vinaigrée.
- Posez les laitances sur la grille d'un couscoussier ou d'un cuit vapeur, et faites-les raidir quelques secondes à la vapeur. Réservez-les.
- Mettez la farine dans une assiette et farinez légèrement les laitances.
- Rangez-les sur une autre assiette et piquez-les sur leurs 2 faces pour qu'elles n'éclatent pas à la cuisson.

Comme pour la recette précédente, à servir sur de petites assiettes, en fleurons d'un apéritif-dîner, ou en hors-d'œuvre, en remettant à l'honneur ce verjus si prisé des cuisiniers d'antan.

- Dans une poêle antiadhésive, faites chauffer 25 g de beurre et un peu d'huile. Lorsque le beurre est bien mousseux, posez les laitances (côté nerf sur le fond), et retournez-les délicatement après 1 minute de cuisson. Assaisonnez-les de poivre et de sel, et laissez-les cuire également 1 minute sur l'autre face. Gardez-les au chaud.
- Mettez 20 g de beurre dans la poêle, augmentez le feu et jetez-y les dés de champignons, faites-les sauter quelques secondes puis ajoutez les dés de pomme, faites sauter pendant 1 minute.
- Ajoutez encore une noix de beurre, salez, poivrez, puis versez les câpres et les dés de tomates, remuez pendant quelques secondes pour les chauffer.
- Sur des assiettes bien chaudes, répartissez les laitances et la garniture.
- Déglacez la poêle avec le verjus, laissez bouillir à grand feu avant d'ajouter 8 cuillerées à café de vinaigre de cidre. Donnez un bouillon et retirez du feu.
- Servez cette sauce avec les laitances et parsemez de persil ciselé.

LA QUEUE

Queue de cabillaud et ses œufs pochés

Pour 6 personnes
Préparation : 45 min
Cuisson : 1 h 25

- 1,2 kg de filets de skrei
- 500 g d'œufs de cabillaud fumés (ou à défaut du tarama au naturel)
- 1 œuf plus un blanc d'œuf
- 20 g de beurre ramolli
- 100 g de foies de morue
- 50 g de mie de pain
- 3 c. à soupe d'huile de foie de morue
- Fleur de sel et poivres mélangés concassés

Pour le bouillon

- 2 carottes
- 2 poireaux
- 2 navets

Il n'y a pas que le caviar. La plupart des poissons produisent des œufs qui méritent d'être cuisinés. On trouve la plupart d'entre eux en poches, dans les poissonneries ou les grandes surfaces.

- Préparez le bouillon de légumes : lavez et épluchez les carottes, les poireaux et les navets. Coupez-les en tronçons puis faites les cuire dans 1 litre d'eau salée pendant 1 heure à couvert. (Vous pouvez aussi employer du bouillon déshydraté.)
- Pendant que le bouillon cuit, taillez les filets de poisson en larges pavés sans retirer la peau.
- Dans un saladier, mélangez les œufs de cabillaud avec le jaune et les 2 blancs d'œufs battus. Salez et poivrez.
- Beurrez une feuille de papier d'aluminium avec un pinceau, garnissez le centre de la feuille avec les œufs, puis roulez la feuille en forme de gros saucisson pour enfermer ceux-ci. Plongez pendant 30 minutes dans le faitout où cuisent les légumes, sur feu moyen. Plongez également les pavés de poisson dans le faitout pendant 25 minutes.
- Écrasez les foies de morue avec la mie de pain, et faites chauffer dans l'huile de foie de morue assaisonnée.
- Prélevez dans le faitout les œufs de cabillaud cuits dans le papier d'aluminium, retirez celui-ci et taillez le saucisson d'œufs en fines tranches.
- Servez les pavés de poisson pochés cuits à point avec les légumes arrosés d'huile de foie de morue, entourés des tranches d'œufs et des foies de morue.

et ses

Pour 4 personnes
Préparation : 30 min
Cuisson : 20 min

- 1,5 kg de queue de lotte
- 2 oignons
- 2 gousses d'ail
- 4 c. à soupe d'huile d'olive
- 5 grandes tranches de jambon de Bayonne
- 2 brins d'estragon
- 1 crépine
- 1 botte de petits oignons nouveaux
- 10 cl de vin blanc sec
- Sel et poivre

Rôti de lotte au jambon

Charnues, goûteuses et sans arêtes, les queues des grands poissons font partie des morceaux nobles. Elles se rôtissent, se mitonnent, la succulente queue de lotte tout particulièrement.

- Demandez au poissonnier de peler le poisson et de retirer l'arête centrale, sans séparer les deux filets.
- Pelez les oignons et les gousses d'ail : hachez-les finement, puis faites-les étuver doucement dans 1 cuillerée d'huile d'olive sans les faire colorer. Hachez grossièrement l'une des tranches de jambon. Ciselez finement les feuilles d'estragon. Dans un bol, mélangez le jambon haché, le hachis d'oignon et d'ail, et l'estragon. Salez et poivrez. Glissez cette préparation dans la cavité laissée par l'arête centrale.
- Enveloppez la queue de lotte avec les tranches de jambon restantes. Et, pour finir, entourez-la avec la crépine. Ficelez-la comme un rôti.
- Épluchez les petits oignons nouveaux, gardez-les entiers, mais découpez les tiges vertes en petits tronçons.
- Dans une cocotte, faites dorer tout doucement le rôti de lotte sur toutes ses faces dans de l'huile d'olive. Versez le vin blanc. Ajoutez les petits oignons.
- Couvrez et laissez mijoter tout doucement pendant une vingtaine de minutes. Retournez le rôti à mi-cuisson.
- Servez très chaud, découpé en tranches épaisses.

Pour 4 personnes
Préparation : 10 min
Cuisson : 30 min

- 4 petites queues de lotte
- 3 gros oignons blancs
- 1 citron
- 1 dosette de pistils de safran
- Huile d'olive
- Sel et poivre

Queue de lotte aux oignons et safran

Facile, rapide, belle couleur, grande saveur, intéressant accord du citron et du safran : très exactement ce que l'on nomme, la mine réjouie, un plat mitonné aux petits oignons.

- Pelez et émincez finement les oignons. Coupez le citron en quartiers.
- Faites revenir les oignons et le citron à l'huile d'olive pendant 30 minutes dans une poêle sur feu moyen. à la fin, ajoutez le safran, salez et poivrez.
- Simultanément, dans une autre poêle, mettez les queues de lotte à cuire dans de l'huile d'olive sur feu vif, durant 15 minutes, en les retournant à mi-cuisson. Salez et poivrez.
- Servez immédiatement les queues de lotte sur le lit d'oignons au citron et au safran.

Pour 6 personnes
Préparation : 15 min
Cuisson : 30 min

- 1,5 kg de queue de lotte
- 200 g de filet de saumon dépouillé
- 12 fines tranches de lard fumé
- 8 feuilles de laurier
- 1 bouquet de thym
- 130 g de beurre
- 15 cl de vermouth
- 15 cl de fumet de poisson
- 1 c. à soupe de moutarde de Meaux
- Sel et poivre

Rôti de queue de lotte et de saumon aux herbes

Le saumon farcit la lotte. Le lard fumé leur ajoute une note intrigante. Le thym et le laurier embaument. Rien de tel pour convertir au poisson ceux qui croyaient ne pas l'aimer.

- Préchauffez le four à 210 °C (th. 7).
- Demandez au poissonnier de retirer la membrane blanche qui entoure la queue de lotte et d'enlever la grosse arête centrale mais sans détacher les filets du poisson. Posez la queue de lotte côté bombé sur votre plan de travail. Salez et poivrez-la.
- Déposez le filet de saumon coupé en fines lanières au centre de la lotte, à l'emplacement de l'arête centrale. Salez et poivrez de nouveau.
- Rabattez les parties minces de la queue de façon à lui donner la forme d'un rôti. En les faisant chevaucher, entourez le rôti de tranches de lard. Ajoutez les feuilles de laurier et les branches de thym, et ficelez le rôti.
- Déposez votre poisson dans un plat beurré. Versez-y le vermouth et parsemez de 50 g de beurre en petits morceaux. Enfournez pendant une trentaine de minutes. Au bout de ce temps, déposez le rôti de queue de lotte sur le plat de service, couvrez celui-ci d'une feuille de papier aluminium et laissez-le à l'entrée du four éteint.
- Mettez le plat de cuisson sur le feu, ajoutez le fumet de poisson, et faites un peu réduire. Incorporez en fouettant le reste du beurre en parcelles, puis la moutarde. Rectifiez l'assaisonnement et versez la sauce tout autour du rôti de lotte.
- Servez aussitôt.

Sauces, coulis

beurres, fumet et court-bouillon

Aux recettes de poisson ou de viandes les plus basiques, grillées, à la vapeur, etc., des ponctuations marines donnent de l'esprit. Les sauces, coulis, beurres maniés et fumets sont alors de précieux alliés. Ici, leur préparation fait largement appel aux algues, précieux légumes et condiments offerts par la mer.

EN PARTANT DE RECETTES CLASSIQUES, ON PEUT LEUR DONNER UNE NOTE PLUS MARITIME EN LEUR AJOUTANT, PAR EXEMPLE, DES ALGUES QUE L'ON TROUVE MAINTENANT SOIT DÉSHYDRATÉES, SOIT SOUS FORME DE PAILLETTES, SOIT FRAÎCHES ET SALÉES. CES PRODUITS SONT VENDUS DANS LES BOUTIQUES BIO, SUR DES ÉTALS DES MARCHÉS BIO, ET POUR LES PLUS COURANTES, CHEZ CERTAINS POISSONNIERS.

Sauce vierge à la bretonne

Son plus : le nori, algue en japonais où l'on appelle ainsi un mélange d'algues cultivées. En France, il s'agit de la *Porphyra tenera* sauvage, riche en fer et en calcium.

Cuisson : 30 minutes • **3 tomates entières • 2 gousses d'ail • 2 c. à soupe de persil plat haché • 1 c. à soupe d'estragon également haché • 1 dizaine de grains de coriandre concassés • 15 à 20 g de paillettes de nori ou de laitue de mer • 10 cl d'huile d'olive**

- Supprimez les pédoncules des tomates et pelez-les après les avoir plongées dans une casserole d'eau bouillante.
- Coupez-les en deux et pressez-les doucement pour en extraire l'eau de végétation ainsi que les pépins, puis coupez-les en petits dés.
- Mettez tous les ingrédients dans une casserole avec 10 cl d'huile d'olive, et faites tiédir très doucement pendant environ une demi-heure.
- Cette sauce peut se consommer tiède ou froide.

*

UNE IDÉE EN PLUS
Ayez sous la main les épices de la mer en concoctant vos propres mélanges d'algues en paillettes. À employer directement dans les sauces, vinaigrettes, marinades et soupes.

QUELQUES IDÉES DE BEURRES COMPOSÉS

PRESQUE INSTANTANÉMENT PRÊTS, LES BEURRES COMPOSÉS SONT AUX MAÎTRESSES ET MAÎTRES DE MAISON CE QU'EST LA BAGUETTE MAGIQUE AUX FÉES. ESSAYEZ CEUX-CI PUIS INVENTEZ LES VÔTRES. CONSEIL AUX AMATEURS : UNE TARTINE DE BEURRE D'ALGUES OU DE BEURRE SALÉ ET SALICORNE AVEC DES HUÎTRES, SIMPLE ET MAGNIFIQUE !

Beurre d'ail

Cuisson : 7 minutes **200 g de beurre • 50 g d'ail sans le germe • 50 g de criste-marine ou de salicorne frais • Sel, poivre**

- Versez de l'eau dans une casserole. Portez à ébullition puis jetez-y les gousses d'ail épluchées. Laissez cuire 6 à 7 minutes.
- Retirez la casserole du feu et égouttez les gousses d'ail.
- Mixez-les en ajoutant le beurre mou fractionné, ainsi que les algues coupées en petits morceaux. Amalgamez bien le tout.
- Salez et poivrez.

Beurre de citron

200 g de beurre • 100 g de criste-marine ou de salicorne hachées, si possible fraîches • 1 filet de citron • 1 pointe de muscade

- Malaxez l'ensemble des ingrédients.

Beurre provençal

Préparation : 10 minutes. Pas de cuisson **125 g de beurre demi-sel • 6 à 8 gousses d'ail pelées et dégermées • 25 cl d'huile d'olive • 1 bouquet de persil plat effeuillé • 3 anchois dessalés • 1/2 c. à café de cognac • Poivre du moulin**

- Mettez tous ces ingrédients dans le mixeur jusqu'à obtention d'une purée onctueuse et lisse.

Beurre d'algues

- Incorporez dans du beurre salé mou un mélange d'algues en paillettes (dulse, laitue de mer, nori), à raison de 25 g de paillettes environ pour 125 g de beurre.

BEURRE D'ALGUES*

NAGES, FUMETS ET COURT-BOUILLONS

À BASE DE PARURES, DE TÊTES ET D'ARÊTES, CES FONDS DE CUISSON SONT CONSTAMMENT UTILISÉS PAR LES GRANDS CUISINIERS. ILS NE COÛTENT RIEN MAIS ILS CHANGENT TOUT.

Les épices de la mer

- Mélangez des algues déshydratées présentées en paillettes.
- Ces épices de la mer s'emploient directement dans une sauce, une vinaigrette, une marinade, une soupe, etc.

Consommé au saumon

Autour du saumon, un consommé astucieux...

Le plus simple des bouillons, mais parfait pour y pocher poissons ou crustacés et les servir à la nage dans ce consommé, en soupière et assiettes creuses.

Cuisson : 45 minutes **1 kg de peau de saumon écaillée • 1,5 l d'eau**

- Lavez la peau du poisson et plongez-la dans une casserole d'eau froide.
- Lorsque l'eau commence à bouillir, laissez mijoter à feu doux pendant 45 minutes. Passez le tout au chinois et linge fin.
- Rectifiez l'assaisonnement, réservez.
- Servez le consommé chaud, comme base de nage de poisson.

Sauce genevoise

Une recette d'Alain Passard, restaurant L'Arpège à Paris

Pour 8 personnes **1 kg d'arêtes de saumon • Le sang et les abats du saumon • 50 g de beurre doux • 300 g d'oignons blancs • 2 carottes • 1 branche de céleri • Le zeste d'1 orange • Le zeste d'1 citron vert • 2 gousses d'ail ciselées • Herbes aromatiques (thym, laurier…) • 1 l de vin rouge • Sel Poivre en grains • 1 c. à soupe de vinaigre balsamique**

- Faites revenir dans le beurre moussant les arêtes détaillées en petits morceaux jusqu'à ce qu'elles atteignent une belle coloration. Ajoutez les oignons ciselés, les carottes et la branche de céleri émincés, les zestes d'agrumes, l'ail, le poivre et les herbes aromatiques. Laissez cuire sur feu moyen.
- Lorsque le mélange atteint une belle couleur caramélisée et colle au fond du sautoir, déglacez avec le vin rouge. Détachez bien les sucs à l'aide d'une spatule et laissez réduire à petits frémissements jusqu'au tiers.
- Passez la sauce au chinois étamine, liez avec le sang et les abats de saumon concassés. Passez de nouveau au chinois, rectifiez l'assaisonnement en sel et vinaigre balsamique. Surtout ne faites pas bouillir la sauce une fois la liaison au sang réalisée.
- Servez cette sauce avec le saumon poêlé.

UN COURT-BOUILLON DE BASE

ON EN TROUVE CERTES DE PRÊTS À L'EMPLOI. MAIS FAIT MAISON, IL EST BIEN PLUS ODORANT. ET COMME IL EST RECOMMANDÉ DE LE PRÉPARER LA VEILLE, PAS DE RAISON DE S'EN PRIVER.

Court-bouillon

Cuisson : 30 minutes **1 carotte • 1 bouquet garni (thym, laurier, tiges de persil, brins de fenouil) • 1 oignon piqué de 4 clous de girofle • 1 poireau • 1 tige de céleri • 1 échalote • 3 étoiles de badiane • 1 c. à café de poivre noir en grains • 1 poignée de gros sel marin • 1 pincée de sucre • 1 écorce d'orange séchée • 1 piment oiseau (éventuellement) • 1 verre de vinaigre de vin rouge ou blanc, ou le jus d'1/2 citron**

- Épluchez et émincez tous les légumes.
- Préparez le bouquet garni.
- Mettez tous les ingrédients, à l'exception du vinaigre, dans 5 l d'eau, et portez à ébullition.
- Laissez cuire 30 minutes à petits frémissements
- En fin de cuisson, goûtez et rectifiez l'assaisonnement.
- Retirez la casserole du feu, ajoutez un bon verre de vinaigre de vin blanc ou rouge, ou le jus d'un demi-citron.
- Laissez refroidir le court-bouillon avant de l'utiliser. Il est même préférable de le faire la veille et de laisser infuser les éléments.

BOTTE FINALE, LE BOUQUET GARNI MARIN

POUR COURTS-BOUILLONS, FUMETS ET SAUCES CÉLÉBRANT L'OCÉAN. IL SE COMPOSE, COMME LE BOUQUET GARNI CLASSIQUE, DE QUEUES DE PERSIL, BRANCHE DE CÉLERI, THYM ET LAURIER MAIS ON LE COMPLÈTE DE LANIÈRES D'ALGUES : WAKAMÉ OU PORPHYRE (DANS LES BOUTIQUES ET RAYONS BIO).

UN FUMET SANS ÉGAL

LÀ ENCORE, ON EN TROUVE PRÊT À L'EMPLOI. MAIS EN BIEN PEU DE TEMPS, ET POUR UN COÛT MINIME, ON PEUT EN PRÉPARER UN, SUBTIL, ET QUI, PLUS EST, SE CONSERVE PLUSIEURS JOURS.

Fumet de poisson

Le fumet de poisson sert à braiser poissons et crustacés, et surtout il sert comme base dans les sauces ou dans le mouillement des cuissons.

Cuisson : 25 minutes **Pour 1 à 2 l de fumet (il se conserve 8 jours dans un bocal au réfrigérateur) • 1 kg d'arêtes de poissons ou de parures de poissons ou encore carapaces et têtes de crustacés • 2 c. à soupe d'huile d'olive • 2 gousses d'ail en chemise • 1 kg de petits légumes mélangés (carottes, racines de persil, blanc de poireau, oignons, champignons de Paris) • 1 l de vin blanc sec • 1,5 l d'eau • 1 bouquet garni • Quelques grains de poivre • 1 clou de girofle • 1/2 citron • Sel**

- Retirez, s'il y en a, les branchies qui rendraient le fumet amer. Rincez bien les parures de poisson. Concassez les arêtes et autres déchets. Faites-les revenir dans l'huile d'olive. Faites suer quelques instants, puis ajoutez l'ail sans l'éplucher et tous les légumes émincés. Remuez, versez le vin blanc sec et l'eau. Ajoutez le bouquet garni, les grains de poivre, le clou de girofle.
- Mettez sur feu moyen et portez à ébullition une vingtaine de minutes. Écumez au fur et à mesure puis passez au chinois ou à la passoire fine. Remettez le fumet sur le feu, assaisonnez, ajoutez le jus du demi-citron. Faites encore réduire pendant 5 minutes, puis passez de nouveau à la passoire fine sans entraîner le fond.
- On peut ajouter à cette recette, afin d'obtenir un fumet encore plus parfumé, des algues, telles que laitue de mer, wakamé ou kombu breton, que l'on trouve soit dans les boutiques soit sur les marchés bio.

INDEX

Festin de

Remerciements

Merci ou plutôt mercis avec un S - mille mercis - merci à la vie de m'avoir permis un jour de réaliser un rêve : créer un restaurant qui m'a ainsi fait découvrir un métier fabuleux, la cuisine. Merci aux chefs avec qui j'ai travaillé, merci aux « grands chefs » que j'ai eu le plaisir de rencontrer, merci à tous ces inspirateurs : cuisiniers - revues - livres (la lecture est ma seconde passion) - la cuisine inépuisable où toujours des passionnés, des créateurs arrivent à réinventer de nouvelles recettes. Toujours la même, toujours recréée, toujours différente... sans limite. **Arlette Sirot**

Iris L. Sullivan dédie ce livre à la chatte Atlantique. Elle remercie Virginie Michelin pour son enthousiasme, son talent et sa collaboration de chaque instant. Sans elle, ce livre n'aurait pas été ce qu'il est. Merci à Valérie Chain d'avoir généreusement prêté certains de ses tableaux (chinus@club-internet.fr). Merci aux poissonniers du marché de la Place des Fêtes : Oléron Marée et Gioia. À Éric pour sa gentillesse ainsi qu'aux boutiques Quartz et CFOC. Les photos des pages 1 et 152 sont un hommage à Irving Penn.

Conception graphique : Laurence Maillet
Connectez-vous sur : www.lamartinieregroupe.com
© 2007, Éditions Minerva, Genève (Suisse)
ISBN : 978-2-8307-0922-3

Tous droits de traduction, d'adaptation et de reproduction, sous quelque forme que ce soit, réservés pour tous pays.

Photogravure : Quadrilaser
Achevé d'imprimer en janvier 2007
Sur les presses de l'imprimerie : Graficas Estellas
Dépôt légal : mars 2007
Imprimé en Espagne